Which Rights Should Be Universal?

Which Rights Should
Be Universal?

WILLIAM J. TALBOTT

OXFORD
UNIVERSITY PRESS

OXFORD
UNIVERSITY PRESS

Oxford University Press, Inc., publishes works that further
Oxford University's objective of excellence
in research, scholarship, and education.

Oxford   New York
Auckland   Cape Town   Dar es Salaam   Hong Kong   Karachi
Kuala Lumpur   Madrid   Melbourne   Mexico City   Nairobi
New Delhi   Shanghai   Taipei   Toronto

With offices in
Argentina   Austria   Brazil   Chile   Czech Republic   France   Greece
Guatemala   Hungary   Italy   Japan   Poland   Portugal   Singapore
South Korea   Switzerland   Thailand   Turkey   Ukraine   Vietnam

Copyright © 2005 by Oxford University Press, Inc.

Published by Oxford University Press, Inc.
198 Madison Avenue, New York, New York 10016

First issued as an Oxford University Press paperback, 2007

www.oup.com

Oxford is a registered trademark of Oxford University Press

Library of Congress Cataloging-in-Publication Data
Talbott, W. J.
Which rights should be universal? / William J. Talbott.
    p.   cm.
Includes bibliographical references and index.
ISBN 978-0-19-517347-5; 978-0-19-533134-9 (pbk.)
1. Human rights—Philosophy.   2. Human rights—Moral and ethical aspects.   I. Title.
JC571.T1445   2005
323'.01—dc22   2004052064

9 8 7 6 5 4 3 2 1

Printed in the United States of America
on acid-free paper

To my parents

ACKNOWLEDGMENTS

This book began as a public lecture at the University of Washington in January 1998. The idea grew to become a chapter, then a book, then two books, of which this is the first. The second volume (*Human Rights and Human Well-Being*) will also be published by Oxford University Press.

The book has benefited from the contributions of many people. I used part of the manuscript in a joint seminar that I taught with my colleague in political science Jamie Mayerfeld in the winter of 2001. I received many good suggestions from the members of the seminar, especially from Katherine Kim and Grace Pastine.

I presented a draft of several chapters to an interdisciplinary group of humanities scholars at the University of Washington's Simpson Center for the Humanities in the fall of 2000. I particularly benefited from the comments of Bruce Burgett, Margit Dementi Rankin, Shannon Dudley, Dianah Leigh Jackson, and Kathleen Woodward.

I have also benefited from discussion in my undergraduate classes, especially from questions asked by Dakota Solberg-Moen and Andrew Ness. I was fortunate to be able to discuss part of the manuscript with an interdisciplinary group of faculty at Green River Community College in February 2002. In the spring of 2003, I had an opportunity to present a partial draft of the book in a series of five lectures to a nonacademic audience in the Wednesday University, a joint program of Seattle Arts & Lectures and the U.W. Simpson Center for the Humanities.

Work on this book has been supported by a summer grant from the U.W. Human Rights Education and Research Center, by a one-quarter release from teaching funded by the U.W. Simpson Center for the Humanities, and by a sabbatical leave from the University of Washington.

I have received valuable comments from many people on drafts of various chapters, including Jeff Clausen, David Keyt, Bruce Kochis, Thomas McCarthy, Tom Nagel, Paul Taylor, Martin Tweedale, Jay Wallace, and an anonymous referee. Elijah Millgram and Liam Murphy provided detailed and very useful comments on several chapters. Jacques Corriveau, Katherine Kim, and John Talbott read and commented on an early version of the full manuscript. Katherine Kim helped with the proofreading of the final version. I also want to thank the following members of the editorial staff at Oxford University Press for their contributions: Stacey Hamilton, Merryl Sloane, Lara Zoble, and especially Peter Ohlin for his encouragement and guidance throughout the publication process.

I owe a special debt of gratitude to Jamie Mayerfeld. Over the years, I have discussed many of these issues with Jamie; in the winter of 2001 we cotaught a course that gave me many ideas for the book; and over the past three years Jamie has commented on many drafts of many chapters. His good advice has helped me in more ways than I can list.

I want to thank my daughters, Kate and Rebecca, for teaching me so much about the rewards of child rearing as well as for being such a good audience for my ideas over so many years. I am grateful to my stepdaughter, Erin Burchfield, who challenged me to articulate the appeal of moral relativism and who also provided me with information about the life of women in Nepal after she spent a semester there. Finally, I want to thank my wife, Judy, who has provided me with the encouragement and emotional support that enabled me to write the book, has proofread the entire manuscript, has provided me with many suggestions that improved the book, and has taught me so much about empathic understanding.

CONTENTS

Which Rights Should Be Universal?

1

INTRODUCTION

The best lack all conviction, while the worst are full of
passionate intensity.
　　　　　　　—William Butler Yeats, "The Second Coming"

Are there any universal rights? Much has been written on this question. A
problem about phrasing the question this way is that the very idea of someone's having a right to something is an idea with a historical lineage. There
were human societies long before anyone even had any such idea.[1] It seems
puzzling to think that someone might claim that rights existed before anyone had ever articulated the idea itself. How could it make sense to think
that the members of a prehistoric human community might have had
rights, when no one had ever had such a thought? Historically, natural
rights theorists typically appealed to God as the source of individual rights
to provide a solution to this puzzle. The suggestion is that even before human beings had the idea of a right, God had it. Thus, God made it true that
human beings have rights, even before the human beings themselves had
any inkling of this fact.

I want to suggest a different kind of defense of universal rights. On my
view, the proposition that human beings *should have* certain legally protected basic rights is a partly moral, partly empirical discovery based on
thousands of years of accumulated experience of human social existence.
Because the necessary discoveries took thousands of years to make, it is a
mistake to think that members of prehistoric human communities *should*
have respected each other's basic rights. However, it is still true that the
members of those communities had characteristics which, once they are
generally recognized and their moral significance generally appreciated,
would explain why certain basic rights should be universally protected.

To allow for this element of discovery in the theory of rights, rather than
consider whether any rights *are* universal, I consider whether, in light of
what we now know about human beings, any rights *should be* universal.
My answer to that question is: We now have sufficient understanding of
the nature of human beings and of the moral constraints on how they
should be treated to realize that governments everywhere ought to guarantee certain basic rights to everyone within their borders. In this book, I

outline what those rights are and explain why they should be universally protected.

Religious Authorities and Moral Philosophers

The discovery that certain basic rights should be universal is the product of thousands of years of human moral development. The earliest stages are shrouded in prehistory. The first historical records are the written documents preserved by various religious traditions, usually documents that believers regard as sacred texts recording the commands of a moral authority, typically regarded as infallible. At least initially, most religions hold that moral truths can be determined simply by accepting without question whatever the moral authority says (or an authoritative interpretation of what the moral authority says).

Suppose we take the defining feature of a religion to be its identification of a moral authority, a person or a text, typically regarded as infallible. On this definition, all of the major religions qualify as religions, but some movements not usually thought of as religions—for example, various twentieth-century Marxist movements—also qualify. In this book, I will use the term *religion* in the broader sense that includes Marxist movements, because I believe their commonalities are more important than their differences.

At least initially, religions typically admonish their adherents to follow the directives of the relevant moral authority unquestioningly, and not to exercise their own moral judgment. Nonetheless, these religious traditions tend to produce at least some people with a capacity for independent moral judgment. People who exercise this capacity will not regard any other person or text as a source of unquestionable moral truth. They can regard people or texts as sources of moral wisdom, to be seriously considered in deciding what to do. However, the ultimate decision about what to do will always depend on their own moral judgment. I will refer to people who develop and exercise their own moral judgment as *moral philosophers.*

Historically, religions have usually regarded moral philosophers, in the sense in which I use the term, as threats. This is understandable, because if people generally were to exercise their own moral judgment, they would almost surely question the religion's designated moral authority on some issues. This would make it very difficult to maintain the relevant authority as an infallible source of moral truth. Thus, moral philosophers have often been classified as heretics, apostates, corrupters of the young, or enemies of the people and dealt with harshly.

It is only relatively recently that some religions have ceased to persecute moral philosophers. Typically, tolerance for moral philosophy depends on the recognition of some sort of right to freedom of religious and political thought, and the recognition of such rights is a relatively recent phenomenon in historical time. Today, moral philosophy is tolerated in more parts of the world than ever before in history, but there are still many places where it is not tolerated.

Since you are reading this book, I assume that you are a moral philosopher, in the sense in which I use the term—that is, you have developed and exercise your own moral judgment. Does this mean you are areligious? No, but it does imply that if you are religious, you are not blindly submissive to a moral authority. Consider an example. The highest moral authority in the Roman Catholic church is the pope. Nonetheless, polls consistently show that large majorities of Catholics in the United States (and in many other countries) disagree with the pope's position on contraception and on the ordination of women. This is powerful evidence that, in the sense in which I use the term, there are a lot of moral philosophers in the Roman Catholic church. Moral philosophers can be found in any religion.

Many people are moral philosophers without realizing it. For example, many people believe that their moral judgments come from moral authorities, without realizing that a large component of their moral judgment involves interpreting what the moral authorities have said in light of their own circumstances. So, for example, most Christians believe that God commanded, "Thou shalt not kill." Yet very few of them are pacifists. Of course, there are religious authorities such as the pope who claim to provide authoritative interpretations of such commands. At one time it was plausible to think that there is a division of moral labor. Religious authorities could announce moral imperatives or fix the interpretation of previously promulgated imperatives and others would simply follow orders. The history of moral development does not fit this pattern.

Time and again, moral development has occurred as the result of a bottom-up process by which the opinions of those who are regarded as moral authorities or those who are members of an elite group of decision makers are overturned by social movements that emerge from below. In this book I discuss a large number of examples of the bottom-up process of moral development involving rights norms. In chapter 2, I explain why this bottom-up social process should be understood as being bottom-up in a further, epistemic sense.

The bottom-up process of moral transformation is not limited to the recognition of individual rights. Consider, for example, the development since the 1970s of the animal welfare movement. This movement developed in the United States in spite of the fact that, at the outset, none of the major religions in the United States endorsed its goals. The movement has been successful, because it has been able to trust that ordinary people exercising their own moral judgment will object to the ways that some animals are treated, if only they are given accurate information about it. The movement is not based on a shared moral principle or moral theory. In fact, the movement's philosophical leader, Peter Singer (1975), bases his advocacy of animal welfare on a philosophical view (utilitarianism) that most people who are active in the movement or who are sympathetic to its goals would reject.[2]

I believe that most important moral developments are due, in large part, to this sort of bottom-up process of social transformation. Because this bottom-up process of moral transformation depends on there being enough people who exercise their own moral judgment, those are the people to whom I address this book.

This bottom-up process of moral transformation would have been even more influential in the past, had it not been for the fact that moral development typically occurs within religious traditions defined by moral authorities. As I have already mentioned, these religious traditions have typically responded to the exercise of independent moral judgment with persecution. Almost as important, when moral reformers have proposed a new moral norm or a new interpretation of an existing one, they themselves have often not understood what they were doing. In chapter 2, I discuss why the authors of the U.S. Declaration of Independence thought they had to claim that basic rights principles were "self-evident," when the only thing close to being self-evident was that they were not. In chapter 3, I discuss one of the most important moral reformers who ever lived, Bartolomé de Las Casas. The development of Las Casas's moral views illustrates how moral judgments about particular cases can lead to changes in one's moral principles, even those antecedently taken to be infallible. There is no evidence that Las Casas himself realized what was going on. Las Casas and the authors of the U.S. Declaration of Independence were moral philosophers, in my sense, but moral philosophers who lacked an adequate framework for understanding how it was possible to be a moral philosopher.[3]

Religious intolerance of independent moral judgment and misunderstanding of how moral philosophy is possible have both greatly retarded the bottom-up process of moral transformation. Even so, the effects of individuals exercising independent moral judgment are pervasive, nowhere greater than in the development of the theory of individual rights.

Universal Human Rights?

In this book I identify nine kinds of basic rights that should be universally guaranteed to all adult human beings who reach a minimum level of cognitive, emotional, and behavioral functioning. I do not wish to imply that minors or human beings with significant impairments or nonhuman animals should have no rights, only that their rights should be different. For example, it seems quite reasonable to think that all sentient beings should be protected against torture, but only beings who exceed a certain threshold of cognitive, emotional, and behavioral functioning should be guaranteed a right to vote.

To avoid the awkwardness of referring to them as *basic rights of adult human beings who surpass a minimum level of cognitive, emotional, and behavioral functioning*, I propose to refer to them as *basic human rights*. However, the term *human rights* is used in many different and conflicting senses in the literature. To avoid misunderstanding, it is important for me to identify the sense in which I use the term. I begin by distinguishing my use from two other established uses of it.

The Coercive Intervention Interpretation of Human Rights

This is the narrowest interpretation of human rights, because, on this interpretation, only those acts so shocking and abhorrent to justify coercive outside intervention qualify as violations of human rights. For example, the International Criminal Court has jurisdiction over war crimes, crimes against humanity, and genocide.

It is understandable why those involved in the prosecution of human rights violations would employ the coercive intervention interpretation of human rights. It is important to draw a line between rights violations that justify breaches of national sovereignty and those that do not. It is not necessary to hold that *only* the former qualify as violations of human rights. Instead, adapting an idea from Kymlicka (1966), we might distinguish between "bad" human rights violations, which do not justify breaches of national sovereignty, and the "intolerable" ones (Kymlicka's examples are slavery, genocide, torture, or mass expulsions), which can justify breaches of national sovereignty. Kymlicka thinks it is important to identify bad human rights violations, even if they are not intolerable, because, for example, there are many noncoercive responses that can be justified, even if coercive intervention is not justified.

The coercive intervention interpretation of human rights has its appropriate place, but it cannot claim to be the only or even the most important interpretation of human rights. It is particularly unsuited to my purposes, because, though I agree that coercive intervention can be an appropriate response to human rights violations, my main focus is on noncoercive responses.

The Overlapping Consensus Interpretation of Human Rights

C. Taylor (1996) suggests that at least some human rights norms could be universal, even if there were no agreement on their justification. Different religious and cultural traditions with different moral authorities might provide their own parochial justifications for similar human rights norms. In such a case, though their justifications would be parochial, the various religious and cultural traditions might agree on some "universal" human rights norms. On this interpretation, the rights that should be universal human rights are either those rights on which there already is an overlapping consensus or those for which there is a reasonable prospect of developing an overlapping consensus from among the moral authorities and moral principles currently guiding the existing cultural and religious traditions.[4]

For those who are attempting to draft and implement international human rights conventions, there is some reason to use the overlapping consensus model of human rights. There is usually no point in drafting conventions for rights that there is no prospect of signing or ratifying. However, it would be a mistake to limit the interpretation of human rights in this way. From a historical perspective, important rights typically develop in *opposition* to the moral views of the relevant cultural and religious authorities. Consider, for example, the right to religious tolerance. Before the seventeenth century, Christian, monarchical Western Europe had no tradition of religious tolerance. On the contrary, it had a tradition of the most virulent religious intolerance (Zagorin 2003). Western Europe sustained crusades against Islam for centuries. After the Protestant Reformation, Catholics and Protestants fought each other in seemingly interminable wars of religion. No matter which side won these wars, it was taken for granted that they would forcibly suppress all religious heterodoxy, so that not only would victorious Catholics forcibly suppress defeated Protestants and victorious Protestants suppress defeated Catholics, but also victorious Protestants would suppress other Protestant denominations. In 1553, Servetus was declared a heretic by both the Roman Catholic Inquisition and by John Calvin for his unorthodox theological writings. He was burned at the stake by Calvinists in Geneva. In the seventeenth century, Protestants persecuted Protestants in the Netherlands and in England. English Puritans fled to Massachusetts to escape persecution by Anglicans, not by Roman Catholics. When they arrived, they established a "Puritan theocracy" that permitted no dissent (Zagorin 2003, 198).

Somehow from this tradition of religious intolerance there emerged a right to religious tolerance. Imagine yourself as a seventeenth-century Christian Western European who has come to the conclusion that your government should enact guarantees of religious tolerance. You could not be under the illusion that your moral tradition endorsed such a right. Nor, in light of the fact that the First Commandment of the Decalogue, your central moral authority, is a commandment not to worship false gods, would it be easy to hold that your moral tradition was in some way committed to or even compatible with such a right. However, there is another alternative open to you. You could believe that your moral tradition should make the necessary *changes* to recognize such a right.

I think we can easily imagine how a seventeenth-century Western European could have come to the conclusion that governments should guarantee religious freedom, even though there was little or no basis for such a guarantee in the religious traditions of Western Europe. If it is true that these intolerant religious traditions should have changed to recognize a right to religious tolerance, then perhaps there are some rights that all traditions should respect, regardless of whether or not they currently endorse them and regardless of whether or not they are compatible with the currently accepted moral authorities and moral principles of those traditions. At the very least, I do not want to exclude such a possibility from the outset.

Donnelly identifies one of the most important functions of the concept of a human right as its role in providing a standpoint from which to criticize existing laws (2003, 12). I would only add that the concept of a human right also provides a standpoint from which to criticize existing human rights documents and whatever the existing overlapping consensus on human rights may be.[5] So when I ask whether a given right should be universal, that question must be understood in a way not limited by the overlapping consensus interpretation of human rights.[6]

The Minimal Legitimacy Interpretation of Human Rights

The most divisive issue in the interpretation of human rights is whether or not human rights should be understood to include the full complement of liberal rights, including democratic rights, freedom of religion, freedom of expression, freedom of assembly, and freedom of the press. Rawls (1999) uses the term *human rights* to designate the minimum rights necessary for a society (or people) to be a "decent" one.[7] Rawls believes that liberal societies have an obligation to tolerate "decent" nonliberal societies. For Rawls, toleration of nonliberal peoples by liberal peoples requires not only refraining from exercising military, economic, or diplomatic sanctions, but also refraining from offering economic incentives to them to change (1999, 59, 85). Thus, Rawls's interpretation is best understood as an extension of the coercive intervention interpretation to what might be called the "generalized intervention" interpretation. On this interpretation, human rights are the rights the violation of which can justify some sort of coercive or noncoercive response by liberal peoples.

Which rights are they? According to Rawls, they include "the right to life (to the means of subsistence and security); to liberty (to freedom from slavery, serfdom, and forced occupation, and to a sufficient measure of liberty of conscience to ensure freedom of religion and thought); to property (personal property); and to formal equality as expressed by the rule of natural justice (that is, that similar cases be treated similarly)" (1999, 65; footnotes omitted).[8] Rawls also places various other requirements on decent peoples, including the requirement that they include a decent consultation hierarchy, in which the interests of all of their members play a substantial role in political decisions (typically, through consultation with representatives of relevant groups) and in which political dissent is permitted (1999, 64, 72, 77).

I believe there is an important role for the minimal legitimacy interpretation of human rights. However, like Beitz (2001), I believe that Rawls has drawn the line between human rights (government respect for which is necessary for minimal legitimacy) and other rights in the wrong place. Why are the rights enumerated by Rawls the only ones necessary for minimal legitimacy? Rawls provides no principled reason for drawing the line where he does.

Beitz (2001) has argued for drawing the line so as to include a right to democratic institutions. I would add other rights, especially a right to education. How are we to adjudicate between these different lists of proposed human rights necessary for minimal legitimacy? In this book, I propose a principled answer to that question.

Principled Standards for Defining the Rights Necessary for Minimal Legitimacy

Here I briefly summarize the account developed in the rest of this book. In human history, the idea of rights develops as a response to the oppression of one group by another. It provides a framework for stating the objections of male property owners in Europe and America to governments in which they had no voice; a framework for Blacks in the United States to object to being enslaved and to object to the system of legally enforced segregation established after slavery was prohibited; a framework for native populations in the Americas and in Africa to object to European colonization; and a framework for women in patriarchal societies to object to their subjugation by men. In each case, the oppressors have attempted to justify their oppression paternalistically, by claiming that members of the oppressed group were not good judges of what was good for them and that the oppressors were really acting *for the good of those they oppressed.* The fundamental idea behind rights is that all adult human beings with normal cognitive, emotional, and behavioral capacities should be guaranteed what is necessary to be able to make their own judgments about what is good for them, to be able to give effect to those judgments in living their lives, and to be able to have an effective voice in the determination of the legal framework in which they live their lives.

Looked at in this way, rights are guarantees of what is necessary for individual autonomy. Rights to religious freedom protect individuals from coercion based on someone else's opinion about how best to secure salvation or avoid damnation. Rights to freedom of thought and expression guarantee that individuals won't be prevented from hearing ideas that others think it would be bad for them to hear. However, these rights, by themselves, are not enough to secure protection against objectionable paternalism. For example, if women are denied an education, it will be much easier for male leaders to convince them that the government knows what is good for them. That would not make the paternalism justifiable.

Isn't autonomy a Western idea? Isn't it morally imperialistic for Westerners to insist that autonomy rights should be universal? This book is an extended answer to those questions.

One of the innovations of my approach is that my case for autonomy rights does not depend on according intrinsic value to autonomy. I believe that the case for autonomy rights can be made entirely in terms of equitably promoting human well-being, without assuming that autonomy is a necessary component of human well-being.[9]

Rawls would object to enlarging the category of human rights to include autonomy rights, because he would object to the implication that only liberal societies can be decent. It is important to emphasize that my defense of autonomy rights does not imply that nonliberal individuals cannot be decent *people.* It is a claim about societies. When societies are so structured that government decisions affecting certain castes, classes, or other groups are made on the basis of paternalistic judgments about what is good for them, it is unlikely that the government's policies will adequately promote their good. No illiberal government can be relied upon to adequately promote the good of the groups it treats paternalistically.

I suspect that Rawls's criteria for a decent society are an attempt to mollify his communitarian critics (e.g., Sandel 1982). Communitarianism can be a useful addition to accounts of individual rights, if it reminds us that, in addition to the rights they have, members of a community also have responsibilities to each other. However, communitarians often champion culturally embedded social identities that are highly paternalistic. Because paternalism toward women is a near cultural universal in traditional societies, communitarians who champion culturally embedded social identities almost inevitably, implicitly if not explicitly, endorse lots of discrimination against women.

Rawls's criteria for a decent society seem to me to be an unstable compromise between communitarianism and liberalism. They include enough conditions (e.g., rights to freedom of religion and thought) to make them unacceptable to many communitarians, but not enough conditions to prevent extreme paternalistic restrictions on women and on other social groups. On Rawls's account, a decent society could exclude women from education and from all social roles outside the family. Rawls does require a decent society to have some way of taking account of women's interests in its laws (that is, a decent consultative hierarchy; 1999, 71–75). Any such process would be highly paternalistic if women lacked the education to be able to make their own independent judgment about those laws.

It is clear that Rawls intends to include societies that treat women paternalistically in his decent societies, because the one example he gives of a decent hierarchical people is an idealized Islamic people (75–78). Rawls makes the example more palatable by imagining that in his imaginary Islamic society "dissent has led to important reforms in the rights and role of women" (78). There are three obvious problems with Rawls's idealization: (1) none of his criteria for decency *requires* such reforms; (2) since nothing in his account of decency requires a right to education for women or a right to freedom of the press, there is little prospect that women themselves will ever even find out about the possibility of other reforms or regard themselves as competent to agitate for them; and thus, (3) even if we suppose some important reforms have been made, there might well be other important reforms that should be made but never will be.

Recall that, for Rawls, if an illiberal society is decent, it is wrong for liberal societies to take any action to promote change in the illiberal society, even if only by offering financial incentives. It is easy to imagine prudential reasons for a liberal society to not want to offend the leaders of an illiberal society by, for example, offering support to groups advocating rights for women. This would probably upset the leaders of the illiberal society and it might be in the interests of the liberal society not to upset them. However, this is a prudential, not a moral, consideration. I am at a loss to understand how, if the prudential considerations were not decisive, there could be an additional moral reason for not offering support to such groups. In chapter 5 I discuss the development of autonomy rights for women.

It might seem that the standard of decency I defend collapses the distinction between decency and justice.[10] This would be a mistake. Guaranteeing the nine basic rights I advocate in this book is not enough to make a society just. However, my nine basic rights do have an important relation to justice. As I explain in chapter 7, they are the rights necessary for a government to be relied upon to make itself more just over time. I do not believe these nine rights exhaust the rights that should be universal. However, they are the most basic rights because, once they are guaranteed, it is reasonable to expect that other rights will be enacted democratically. This is a second reason for regarding these nine rights as the basic human rights that define a decent, if not fully just, society.

There is a third reason for regarding them as basic human rights. Rawls himself acknowledges that there would be no way to justify illiberal societies if, as a matter of fact, illiberal regimes are almost always oppressive and violate the human rights on his list (1999, 79). How many illiberal societies protect women against violence perpetrated by their partners, or even acknowledge the responsibility to do so? How many adequately defend the rights to freedom of religion and freedom of thought? And even if they do respect those rights now, what kind of institutional guarantee is there that they will continue to do so in the future? In chapter 6 I explain why benevolent autocracies tend to be oppressive. In chapter 7 I explain the role of democratic rights in the protection of other rights.

For all of these reasons, I believe the standard of minimal legitimacy that all decent societies should satisfy includes guarantees of the nine basic rights I discuss in this book. These nine basic rights are not the only rights that should be universally respected. However, because of their special importance, it makes sense to think of them as basic human rights.

Going Beyond Defensive Arguments for Universal Rights

As I use the term, the very idea of moral philosophy was at one time a radical one: that there is no elite with special insight into moral truths; that everyone's opinion deserves serious consideration; and that moral progress is generally bottom-up, rather than top-down. Unfortunately, this idea has often been thought to entail some form of moral relativism. So one of the goals of this book is to explain why the allure of moral relativism is meretricious.

In "How to Argue for a Universal Claim," Jeremy Waldron (1999) identified three argumentative strategies for defending universal moral claims against moral relativists. The three strategies identified by Waldron are fine as far as they go, but they don't take us very far. Waldron's first strategy is to identify practices, such as torture, that horrify universally. His second strategy is to identify practices, such as foot binding and infibulation (the most severe form of female genital cutting), that, though approved by some cultures, are so shocking as to undermine relativist neutrality (Waldron 1999, 306). Even if successful, these two strategies would never produce arguments for more than a relatively small number of rights against a small number of horrific practices.

Waldron's third strategy addresses relativist responses to the first two strategies and undermines them. Because the third strategy is only a buttress for the first two, it does not provide support for any more rights than can be gotten out of the first two strategies.

Whether taken individually or in concert, it is striking how defensive these strategies are. Waldron, like many other philosophers, frames the advocacy of universal human rights as a kind of intellectual combat: the universalist versus the relativist. The universalist wins by putting together an argument so compelling that the relativist is forced to surrender.

As I discuss in chapter 2, it is a legacy of what I call the *Proof paradigm* in Western philosophy that philosophical discussions of human rights (and of so much else) are often framed in this way. Even to describe the project as "arguing" for a universal claim almost inevitably imports the combat framework.

Waldron's three strategies may be good ones for winning (or at least, not losing) a kind of rhetorical combat with a relativist. They are not promising strategies for understanding the distinctively human rights. Most of the distinctively human rights go beyond rights against such horrific practices as torture, foot binding, or infibulation. These are indeed horrific practices and it is true that people should be protected against them. However, a good case can be made that practices such as torture, foot binding, and infibulation are wrong if done to any sentient being.[11] Thus, rights against them do not even seem to qualify as distinctively *human* rights. If we want a better understanding of the distinctively human rights (e.g., the right to do moral philosophy), we will need a different kind of strategy.

In this book, though I address the relativist, my goal is not to show the relativist's position to be logically untenable nor to construct the most logically impregnable defense of universalism I can. Instead, my goal is to contribute to the long-term, cooperative project of trying to work out what it is reasonable to believe on these matters. In this project, there is a role for argument, but not argument understood as a form of combat where the goal is to compel the other side to surrender. In this project, I use arguments to explore the implications of various positions in order to better evaluate them. In the end, there is no substitute for having the capacity to make moral judgments, at least in relatively clear-cut cases, and for having the capacity to evaluate competing explanations of those judgments on the basis of which ones are more reasonable.

Epistemically Modest, Metaphysically Immodest Moral Philosophy

Anyone who claims that at least some moral truths are universal should be concerned about *moral imperialism*. There are two ways I could be a moral imperialist:

1. *Moral infallibilism.* I could say or imply that anyone who disagrees with me on moral matters must be mistaken. I avoid moral infallibilism by acknowledging my own fallibility. Human beings do not have direct, rational access to moral truths. We depend on other people to help us to acquire moral judgment, and we depend on interactions with others to expand our moral awareness and to help us to identify our moral blindspots. Moral philosophy is a fallible social enterprise.

2. *Moral paternalism.* Even if I don't claim to be infallible on moral questions, I may think I am morally justified in using force to impose my moral judgments on others for their own moral or nonmoral good, even if they disagree.[12] Suppose I force other people to practice my religion, because I am convinced it will save them from eternal damnation. Eternal damnation is a nonmoral bad and avoiding it is a nonmoral good. My use of force would be morally paternalistic. Or suppose I threaten to punish consensual sexual relations between homosexual adults solely on the grounds that such acts are morally bad for them (and morally bad for any other autonomous adults they might persuade to engage in them). My use of force would be morally paternalistic. In chapter 5, I explain how my advocacy of universal human rights avoids moral paternalism.

I will say that a moral philosophy is *epistemically modest* if it acknowledges its fallibility. I call the modesty *epistemic* because it is a reflection of the limitations on ourselves as knowers, not on the scope of what can be known.

Although my view is *epistemically* modest, there is a different sense in which it is immodest. It is immodest because it holds that there *are* universal moral truths—that is, moral truths that apply to everyone, even those who disagree with them. Moral relativists deny this. Moral relativists are *metaphysically modest*, because they place limits on the scope of moral truth. Because I do not limit the scope of moral truth in this way, my view is *metaphysically immodest*.

On the face of it, it is not at all clear that a metaphysically immodest moral philosophy can avoid moral imperialism. I believe that the desire to avoid moral imperialism is an important part of the appeal of moral relativism. The relativist who claims that all moral judgments are equally valid will never be accused of moral imperialism. The problem with moral relativism is that it goes too far in the other direction: It is too wishy-washy. As I explain in chapters 3 and 4, it is simply not true that all moral judgments are equally valid. If I were to rewrite Yeats's famous line that serves as the epigraph to this chapter to make it more precise, I would say: Often the best are morally wishy-washy, while the worst are morally imperialistic. One of the goals of this book is to show how an advocate of universal rights can avoid moral wishy-washiness, without being morally imperialistic.

Because I don't claim to have any special insight into moral truth, you might wonder how I could be qualified to write this book. There is now a sufficient history of human moral development that it is possible to review it and to theorize about it. I believe we have enough evidence about the process to enable us to project, at least in rough outline, where, if unimpeded, the process would go and to understand, again in rough outline, why it would go there.

In this book I focus on distinctively human rights—that is, rights that should be guaranteed to normal, human adults. When I say that some basic human rights should be universal, I mean they should be legally protected everywhere. The universality extends to all normal adult human beings, but it does not necessarily stop there. Basic rights should be guaranteed to normal adult human beings not because they are a member of the species *Homo sapiens*, but because they have certain capacities, especially what I refer to as the *capacity for judgment*. I illustrate this idea with a discussion of the development of women's rights in chapter 5. I discuss the capacity for judgment in more detail in chapter 6. If there are other beings anywhere in the universe who have the capacity for judgment, these basic human rights should be guaranteed to them also.

Consequentialism and Nonconsequentialism

Some advocates of universal human rights believe that the reason that human rights should be universally protected is that a society in which human rights are guaranteed will do a better job of promoting well-being (perhaps appropriately distributed well-being). They are *consequentialists*. *Nonconsequentialists* believe that the protection of human rights has moral importance independent of its contribution to human well-being—for example, that it is required in order to show the proper respect for autonomous moral agents. Most defenders of universal human rights are nonconsequentialists.

Because the issues between consequentialist and nonconsequentialist defenders of human rights are so deep and complex, I have decided to address them in a companion volume to this one (Talbott forthcoming). For the purposes of this book, I have tried to remain neutral between the two points of view. Each account helps to strengthen our understanding of the importance of human rights.

Even if the nonconsequentialist is correct that the case for human rights protections does not depend on their contribution to human well-being, if it is true that societies that protect basic human rights do a better job of promoting human well-being than societies that do not, that would be important information to have. It would undermine what is surely the most influential form of argument *against* human rights, arguments that people are generally better off in an autocracy that does not respect them. The *locus classicus* of this argument is Plato's *Republic*. It was updated by Thomas Hobbes in *Leviathan*. I respond to the Platonic defense in chapter 6 and the Hobbesian defense in chapter 7. In recent times, the most influential argument against human rights is due to Lee Kwan Yew and others who oppose universal human rights by appeal to "Asian values." I introduce the Asian values objection to universal human rights in chapter 3 and respond to it in chapter 8.

If these defenses of autocracy are mistaken, if there is good reason to believe that people are better off when basic human rights are protected, then the most influential arguments against making them universal would be discredited. This would be an important result for nonconsequentialists as well as for consequentialists.

In this book, I outline a consequentialist defense of basic human rights. One of the novelties of my consequentialist defense is this: Though I argue that basic human rights can be justified by their contribution to human well-being, I do not claim to be able to define "well-being." I believe that the historical process that leads to the discovery of basic human rights is a process of discovering what kind of life is a good life for human beings. We have learned a lot about human well-being, but there is much more to be learned. Societies that guarantee the basic human rights enable their citizens to conduct "experiments in living." Over time, these experiments lead to general improvements in well-being.

What is the ground of basic human rights? I believe it is the capacity for making reliable judgments about one's own good. All normal human beings have this capacity. Basic human rights provide the background conditions that enable them to develop and exercise it. Though the capacity for making reliable judgments about one's own good plays a central role in my conse-

quentialist defense of basic human rights, I do not believe that human beings only care about their own good or even that caring only about one's
own good is a good way to live one's life. In addition to the capacity for
making reliable judgments about one's own good, a related capacity plays
an important role in making rights-respecting democracies stable and in
enabling them to improve themselves over time. This is the ability to make
judgments of fairness from the moral standpoint and the willingness of most
people to incur small costs to promote fairness. I explain the moral standpoint in chapter 4 and explain how it makes rights-respecting democracies
stable and enables them to improve themselves over time in chapter 7.

In this book I have used broad strokes and a large canvas to paint a big
picture of the basic human rights that should be universal. I work out some
details and respond to various objections when doing so contributes to
seeing the big picture. Many more details and much more extensive consideration of potential objections will be found in the companion volume (Talbott forthcoming), where I broaden the focus to consider the various nonbasic rights that should also be universal.

If I am right that you are a moral philosopher, in the sense in which I
use the term, you will not read this book uncritically as an infallible source
of moral truth. Instead, you will exercise your own judgment to decide what
seems reasonable to you. Almost surely, you will disagree with some of
what I say. In many cases, you will think of considerations that did not
occur to me. So after you have read the book, why don't you send me your
thoughts? Because e-mail addresses often change, I cannot be sure what my
e-mail address will be when you have finished reading this book. If you use
a good Internet search engine, you should have no trouble finding a current
e-mail address for me, or you can write to me in care of the publisher.

2

THE PROOF PARADIGM
AND THE MORAL DISCOVERY
PARADIGM

> Democracy countered Communism by sponsoring what has been
> advanced as the axiomatic truths of free society, which includes
> freedom of the press and human rights. But are they universal
> values? Can you prove their universality?
>
> —Lee Kwan Yew, former prime minister of Singapore

Universal Human Rights
and Moral Imperialism

To say that some basic human rights should be universal is to make a
normative moral claim. It is different from the purely descriptive (and false)
claim that basic human rights are universally respected; and it is different
from the purely descriptive (and also false) claim that everyone agrees that
basic human rights should be universally respected. In making the normative moral claim that certain basic human rights should be universal, I am
not under the illusion that human beings always act on their moral beliefs.
However, I do believe that most people's choices are based in part on moral
considerations. Nonmoral factors also play a role. I refer to these nonmoral
factors as *pragmatic* factors.

There is no theoretically neutral way to distinguish moral from pragmatic factors. I believe almost everyone can easily distinguish them in clear
cases.[1] For example, when Christopher Columbus arrived in the New World,
he was eager to obtain as much gold as possible, so he established a capita-
tion tax on the natives to be paid in gold. Those who did not pay it were
punished by having their hands cut off and being left to bleed to death (Sale
1990, 155). Because many of the natives could not find enough gold to pay
the tax, many natives were killed. It is easy to understand how Columbus's
tax was pragmatically motivated by his desire for gold. From a moral standpoint, the tax is shocking. The Spanish colonists and their apologists did
attempt to provide moral rationalizations for this sort of treatment of the

natives. Their example reminds us that not only non-Westerners, but also Westerners have argued that basic human rights do not extend to non-Western peoples.

Many people are reluctant even to entertain the possibility of universal moral claims, because they feel it is morally objectionable for anyone to extend their own moral judgments to different cultures or moral traditions. To do so smacks of *moral imperialism.* There are many historical examples of moral imperialism. Here is an example that will be important later. In the sixteenth century, Spanish colonists in the Americas announced their arrival at a native village with the reading in Spanish of what was called the *Requirimiento.* This document required them to "recognize the Church and its Pope, as rulers of the universe, and, in their name the King and Queen of Spain as rulers of this land." It threatened that if they failed to comply, "we shall enslave your persons, wives and sons, sell you or dispose of you as the King sees fit; we shall seize your possessions and harm you as much as we can."[2] The sixteenth-century Dominican priest Bartolomé de Las Casas reports that when the natives failed to comply, the Spaniards established a regime of forced labor that eventually killed 90 percent of the native population.

I believe it was wrong for the Spanish colonists to simply assume that the American natives should be bound by Spanish religion and Spanish morality. If I believe that was wrong, how, in good conscience, can I advocate making basic human rights universal? If I insist that human rights norms apply to cultures that do not recognize them, doesn't that make me as much of a moral imperialist as the Spanish colonists chronicled by Las Casas? No, though it will take the rest of this book to explain why not.

In chapter 1, I identified two elements of moral imperialism: infallibilism and moral paternalism. The *Requirimiento* of the Spanish colonists exhibits both elements in an extreme form. The Spanish believed they had an infallible source of universal moral norms, and they were ready to use coercion to enforce them on the natives without any attention to the natives' own judgments about how they should live or what would be good for them.

So my diagnosis of what is morally objectionable about the moral imperialism of the Spanish colonists is their *epistemic immodesty,* that is, their infallibilism, and their *moral paternalism.* Why only their epistemic immodesty? Why not hold that both sorts of immodesty—metaphysical *and* epistemic—are morally objectionable? I answer this question in detail in chapters 3 and 4.

Recall that someone who is metaphysically modest denies that there are any universally true moral norms. However, my diagnosis of what is wrong with moral imperialism immediately suggests a universal moral norm—roughly, a norm that requires giving appropriate consideration to or having appropriate respect for other people's judgments about how they should be treated or about what is good for them. Indeed, my diagnosis of what is wrong with moral imperialism will lead me to articulate and defend a number of universal moral norms, including human rights norms, so it cannot be part of my diagnosis that it is a mistake to articulate and defend universal moral norms.

This explains why my diagnosis of the moral problem with moral imperialism cannot be relativistic. It does not imply that moral relativists cannot have their own, alternative diagnoses of what is wrong with moral imperialism. Thus, it may come as a surprise that they cannot. As I explain in the next chapter, no acceptable explanation of what is wrong with moral imperialism can avoid some nonrelative moral judgments. The reason is that although moral relativists are not themselves moral imperialists, moral relativism itself is incompatible with judging many paradigmatic cases of moral imperialism, including the moral imperialism of the Spanish colonists, to be wrong. This is not a refutation of moral relativism. However, as I explain in chapter 3, it does cut off one of the most attractive lines of argument for moral relativism.

Infallible Moral Authorities and the Proof Paradigm

The awareness of the need for epistemic modesty about moral claims is a relatively recent phenomenon. It has emerged in spite of the fact that almost all religious traditions, which are the source of most people's moral training, typically claim to serve as infallible authorities on moral principles. Although almost all religious traditions are infallibilistic, anyone familiar with the historical development of world religions cannot help but notice an evolutionary development in the moral principles endorsed by those religions, or at least an evolution in their interpretation. For example, the highest religious authorities in Judaism, Christianity, and Islam have all at one time endorsed slavery. There is now a consensus among Jews, Christians, and Muslims that slavery is wrong. So there has been a transformation from a consensus endorsing slavery to a consensus opposing it.[3]

This process of evolution of moral beliefs is undoubtedly a slow one, in part because the need to preserve belief in an infallible moral authority often leads to the religious persecution of moral reformers as heretics. Moreover, even when they are not subject to religious persecution as heretics, moral reformers have typically risked persecution by authoritarian governments that regarded them as threats to political stability. Still today, in many parts of the world, religious or political authorities threaten death to those who simply advocate rights for women or advocate the right to advocate rights for women. No wonder then, on a historical scale, moral development has been slow.

There is another reason that moral development in the West has been slow. In Western philosophy, for hundreds if not thousands of years, a great shadow has been cast over moral philosophy by what I refer to as the *Proof paradigm*. The Proof paradigm is a model of reasons for belief. As a model of reasons for belief, it has had disastrous effects in every area of philosophy, none worse than in moral philosophy. In moral philosophy, the Proof paradigm has led generations of philosophers to conclude that there can be no good reasons for believing a moral statement to be true. Within the Proof paradigm, it is difficult to see how to combine universality with epistemic modesty. How to do so is a puzzle I wrestle with in the remainder of this chapter and in the next two chapters. To solve it, I must disavow the Proof paradigm and adopt an alternative model of reasons for belief. Fortunately, there is an alternative available, an *equilibrium model*, which I trace back to J. S. Mill. In more recent times, it has been articulated in an individualistic form by John Rawls and later given a nonindividualistic interpretation by Jürgen Habermas. I outline my own variation on the Mill-Rawls-Habermas model later in this chapter.

Moral Justification and Epistemic Justification

The main goal of normative moral theory is to articulate the principles that explain why particular actual or hypothetical social arrangements, practices, or actions are justified or not justified. The kind of justification involved is *moral* justification. For example, to ask about the justification of the Hindu caste system or a system of hereditary slavery is to ask whether the system is morally wrong or not.

One distinctively human characteristic is that human beings tend to try to show that their actions are morally justified. To successfully show that an act, system, practice, or social arrangement is morally justified, it is not sufficient merely to *claim* that it is not wrong, nor is it sufficient merely to *believe* that it is not wrong. One must be *justified* in believing that it is not wrong, where the relevant notion of justification is not *moral* justification, but the kind of justification that is appropriate for beliefs: *epistemic* justification. So, for example, for a slaveowner to be *morally* justified in the action of treating his slaves as his property, the slaveowner must be *epistemically* justified in believing that treating his slaves as his property is not wrong.[4]

What is epistemic justification and how does one acquire it? Until recently, the Proof paradigm provided the theoretical framework for answering that question in Western philosophy.

The Proof Paradigm

When the authors of the U.S. Declaration of Independence wrote the words: "We hold these truths to be self-evident . . . ," they were under the influence of the Proof paradigm for epistemic justification. The Proof paradigm takes the model of proof in mathematics as the paradigm for all epistemically justified beliefs. Taking mathematical knowledge to be rationally unquestionable, the Proof paradigm requires that all epistemically justified beliefs be rationally unquestionable. Interpreting mathematical proofs as starting from premises that can be directly seen to be rationally unquestionable (e.g., self-evident premises) and proceeding by rules of inference that can be directly seen to be deductively valid, the Proof paradigm requires that all epistemically justified beliefs fit this model.

The Proof paradigm has been an almost unmitigated disaster in Western moral philosophy, because it holds that a moral principle cannot be epistemically justified unless it is directly, rationally unquestionable or provable from directly, rationally unquestionable premises. Because they were operating within the Proof paradigm, the authors of the Declaration of Independence had only three alternatives: (1) assert that the claim of universal human rights is directly epistemically justified—that is, that it is self-evident; (2) assert that the claim of universal human rights is indirectly epistemically justified, by proving it from self-evident premises; or (3) don't assert that the claim of universal human rights is epistemically justified.

To adopt alternative 3 would have been to treat the claim of universal human rights as a mere bias or prejudice. For obvious reasons, the authors of the Declaration of Independence did not favor this alternative. I agree with them that it is a mistake to think of it as mere bias or prejudice.

To adopt alternative 2 would have required that they actually come up with a proof of the claim of universal human rights from other premises that were self-evident. What could those other premises have been? I conjecture that the authors of the Declaration of Independence would not have been able to agree on any other premises from which the claim of universal rights could be derived. If they could not themselves agree on any other premises from which it could be derived, they could hardly claim that any such premises were rationally self-evident. Therefore, because they were operating within the Proof paradigm, the only way they could hold that the claim of universal human rights was epistemically justified was to adopt alternative 1—that is, to hold that the claim itself was rationally self-evident and therefore not in need of proof. And that is what they did.

The short-term effect of this choice was to rally the American colonists around the claim of universal human rights. The longer-term effect was to make the job for philosophical defenders of human rights much harder and to make the job for opponents of human rights much easier. Today it seems simply incredible that anyone could hold that the claim of universal human rights is self-evident. At the time the Declaration of Independence was written, a greater number of educated people in Europe would have held that the claim was self-evidently *false* than that it was self-evidently *true*, because to most educated people in Europe the evident differences among people seemed to justify their having very different rights. What is worse, today, more than 200 years later, there can be no doubt that the authors' moral claims were not self-evident, because they interpreted those claims in such a way as to permit racial slavery and in such a way as to permit granting women different rights from men. Most reasonable people today would not agree with the authors' interpretation of their own claims. If the claims were self-evident, there would not be so many reasonable people who disagree with them.

It is difficult to overestimate the damage that the Proof paradigm has done in Western philosophy. Under the influence of an early version of the Proof paradigm, Plato came to the conclusion that absolute rule by a philosopher-autocrat was the best form of government for human beings, because, just as a mathematician without any experience of physical triangles can know the Pythagorean theorem is true by proving it, a philosopher-autocrat would be able to know what was best for his subjects without having to have any experience with government and certainly without having to consult any of them about what they thought would be good for them. On Plato's view, the philosopher-autocrat would know purely on the basis of reasoning, and better than the citizens themselves, what was good for them.

It was under the influence of the Proof paradigm that David Hume issued his famous challenge to moral philosophy, usually abbreviated by saying that you cannot derive an "ought" from an "is" (Hume [1734], 469). Under the influence of the Proof paradigm, Hume ultimately came to the conclusion that our moral principles were an expression of our own feelings; Jean-Paul Sartre (1956) came to the conclusion that moral principles are simply choices or personal commitments one makes without reasons; John Mackie (1977) concluded that they were simply a communal invention.[5]

Although it is possible to accept the Proof paradigm for epistemic justification and also hold that one's moral beliefs are epistemically justified, I believe it is no accident that the Proof paradigm often leads to moral skepticism (and to skepticism about so much else). To understand the epistemic justification of moral principles, we need an alternative model of epistemic justification. Fortunately, there is an alternative, an equilibrium model of epistemic justification, which I trace through Habermas and Rawls back to J. S. Mill. In the remainder of this chapter, I outline the version of the equilibrium model of epistemic justification that I favor. The model is worked out more fully in subsequent chapters.

Attempts to justify moral principles by appeals to religious authority and by the Proof paradigm have one feature in common. Both require, or at least invite us to believe, that our epistemically justified moral beliefs must be infallible.[6] Thus, both accounts are undermined by the overwhelming evidence that human moral beliefs are not infallible. In addition, as I illustrate in chapter 4, particular examples, actual or hypothetical, can lead us to give up or modify a previously accepted moral principle. We need an explanation of how our epistemically justified beliefs in moral principles can be fallible and of how judgments about particular cases can make it reasonable to give them up or modify them.

It should be said in the defense of the Proof paradigm that at least some justificatory arguments have the deductive logical structure of a proof. Consider, for example, a potential justificatory argument I might give for the conclusion that it is wrong for you to shoot me (see example 2–1).

PREMISES: MN1. It is always wrong to kill another person.
                P2. I am a person, and not the same person as you.
CONCLUSION: PMJ1. It is wrong for you to kill me now.

Example 2–1. A Potential Justificatory Argument with Two Premises (P), Including a Moral Norm (MN), the Conclusion of Which Is a Particular Moral Judgment (PMJ).

Because of its deductively valid structure, the argument in example 2–1 sure looks like an attempt at a proof. If it is not an attempt to prove its conclusion, what is it trying to do? To answer this question, I must say something more about the Proof paradigm.

On the Proof paradigm, deductive arguments such as the argument in example 2–1 always transmit epistemic justification in one direction only, from premises that include moral principles or norms (e.g., MN1) to particular moral judgments (e.g., PMJ1). *Particular moral judgments* are judgments that a particular actual or hypothetical act, practice, or social arrangement is morally wrong, morally permitted (not morally wrong), or morally required (anything else would be wrong). *Moral principles* or *norms* are generalizations about what sorts of acts, practices, or social arrangements are morally wrong, morally permitted (i.e., not morally wrong), or morally required. Because, on the Proof paradigm, epistemic justification is transmitted in one direction: from the premises to the conclusion. I refer to this as a *top-down* model of moral reasoning.

On the Proof paradigm, a justificatory argument such as the one in example 2–1 can only epistemically justify its conclusion if the premises are justified. What sort of epistemic justification could the moral norm MN1 have? On the Proof paradigm, either its justification must be immediate (e.g., it must be self-evident) or it must be derivable from some more basic beliefs that are self-evident. This is a quite restrictive picture of how moral norms could be epistemically justified. To see how restrictive it is, consider an alternative picture of epistemic justification, which I refer to as the *inductivist model*.[7]

The Inductivist Model of Epistemic Justification

On the inductivist model of epistemic justification, particular moral judgments have immediate epistemic justification, and other moral beliefs, including moral norms, acquire their epistemic justification by their role in *explaining* particular moral judgments. Because the standard model of explanation is one in which the explainers deductively imply the evidence to be explained, on the inductivist model, deductive arguments such as those in example 2–1 have the potential to epistemically justify one or more of their premises, when the premises explain epistemically justified particular moral judgments (and explain them better than any of the alternatives).[8] The direction of moral reasoning is bottom-up, from immediately epistemically justified particular moral judgments to moral principles or norms and other beliefs that play a role in explaining the particular moral judgments. Thus, on the inductivist model, the conviction that it would be wrong for you to kill me would be the source of epistemic justification, which would flow to the moral norm MN1 that explained it.

This bottom-up model of moral reasoning has much to be said for it. For one thing, it can explain not only how particular moral judgments can help to support moral principles and norms, but also how they can undermine them. Suppose we ask whether it would be wrong for you to kill me if I were trying to kill you and there were no other way for you to prevent me from killing you. It is easy to see that MN1 from example 2–1 implies that killing me would be wrong even in this case (see example 2–2).

PREMISES: MN1. It is always wrong to kill another person.

P2. I am a person, and not the same person as you.

P3. I am trying to kill you.

P4. There is no way for you to prevent me from killing you except to kill me.

CONCLUSION: PMJ2. It is wrong for you to kill me now (even though I am trying to kill you and there is no way for you to prevent me from killing you except to kill me).

Example 2–2. How a Particular Moral Judgment Can Undermine a Moral Norm.

Most people would not accept the conclusion of the example 2–2 argument. Let PMJ2′ be the particular moral judgment that it is *not* wrong for you to kill me in the hypothetical circumstances of the example. If, on reflection you accept PMJ2′ (e.g., you believe that killing in self-defense can be justified when it is necessary to save one's own life), then on the inductivist model, you have good reason to give up MN1.

On the Proof paradigm, the possibility of making a mistake in one's moral principles or norms is a threat to the possibility of moral inquiry. It should not be. It is not easy to formulate exceptionless moral principles or norms. The inductivist model helps to explain why. Even if a moral norm or moral principle is epistemically justified by its role in explaining the actual and hypothetical particular moral judgments that have been made so far, there will always be other future actual cases and other hypothetical cases that have not yet been imagined. It is always possible that reflection on those cases would lead to particular moral judgments that are incompatible with the accepted norms and principles. So on the inductivist model, fallibility of accepted moral norms and principles is to be expected.

Another advantage of the inductivist model is that it undermines the presumption that moral principles should be self-evident. In science, the attempt to find theories that adequately explain the experimental evidence has led to the formulation of principles (e.g., $E = mc^2$) that are far from obvious. The same should be expected in moral inquiry.

What should we do if we accept PMJ2′ and reject PMJ2, the conclusion of the example 2–2 argument? On the inductivist model, we need to find other moral principles or norms that will explain both PMJ1 and PMJ2′. So we must ask ourselves: Why is it usually wrong to kill other people, but not in cases of self-defense? Consider the principle that everyone has a right to life (i.e., a right not to be killed). This principle is sometimes interpreted as though it is just another way of asserting MN1, that it is always wrong to kill another person. Interpreting human rights principles in this way makes them just fancy ways of saying something that could be said without talking about rights at all. This seems to me to be a mistake. The claim that everyone has a *right* to life does not imply that killing another human being is *always* wrong. It is an attempt to articulate a more complicated idea. To a first approximation, the idea is this: It is wrong to kill another person, unless that other person is failing or has failed to respect another person's right to life.

This example illustrates in brief how the attempt to explain particular moral judgments could lead us to the discovery of human rights principles by bottom-up reasoning. The initial idea that killing another human being is always wrong must be given up in light of justifiable examples of self-defense. Then the idea of a right to life is introduced to explain why killing another person is usually, but not always, wrong. This is the sort of process that led to the discovery of human rights principles.

If this is correct, then we should not expect human rights principles to be simple (e.g., not as simple as the norm MN1, that killing another person is always wrong), and we should not expect them to be self-evident. On the contrary, it is difficult to discover them.

Though I believe that the bottom-up structure of the inductivist model is an improvement over the top-down structure of the Proof paradigm, neither by itself is adequate. One reason for thinking that the inductivist model is not an adequate model is that, at least in its most extreme form, it would imply that our epistemically justified particular moral judgments are infallible.[9] While it is more plausible to think that some particular moral judgments are infallible (e.g., that certain gruesome tortures of young children merely for the fun of it would be wrong) than it is to think that any of our substantive moral principles or norms is infallible, I believe it would be a mistake to hold that any moral judgments of any kind are infallible.[10]

How can particular moral judgments provide a basis for justifying moral norms and moral principles, if they are not infallible? Consider the analogy to science, where theories are justified by their role in explaining experimental observations. The experimental observations are not regarded as infallible and do not have to be infallible in order to provide epistemic justification for accepting a theory that explains them. They only have to be reasonably reliable. I think that the same is true of particular moral judgments, which, so long as the analogy is not taken too strictly, can be thought of as a kind of *moral observation*. The justification of our moral norms and even our most fundamental moral principles depends on their role in explaining our fallible but reasonably reliable moral observations (i.e., our particular moral judgments).

The Equilibrium Model
of Epistemic Justification

On the Proof paradigm, moral reasoning is always top-down; on the inductivist model, moral reasoning is always bottom-up. The main reason I am dissatisfied with both of them is that moral reasoning seems to go in both directions, bottom-up and top-down. I have already illustrated bottom-up reasoning. An example of top-down moral reasoning is the following: Some people have a visceral reaction to homosexuality. Their particular moral judgments condemning homosexual activity seem unshakable. Nonetheless, over time it is possible for them to come to accept principles that lead them to reconsider their particular moral judgments condemning homosexual activity. In this case, the principles lead them to give up what at one time seemed to be unshakable particular moral judgments. I discuss this example further in chapter 6.

A model that combines top-down and bottom-up reasoning and holds that no moral beliefs of any kind are infallible is an *equilibrium model*. I illustrate the equilibrium model with a more fully developed example in chapter 4.

I trace the equilibrium model for epistemic justification to Mill, although the term *equilibrium* comes from Rawls.[11] Thus far, my description of the equilibrium model has been individualistic in the way that Rawls's own model is: For Rawls, the equilibrium model is an intrasubjective one, in that it involves the beliefs of a single individual.[12]

Habermas has proposed a variation on the equilibrium model that he refers to as "discourse ethics," in which the equilibrium is irreducibly intersubjective or social. It is an equilibrium reached by an ideal process of "inclusive and noncoercive rational discourse among free and equal participants, [where] everyone is required to take the perspective of everyone else, and thus project herself into the understandings of self and world of all others" (Habermas 1995, 117). It is not necessary to choose between the individualistic Rawlsian model and the social model of Habermas, if the individualistic model is understood to require that one's epistemically justified beliefs about other people's beliefs play a crucial role in the epistemic justification of one's own moral beliefs.[13] It is important to acknowledge the role that the past history of moral discourse and the free and open ongoing discussion of moral issues should play in the equilibrium model. This dependency of epistemic justification of moral beliefs on the history of moral discourse and on the free and open ongoing discussion of moral issues was first emphasized by Mill ([1859], chap. 2).

How *does* the equilibrium model apply to the moral skeptic—that is, to someone who rejects all moral beliefs, both particular moral judgments and moral principles? For a moral skeptic, the bottom-up epistemic justification of moral principles could not even get off the ground, because the moral skeptic never accepts any particular moral judgments of rightness or wrongness. From within the Proof paradigm, moral skepticism has often seemed to be the default rational position, to be dislodged only by some sort of *proof* that one should be moral. This seems to me to completely misunderstand the nature of rational belief in ethics and in other areas. On the equilibrium model, the goal is to have one's beliefs make the most sense, all things considered. On this standard, moral skepticism is not the default position. It must be justified as making more sense than any of the alternatives. I myself do not see how it could make more sense to believe that nothing (e.g., not even typical cases of genocide or torturing children) is morally wrong than to believe that at least some things are morally wrong.[14] However, if people truly believe that nothing is morally wrong, I would not expect my arguments in this book—or any other arguments, for that matter—to change their minds.

Metaphysical Immodesty (Strong Universality)

Immanuel Kant thought that the fundamental moral norms or principles had the strongest kind of universality—that they applied to all morally responsible beings in all possible worlds. Strong universality is a breathtaking claim. It insists that there are concepts of moral rightness and wrongness and of moral responsibility that apply to every culture and in every possible world (though beliefs involving them may vary considerably) and that the fundamental principles of moral rightness and wrongness employing those concepts apply to all morally responsible beings in all possible worlds. Another way of formulating this claim of strong universality for fundamental moral principles is to say that the fundamental moral principles are *metaphysically necessary*. I refer to this claim of strong universality as *metaphysical immodesty* about the fundamental moral principles. Although I have disavowed the Proof paradigm upon which Kant relied to support his metaphysical immodesty, I agree with him that fundamental moral principles are strongly universal.

Let me clarify what I am claiming. I do not claim that *all* moral norms are strongly universal. For example, there is no one universally correct system of norms governing care for the elderly. What I claim to be strongly universal are the fundamental principles that ultimately *explain* why there are various equally good systems of norms governing care for the elderly. In this book I argue that, in combination with what we are now justified in believing about human beings and human societies, those fundamental principles require that certain human rights be universally respected.

It would not be surprising that an advocate of the Proof paradigm would hold that the fundamental moral principles are strongly universal, because an advocate of the Proof paradigm believes we have the ability to directly access metaphysically necessary truths (e.g., those that are self-evident). It is more surprising that an advocate of an equilibrium model would hold that we can be justified in believing moral principles to be strongly universal. Thus, for example, Rawls became so averse to drawing any metaphysical consequences from his account that he gave up any claim to truth and referred to his principles of political liberalism instead as "reasonable," which for Rawls is only to claim that they are "implicit in the public culture of a democratic society" (Rawls 1993, 15).[15] The metaphysical modesty of Rawls's "political" liberalism is extreme. Nothing in his account rules out the possibility that the most extremely intolerant normative moral and political views could be true.

Habermas is less metaphysically modest than Rawls because he is not satisfied with the idea of articulating an implicit consensus in modern democracies or in any other particular form of life. He insists that "anyone who seriously engages in argumentation must presuppose that the context of discussion guarantees in principle freedom of access, equal rights to participate, truthfulness on the part of participants, absence of coercion in adopting positions, and so on" (Habermas 1993, 31). These presuppositions implicitly commit all participants to a universal concept of validity (roughly, the concept of what is supported by the weight of reasons) that is "context-transcending" (Habermas 1996, 323).[16] He insists that although all communicative interaction takes place within a historical and cultural context (in his term, a *lifeworld*), in communication oriented toward reaching understanding (rather than toward exercising coercion, for example), "arguments by their very nature point beyond particular individual lifeworlds; in their pragmatic presuppositions, the normative content of presuppositions of communicative action is generalized, abstracted, and enlarged, and extended to an ideal communication community encompassing all subjects capable of speech and action" (Habermas 1993, 50). And the moral point of view "requires that maxims and contested interests be generalized, which compels the participants to *transcend* the social and historical context of their particular form of life and particular community and adopt the perspective of *all* those possibly affected" (24; emphases in original).

There are two ways of interpreting the universality in Habermas's reference to "all subjects." The universality would be *weak* if Habermas were understood to be referring to subjects who are members of the species *Homo sapiens* and to other subjects who happened to participate in forms of life (or lifeworlds) recognizably like those of the members of the species *Homo sapiens*. The universality would be *strong* if Habermas were understood to be referring to all beings capable of offering and considering reasons, where human beings were just one example of the variety of possible beings with that capacity. It is not clear to me which sort of universality Habermas claims for normative validity. McCarthy has interpreted him as committed to only weak universality, in part on the grounds that the philosophical reconstruction of norms of validity is part of the explanation of *human* communicative interaction.[17] Because *Homo sapiens* is the only species we know of that has developed forms of life that include offering and considering reasons, the fact that our evidence is limited to *Homo sapiens* does not settle the interpretive question. It is still possible to interpret "all subjects capable of speech and action" in the strongly universal way.

I don't know how Habermas himself would come down on this issue. I can tell you where I stand. I believe that the fundamental norms of rationality and of morality are *strongly universal*—in that they apply to all possible beings with the requisite capacities in all possible worlds. This makes my position *metaphysically immodest*. But this raises a puzzle: How could an equilibrium model of epistemic justification for moral beliefs, according to which the epistemic justification for fundamental moral principles is primarily bottom-up, provide any basis for making metaphysically immodest, strongly universal, moral judgments?

On such a model, moral principles are epistemically justified primarily by their role in explaining epistemically justified particular moral judgments. Those particular moral judgments include judgments about actual and hypothetical cases. For example, it is easy to find actual and hypothetical examples involving torture of the innocent that would strike most people as clearly wrong.[18] What is central to my position is that when we make those clear-cut judgments of wrongness, typically we are not merely judging something to be wrong from our own personal or cultural or species point of view. We are judging that those particular acts are wrong from the point of view of *any* morally responsible being, actual or hypothetical. I express this by saying that particular moral judgments are, at least implicitly, *strongly universal*. This is not to say that everyone would agree with us or that we ourselves are infallible in judging them to be wrong. However, anyone who denied they were wrong would have to sustain the burden of explaining why acts that seem so clearly to be wrong are not.

It is surprising to think that the members of the biological species *Homo sapiens* could, on the basis of our native capacities and culturally specific moral training, acquire an ability to make reliable, though not infallible, particular moral judgments that are, when true, universal in the sense that they are true from any possible point of view.[19] I discuss how we are able to do so in chapter 4, where I also discuss some of the factors that make those judgments more or less reliable.

The Historical-Social Process of Moral Discovery

On the assumptions that we are able to make strongly universal particular moral judgments and that, over time, those judgments become reasonably reliable, though not infallible, it is possible to see how we can aspire to articulate strongly universal fundamental moral principles. In the most favorable case, if we could identify moral principles that explained all true actual and hypothetical particular moral judgments, those principles would be strongly universal, in the sense that they would cover all possible situations and apply to all possible moral points of view. If we had ideal imaginations that enabled us to imagine all relevant possibilities, it would be easy to see how we could have bottom-up justification for believing moral principles to be strongly universal, because they could be tested by thought experiments involving all of the relevant possibilities.

Given the limited imaginations of human beings, claims to strong universality for fundamental moral principles should be made with considerable caution. Given what we know about the limitations of human imagination, it would be foolhardy, for example, for a single individual to claim to be epistemically justified in believing a moral principle to be strongly universal on the basis of the relatively few actual situations a single individual would confront in a single life or on the basis of the cases that a single individual could imagine. The only way to obtain a nonnegligible degree of epistemic justification for the strong universality of a moral principle would be to test one's moral principles against something approaching the full variety of actual social practices that exist or have existed and against something approaching the full variety of hypothetical examples that have been imagined by others. This makes the justification of strongly universal moral principles a social rather than an individualistic project, for we depend on others for information about the various social practices that exist and have existed, and even more, we depend on others to imagine possibilities that, by ourselves, we never would have imagined.

Anyone who claims there are strongly universal fundamental moral principles ought to be challenged to identify at least one. Here I have to acknowledge my epistemic limitations and admit I am unable to do so. As I see it, for thousands of years human beings have been attempting to articulate such principles. In that time, a great deal of progress had been made—

for example, almost every major religious tradition has endorsed some version of what is called the Golden Rule (Wattles 1996). And the versions of the Golden Rule have themselves undergone changes in interpretation to improve them.[20] This process has been greatly retarded by the fact that in most of the world during most of those thousands of years, even to raise a question about the adequacy of the moral principles of one's culture has been regarded as a capital offense.

The utilitarian movement in philosophy can be seen as a natural way of making more precise one of the main ideas underlying the various versions of the Golden Rule. The fundamental utilitarian idea is that we should maximize overall well-being. This seems to me to be an important advance in moral understanding, even though all versions of utilitarianism seem to me to be inadequate, for reasons that have been widely discussed.[21]

The failure of the utilitarian idea to provide the fundamental principle of morality should discourage an advocate of the Proof paradigm, because never again in moral or political philosophy will there ever be such a simple and elegant principle as "Maximize overall well-being." This principle is so simple and elegant, one could almost think it was self-evident. To an advocate of the equilibrium model, like me, utilitarianism provides not an example of a self-evident principle, but rather an example of how a fundamental explanatory principle could be strongly universal, in the sense that it would apply to all morally responsible beings in all possible worlds. What is striking about the utilitarian idea is that it does not have any built-in relativity to culture, biology, or ideology. Maximizing overall well-being requires that the well-being of all be given equal consideration, no matter what their cultural background or biological make-up. Thus, utilitarianism provides a model of what a strongly universal fundamental moral principle might be like.

As I see it, we are part of an ongoing historical-social process of moral discovery of universal moral principles. The process involves equilibrium reasoning that is largely bottom-up, because it typically moves from judgments about particular actual and hypothetical cases to attempts to formulate moral principles that explain them. Furthermore, the process is often bottom-up in a social sense, because moral progress is often the result of social movements from below whose response to particular practices (e.g., slavery) leads them to challenge the judgments of the reigning moral authorities. It is not necessary to discover exceptionless, universal moral truths to make progress in this process of moral discovery. The discovery that a moral principle has previously unknown exceptions is itself progress.

If no one were ever able to formulate any plausible universal moral principles, then perhaps it would be necessary to limit our notion of moral progress to improvements in our particular moral judgments. This is not what we find. Only by the most stringent standards of success can the development of the most general version of the Golden Rule or the development of utilitarianism be judged a failure. If these developments are understood as making progress in getting closer to the fundamental principles of morality, they can and should be seen as important successes.[22]

I need a name for this picture of moral development. I will call it the *Historical-Social Process of Moral Discovery paradigm* or, more briefly, the Moral Discovery paradigm. The term *discovery* is a reminder that I am committed to there being universal moral truths; the term *process* is a reminder that exceptionless universal moral principles are not easy to find. Our best hope is to continue to make progress in discovering them.

Even if we are not in a position to articulate the fundamental principles of morality, I believe that, building on past successes, we can discern enough of their shape to understand why, in combination with what we know about human beings and human societies, they will require that certain basic human rights be universally respected. That is the project I undertake in this book.

Rewriting the Declaration of Independence to Accommodate Moral Discovery

I hope it does not sound as though I am critical of the authors of the Declaration of Independence for their implicit commitment to the Proof paradigm. At the time they wrote, there was no alternative available. It is worthwhile for us to consider how, with the benefit of developments in the past 225 years, we might update what they wrote. Here is what I would propose:

> Although for most of human history it has seemed to most people to be almost self-evident that human beings have very different capacities that justify their being treated in very different ways, we have discovered through a long process of trial and error in human social practices that all normally functioning adult human beings ought to be treated in such a way that respects certain basic and inalienable human rights. Any attempt to list these rights should be understood to be fallible and subject to correction in the future, and the interpretation given to the items on the list should also be understood to be fallible and subject to correction in the future. Our best hope is that, over time, we will gradually make progress in defining the basic human rights that should be guaranteed to all normally functioning adult human beings. Right now, the best we can do is to offer the following list: . . .

I have to admit that the original is much more inspiring. What is most remarkable to me about the founding documents of the United States is that by 1789, with the proposal to add the Bill of Rights to the U.S. Constitution, even without an explicit alternative to the Proof paradigm, the founders had implicitly moved toward a new epistemically modest model of justification for human rights claims.

In order to understand the significance of the change from the Declaration of Independence to the Constitution with the Bill of Rights, it is useful to state the problem that had to be solved. If human rights principles had been self-evident, the Declaration of Independence would not have been such a revolutionary document. It is because human beings don't have direct rational insight into fundamental moral principles that their discovery was literally revolutionary.

Self-Improving Self-Regulating Systems

The American Revolution represents the discovery of a design for a government based on the recognition that we have no direct rational insight into self-evident principles of justification. When we investigate the moral justification of government action, the primary considerations are considerations of justice. Described abstractly, the main design problem of politics is to design a system of government that will be appropriately sensitive to the factors that determine the justice or injustice of its actions, so that it will tend to act in ways that are just and not to act in ways that are unjust. This design problem has two parts: (1) how to design a system that receives *reliable feedback* about the factors that determine whether or not the system itself is acting justly; and (2) how to design a system that is *appropriately responsive* to the feedback it receives. Call these the *reliable feedback problem* and the *appropriate responsiveness problem*. A solution to these two problems would be a *self-regulating system* that functioned to make itself more just over time.

A simple example of a self-regulating system is the cruise control available on most cars. Once the driver sets the speed and engages the cruise control, the cruise control will use feedback from the speedometer to control the engine throttle to maintain the desired speed as the external conditions change (e.g., as the car goes up or down a hill). Like the cruise control system, human rights are the main elements of a servomechanism that keeps governments at least roughly aimed at justice. This is not self-evidently true. It is an important moral discovery.

Because of their relative inexperience in designing a government, the founders had to realize that their design of a self-regulating system would be less than ideal. Thus, they had to design a system that would also be able to improve itself over time, that is, a *self-improving self-regulating system.*

For the founders of the United States, this design problem was a particularly daunting one, because they had to design a system of government that would be appropriately sensitive to the factors that determine whether or not the system itself is acting justly and that would improve its sensitivity to them *without knowing exactly what those factors were.* Lacking direct rational insight into the principles of justice, they had to design a system with only the limited understanding of those factors that had been developed at the time they were writing.

If they had had direct rational insight into moral truth, the founders could have simply used their insight to determine the characteristics of a morally ideal state and then they could have implemented the morally ideal state in the U.S. Constitution. In that case, there would have been no need for the Constitution to contain any provisions for amending it, because it would not make sense to change a document that was already morally ideal.

In fact, the original U.S. Constitution was far from morally ideal. Its provisions for maintaining the institution of slavery are moral embarrassments. What is most remarkable about it is that it provides the framework for the system to become more just over time—indeed, it even provides the framework for the system to improve the processes by which it becomes more just. It is a constitution that regards no agent or branch of government as infallible. *Nothing,* not even the Constitution itself, is immune to revision. The procedures for amending the Constitution even apply to themselves.[23] Thus, perhaps without being aware of it, the authors of the Constitution came up with a design for a government of fallible human beings who do not have direct rational insight into self-evident moral principles.

The moral problem the founders were attempting to solve was not a parochial one—for example, a problem that only arose in the West. They were addressing a moral problem that is culturally universal: government abuse of its coercive powers. They began the development of an alternative form of government that would function as a self-improving self-regulating system. The basic human rights are the rights necessary for a government to so function. There are other rights, not on the list of basic rights, that also should be universal—for example, economic rights, including property rights, contract rights, and rights to economic opportunity. These other rights are not basic, because if the basic rights are guaranteed, these others can be defined democratically. I discuss the nonbasic human rights in the companion volume (Talbott forthcoming). In this book, I focus on the basic rights. Because basic human rights are essential to the solution of a universal moral problem—government abuse of its coercive powers—the basic human rights *should be* universal.

In this chapter I have not yet tried to argue for universal human rights. Rather I have set the stage for the kind of argument that you, the reader, should expect: not a logical deduction from self-evident premises, but rather (1) bottom-up reasoning from widely shared particular moral judgments on actual and hypothetical cases to moral principles and norms that explain them; and (2) bottom-up reasoning from facts about the actual history of moral inquiry and judgments about hypothetical histories to principles that explain them. On this picture, philosophical argument is more a matter of considering relevant examples and evaluating competing explanations of them than it is drawing deductive conclusions from antecedently justified premises. For this reason, I think of this book as a whole as an extended explanation rather than as an argument.

3

CULTURAL RELATIVISM
ABOUT HUMAN RIGHTS

The Europeans have scarcely visited any coast but to gratify
avarice, and extend corruption; to arrogate dominion without
right, and to practice cruelty without incentive.
—Samuel Johnson

The true "Westerner" is the man who accepts nothing
unreservedly in our civilisation except the liberty it allows him
to criticize it and the chance it offers him to improve it.
—Raymond Aron

Anyone from a democratic country who claims human rights ought to be
universal can expect to be accused of cultural imperialism. Lee Kwan Yew,
the former prime minister of Singapore, is probably the best-known contemporary exponent of this argument.[1] Under Lee, Singapore was nominally a
democracy with a democratically elected government, but Lee was un-
abashed in imitating the techniques of the communists and even the Roman
Catholic church for securing a one-party state. This included not only the
suppression of any political opposition, but also the suppression of any criticism of the government in the press. In Singapore under Lee, almost all of
the domestic news media were owned by the government, and all foreign
news media were subject to strict regulation.

When criticized for limiting the freedom of the press to question his government and for limiting the freedom of citizens to express dissatisfaction
with his government or to organize opposition parties to try to change it,
Lee charged his critics with arrogance and insensitivity to "Asian values."
What does Lee mean by "Asian values"? Not surprisingly, he favors what
he regards as the Confucian tradition of placing the community above the
individual and its emphasis on obedience to authority.[2]

Lee's defense of Asian values is based on a moral position that has an
undeniable intuitive appeal. *Cultural relativism* is the position that moral
norms apply only to those whose cultures endorse them. The cultural relativist holds that human rights norms apply only to those whose cultures
have a tradition of endorsing human rights. Call this position *cultural rela-*

tivism about human rights. Cultural relativism about human rights was enunciated even before the United Nations formally adopted its Universal Declaration of Human Rights in a statement issued by the American Anthropological Association (1947).[3] Lee's defense of Asian values is a special application of cultural relativism about human rights to Asian societies.

Human Rights Are a Relatively Recent Discovery

Before considering whether cultural relativism about human rights is true, it is important to mention that some of the empirical claims on which it is typically based are simply false. It is sometimes suggested, for example, that human rights apply to Western societies, because Western societies have a tradition of respecting human rights. However, Western societies do not have a tradition of respecting human rights. Human rights are a relatively recent development, even in the West. Consider, for example, the right to religious freedom. It is true that many Western democracies *now* recognize such a right. However, it is a mistake to think that Western Europe has a *tradition* of religious tolerance. On the contrary, as Zagorin says in a history of the development of religious toleration: "Of all the great world religions past and present, Christianity has been by far the most intolerant" (2003, 1). I believe it is this tradition of religious *intolerance* in the West that set the stage for the discovery of a right to religious tolerance.

The first known advocates of religious tolerance were from the East, not the West. Sen points to the Indian emperor Ashoka, who ruled in the third century B.C. (1999, 236). Ashoka was an eloquent advocate of religious tolerance who guaranteed it for all of his subjects. Perhaps the earliest known advocate of religious tolerance was Cyrus the Great, king of Persia in the sixth century B.C.E. Cyrus also opposed slavery and freed thousands of slaves. These facts do not make Cyrus or Ashoka an advocate of human rights. They do show that the ideas that led to the development of human rights are not limited to one cultural tradition.

What about democratic rights? It is true that today the Western European countries are all democracies. However, it is a mistake to think that Western Europe has a *tradition* of democracy. Quite the contrary. Until relatively recently, Western Europe was ruled by hereditary monarchs who claimed and effectively exercised absolute power over their subjects. Those Western Europeans who first advocated democratic rights often did so at the risk of their lives, because such ideas were not looked upon with tolerance by most absolute monarchs. When Benjamin Franklin wanted to demonstrate the possibility of a stable democratic system for the American colonies, he pointed to the example of the Iroquois confederacy (Josephy 1994, 251–252). So it is a mistake to distinguish Western European culture from other cultures in terms of a tradition of religious or political tolerance or a tradition of democratic rights.

Moreover, there is nothing especially Asian about a tradition of obedience to authority. One of the most eloquent defenses of absolute rule is from the Western philosophical tradition, the *Republic* of Plato. It seems to me that the true history of human rights in the West naturally suggests the following question: If respect for human rights can emerge from one of the more despotic and intolerant cultural traditions (e.g., the Western European tradition), are there some characteristics of human beings in virtue of which *any* cultural tradition should respect human rights?

The Cultural Imperialism Argument

Cultural relativists about human rights need not base their case on inaccurate history. Anyone familiar with the history of Western European colonization should acknowledge that it was accompanied by, and indeed justified or at least rationalized by, arrogance and insensitivity to native religious practices and customs. For example, Native American peoples were often forcibly prohibited from practicing their traditional religious rituals and even from speaking their native languages. There is now general agreement—even among those whose ancestors did the colonizing—that this forcible imposition of Western practices on American natives was morally wrong.

Why was it wrong? There is a natural answer to this question, which goes like this: The Western European colonizers were cultural imperialists. They thought their religion was the only true religion; their culture had all of the right answers; and all other cultures were mistaken. Now we find that sort of cultural imperialism morally objectionable. Each culture has its own norms and values. It is inappropriate to judge the members of one culture by the norms of another; members of each culture should be free to act on the norms of their own culture.

Call this argument the *cultural imperialism argument*. The conclusion of the cultural imperialism argument is *extreme moral relativism*. If the argument is correct, no one could ever be justified in objecting to or criticizing the moral norms of another culture. This leads directly to cultural relativism about human rights, because extreme moral relativism implies that it is inappropriate to apply human rights standards to cultures that do not already acknowledge human rights. So, if it were sound, the cultural imperialism argument would support cultural relativism about human rights.

Is the cultural imperialism argument sound? No, on the contrary, it is deeply incoherent. To understand the incoherence, notice that the argument begins from the claim that it was *wrong* for the Western Europeans to forcibly impose their norms on the American natives. This is itself a moral criticism of the Western Europeans' norms for the treatment of the American natives. The conclusion of the cultural imperialism argument is that it is *never* appropriate to criticize a culture's norms. So the argument undermines the very insight that motivated it. If you believe the cultural imperialism of the Western European colonizers really was wrong, you should not be an extreme cultural relativist. What should you be? I return to this question after exploring further the incoherence in the cultural imperialism argument.

Why Extreme Moral Relativism
Is Unacceptable

If it *really* was morally wrong for Western colonizers to forcibly impose their religious practices on native populations, this suggests that native peoples had some sort of *right* to engage in their traditional religious practices, which was violated by the Western colonizers. If there is such a right, it would seem to be a universal right, applicable to all cultures. If Western colonizers ought not to have imposed their religious practices on native peoples, that moral insight cannot be captured within a thoroughgoing relativistic framework that denies any universal moral standards. To see why not, suppose you came upon a sixteenth-century Spanish conquistador threatening to kill any native who did not convert to Catholicism. Appalled, you might try to persuade him that the natives had their own religions and customs, which should be respected by outsiders.

Here is one reply the conquistador might make: You may come from a culture with a norm of tolerance, which explains why you believe that *you* ought to respect native religions and customs. My culture has no such norm of tolerance. As a matter of fact, my culture has a norm of *intolerance*, according to which we are expected to forcibly convert those of different religions to our religion or kill them. Surely, you would not presume to impose *your* norms (of tolerance) on someone whose culture does not have a norm of tolerance.

A cultural relativist who holds that each culture should be free to act on its own norms would find the conquistador's reply unanswerable. That is because the strongest norm of tolerance that can be justified within a relativist framework is what I refer to as a norm of *wishy-washy tolerance:*

Members of cultures with a norm of tolerance ought to be tolerant; but it is inappropriate to apply a norm of tolerance to members of intolerant cultures.

As the reply that I made on the conquistador's behalf illustrates, wishy-washy tolerance cannot be a basis for objecting to the treatment of American natives by Western European colonizers. This shows that the moral insight that cultures should be tolerant of the religious practices and customs of other cultures cannot be captured within a thoroughgoing relativist framework. To express it, we must make a moral claim that applies to *all* cultures—that is, a *universal* moral claim.[4]

Am I being fair to the relativist? It is not possible to canvass all possible relativist positions, so let me try to identify what they have in common. Relativists wish to be sensitive to other points of view and to acknowledge the value of what other people believe. This is an admirable idea. But they express it by saying things like "All moral views are equally valid" or "All cultural norms are equally valid." Views of this kind I call *wishy-washy.* The conquistador example reveals a problem for all wishy-washy views.[5] Suppose the relativist claims that all moral views are equally valid. What will she say to someone whose moral view includes the proposition that all moral views are *not* equally valid? In the extreme case, the interlocutor may believe that those who believe that all moral views are equally valid should be killed. This is not just an idle possibility. People have been put to death for asserting that there is more than one equally valid religious view.

Of course, the relativist can always respond: "When I said all moral views are equally valid, I was only expressing my own moral view, one that is valid for me. When you disagreed with me, you were expressing your own moral view, one that is valid for you." And that is why a wishy-washy moral view could never explain what is wrong with the Spanish conquistador's treatment of the American natives. If we are justified in claiming that the treatment really was wrong, then the conquistador's belief that it was morally obligatory cannot have the same validity as our belief to the contrary.

Cultural Relativism about Internal Norms

The upshot of the preceding discussion is that even to think it appropriate to morally criticize the Western Europeans' intolerance of native cultures, one must give up extreme moral relativism and accept at least one strongly universal moral principle. In order to formulate the principle precisely, I need to make some further distinctions: first, a distinction between *internal* and *external* interactions or practices, then a distinction between *internal* and *external* norms. *Internal interactions* or *practices* are interactions or practices involving only members of the same culture. *External interactions* or *practices* are interactions or practices involving members of different cultures. When a cultural norm applies to internal interactions or practices, I refer to it as an *internal norm*. When a cultural norm applies to external interactions or practices, I refer to it as an *external norm*.

Then, one plausible candidate for a universal moral principle is the principle of *cultural relativism about internal norms*: The members of each culture should be free to act in accordance with their culture's internal norms and, thus, there is no moral basis for the members of one culture to criticize the internal norms of another culture.[6] Cultural relativism about internal norms would explain why it was wrong for the Western European colonizers of the Americas to interfere with the religious and other internal practices of the American natives. It provides the basis for some universal rights. However, they would all be group rights, not individual rights, because they would be rights of the group to noninterference with its religious and other practices governed by its internal norms. Respect for internal norms does not imply respect for individual rights, because the internal norms of some groups do not themselves endorse individual rights. Thus, someone who accepts cultural relativism about internal norms will not be an advocate of any universal individual human rights. In combination with the fact that some cultures have internal norms that do not respect individual human rights, cultural relativism about internal norms directly implies cultural relativism about human rights, because if there is no moral basis for criticizing the internal norms of another culture, then, in particular, there is no moral basis for criticizing on human rights grounds the internal norms of cultures that do not have human rights norms.

So the defender of universal human rights has a difficult task. In order to deny cultural relativism about human rights, she must somehow find a way to challenge cultural relativism about internal norms, without becoming a moral imperialist. Although I am going to argue that cultural relativism about internal norms is a mistake, I do not deny that it represents a significant moral improvement over the cultural imperialism that it is a reaction against.

The main problem for cultural relativism about internal norms is that the reasoning that leads to it almost inevitably leads beyond it. The advocate of cultural relativism about internal norms acknowledges that it is possible to criticize the external norms of another culture, but denies that it is possible to criticize another culture's internal norms. How could this be? Why would internal norms be immune to outside criticism if external norms are not?

Three Defenses of Cultural Relativism about Internal Norms

I can think of three responses that the advocate of cultural relativism about internal norms might make:

1. The Infallibility Thesis. This is the claim that it is not possible for a culture to make a mistake about its own internal norms. If this were true, there would obviously be no basis for criticism of a culture's internal norms. How could the infallibility thesis be defended? Somehow it would have to be shown that, though one culture can have external norms that license the oppression of members of other cultures, no culture could have internal norms that would license the oppression of a subgroup within the same culture. This seems overly sanguine. Like external norms, internal norms can be used to justify hereditary hierarchies of power, status, and privilege. The hierarchies supported by internal norms can involve very great inequalities—as great as the inequalities in hierarchies supported by external norms. So the possibility of oppressive internal norms cannot be ruled out in advance.

2. The Incommensurability Thesis. This is the claim that different cultures have incommensurable fundamental moral principles or incommensurable fundamental moral outlooks. To say they are incommensurable is to say that each culture's moral principles are sui generis and not susceptible to evaluation by any other principles. This is the view of Alasdair MacIntyre (1984, 8). If the incommensurability thesis were true, then only insiders could make reliable judgments about the internal norms of a culture; outsiders would simply not be able to understand the internal norms of another culture well enough to be able to make a moral evaluation of them.

   Is the incommensurability thesis true? Are the internal norms of different cultures incommensurable? If the incommensurability thesis were true, other cultures' norms should be completely opaque to us. I would be inclined to think the incommensurability thesis were true if our best attempts to translate other cultures' internal norms led us to attribute to them moral beliefs that seemed completely arbitrary. Suppose, for example, that our best translation of another culture's justification for their class hierarchy was: Grass is green. That would seem like such a strange justification that we would have to at least consider the possibility that their moral principles really were incommensurable with ours. In the real world, that is not what we find.

   Consider an example. Traditional Hinduism is perhaps the most commonly cited instance of a culture with internal moral norms that cannot be understood from outside—at least, not by a Westerner. What is ironic is that these authors often then proceed to explain why the caste system is justified by the internal norms of traditional Hinduism.

According to the defense of cultural relativism about internal norms I am now considering, if Hindu internal norms and Western internal norms were incommensurable, Westerners should not be able to understand the Hindu justification of caste system norms. In fact, once the explanation has been presented, it turns out that the Hindu internal norms of justice are not very different from Western norms of justice. To see this, it is necessary to briefly review the Hindu justification of the caste system.

Roughly, the Hindu doctrine is that people (and indeed other living things) have many lives (transmigration of souls), and their position in this life is the one that they deserve based on their actions in previous lives (karma). This is a quite ingenious potential moral justification of the Hindu caste system, because it implies that everyone's current position in life is based on what was *earned* in previous lives. Untouchables need only perform their duties well to progress up in the hierarchy, and eventually, by performing their duties well in each life, they, too, will reach enlightenment. Walzer describes the Hindu system as one that promises "equality of opportunity, not in this life but across the lives of the soul" (Walzer 1983, 27). In fact, the principles of justice involved in the Hindu world view go far beyond equality of opportunity. First, there is a principle of *just desert*, which guarantees that all living things get what they deserve. Second, there is a principle of *equitable distribution*, which assures that those who reap the benefits of being in the upper castes must have previously borne the burdens of life in the lower castes and discharged their duties well. So the Hindu caste system, one of the prime examples used to support the relativity of concepts of justice, seems to provide support for transcultural norms of justice governing the fair distribution of the benefits and burdens of social life.

It is not the norms of justice presupposed by the Hindu justification of the caste system that some Westerners find foreign. Rather it is the Hindu doctrines of transmigration of souls and karma. But the foreignness of these doctrines does not interfere with understanding them. It is necessary to understand those doctrines to be able to appreciate how the Hindu justification of the caste system *satisfies* what have been thought of as Western norms of justice. What is foreign about the doctrines of the transmigration of souls and of karma is that Westerners are not used to thinking about the world in such terms. But this is hardly the kind of foreignness that would support incommensurability. The incommensurability thesis is much too pessimistic.

3. The Claim of Distorting Bias. This is the claim that the members of a culture are inevitably so biased against other cultures that they are unable to impartially evaluate the internal norms of other cultures. Before questioning whether the claim of distorting bias is always true, I should acknowledge that it sometimes is. Most of the Spanish colonizers of the

Americas were so biased against the natives that they could never have recognized the value of native culture and native norms. But the claim of distorting bias is much too strong. Indeed, sometimes the distorting bias works in the other direction. When a culture oppresses a subclass of its own members, I say that the culture practices *internal oppression*. When there is internal oppression, those who benefit from the oppression usually have powerful biases in favor of the status quo. Often it is easier for an outsider than it is for an insider to recognize internal oppression. It turns out that there is one kind of internal oppression that is a near cultural universal—the oppression of women. In chapter 5, I explain how an outsider can be in a better position to recognize this sort of oppression than an insider and show how it is possible to identify such oppression and to try to change it without being a moral imperialist.

None of the three responses of the advocate of cultural relativism about internal norms seems compelling. But it is not enough to cast doubt on the positive arguments. I need to find a more plausible alternative. In the next chapter, I explore the transition from moral imperialism to cultural relativism about internal norms by considering the life of one of the first people ever to make the transition: Bartolomé de Las Casas. To make the move to cultural relativism about internal norms, Las Casas had to be able to reach a standpoint from which he could morally criticize the external norms of his culture. In the next chapter I try to say how he was able to do so. In the following chapter, I show how, from exactly the same standpoint, it is also possible to morally criticize a culture's internal norms.

4

AN EPISTEMICALLY MODEST
UNIVERSAL MORAL STANDPOINT

It is a wonder to see how, when a man greatly desires
something and strongly attaches himself to it in his imagination,
he has the impression at every moment that whatever he hears
and sees argues in favor of that thing.

—Bartolomé de Las Casas

It is said, by Las Casas, among others, that what perplexed the
[natives] of Espanola most about the strange White people from
the large ships was not their violence, not even their greed, nor
in fact their peculiar attitudes toward property, but rather their
coldness, their hardness, their lack of love.

—Kirkpatrick Sale

In this chapter, I take up the challenge to explain how it is possible to make
universal moral judgments. To make such judgments requires that we be
able to attain a *universal moral standpoint*. I do not believe that aspiring to
attain such a standpoint guarantees we will attain it, because we can be
blind to our own biases and to the biases of those who influence us. Fortunately, the situation is not hopeless. When we are not overly influenced by
our own interests and prejudices or those of others, we are able to make
fallible, but reasonably reliable, universal moral judgments. In this chapter,
I try to explain how we do so.

In the philosophical literature, there are many arguments for skepticism
about all moral judgments—that is, arguments that all moral judgments
are false or that there can be no rational basis for any moral judgment. I
believe that these arguments are typically based on misconceptions about
the nature of universal moral judgments. Already I have considered why
any account of moral judgment that requires us to begin with exceptionless,
universal moral principles is doomed to fail. However, it is not so hopeless to
think we might be able to make some universal particular moral judgments.
Consider, for example, the particular moral judgment that it was wrong for
the Spanish colonists to force the American natives to give up their traditional religions and to convert to Christianity. For this judgment to be uni-

versal, it is not necessary that there be an exceptionless principle to the effect that forcible conversions are always wrong. All that is required is that this particular instance of forcible conversion be wrong from any point of view. To attribute universality to a particular moral judgment is to insist that it is not true merely from some personal or cultural point of view, but that it is true from the point of view of any morally responsible being.

Universality does not imply infallibility. However, it would not be reasonable even to try to make universal particular moral judgments if we discovered that they were completely unreliable. So one of the goals of this chapter is to uncover some of the factors that make our particular moral judgments fallible, without making them completely unreliable.

In this chapter, I discuss some of the misconceptions that contribute to moral skepticism, but it is beyond the scope of the present work to review and respond to all of the arguments for moral skepticism. In this work, my focus is not on *skeptical* arguments against applying human rights norms— that is, arguments claiming that no one can ever have any good reason for making a moral judgment at all. My focus is on *moral* arguments against applying human rights norms to the internal practices of other cultures that do not already espouse them—that is, arguments that it is *morally wrong* to apply human rights norms to the internal practices of traditional cultures. Anyone who believes that it really was wrong for the Western European colonizers to forcibly impose their internal norms on the American natives cannot rely on skeptical arguments to support that position. On the contrary, it seems to me that anyone who agrees that the European colonizers acted wrongly is committed to the possibility of a universal moral standpoint from which to make reliable, universal, particular moral judgments. In this chapter, I explain how there could be such a standpoint and how human beings can aspire to attain it.

The advocate of cultural relativism about internal norms believes that it is objectionably presumptuous for outsiders to suppose that they could be in a position to morally question the internal norms of another culture; to do so is to engage in a kind of moral imperialism. As I explained in chapter 1, I think there *is* a kind of moral imperialism that is morally objectionable: I would be a *moral imperialist*, in this morally objectionable sense, if I held that anyone who disagrees with me on a moral question must be wrong (infallibilism) or if I were willing to impose my own moral judgments on other adults for their own good (moral paternalism). To avoid moral imperialism, we must acknowledge our fallibility and refrain from moral paternalism. This does not mean that we should always retract our moral judgments whenever anyone disagrees or that we should limit our moral claims only to those who agree with us or hold that all moral views are equally valid. In short, we need not be morally wishy-washy. One of the goals of this book is to explain how we can make universal moral judgments that are neither wishy-washy nor morally imperialistic.

The idea of a universal moral standpoint emerges naturally from thinking about what is involved in taking seriously particular moral judgments about particular acts in particular circumstances. Consider, for example, the starting point of the cultural imperialism argument, that it really was wrong for the Western European colonizers to forcibly impose their internal norms on the American natives. As I use the term, to understand that moral judgment as a *universal* one is not to think that the actions of the Western European colonizers could never have been justified under *any* circumstances (though it is difficult to imagine circumstances that would have justified them). It is to hold that those actions in the circumstances in which they were performed by those who performed them *really were wrong* and that their being wrong is true not just from some personal or cultural point of view, but from the point of view of any morally responsible being.

Recall again the Spanish conquistador whose culture had a moral norm of intolerance of other cultures. To make a universal judgment that the conquistador's treatment of the American natives was wrong is to assert that the conquistador and his culture were mistaken about how they should have treated the American natives. As I view it, the universality is unqualified. Suppose there are other intelligent beings in another galaxy somewhere in the universe who are capable of judging right and wrong. Suppose they were to travel to Earth and find out about the Western Europeans' treatment of the American natives. If they did not recognize that it was wrong, they, too, would be mistaken. The wrongness of the Western Europeans' treatment of the American natives is not limited to beings with the same chemistry or the same evolutionary heritage as *Homo sapiens*. It is wrong from every possible point of view.

To understand a particular moral judgment as universal is different from understanding it as infallible. As I explained in chapter 2, I believe that all of our judgments, including all of our particular moral judgments, are fallible, in the sense that there is no way to guarantee them to be true. I have already mentioned that the Proof paradigm of epistemic justification has done tremendous damage in moral philosophy. One of my main goals in this chapter is to try to undo some of that damage by explaining why it is reasonable to regard at least some of our moral judgments as reliable, though not infallible, and why the acknowledgment of our own fallibility does not make it unreasonable, at least in some situations, to hold that those who disagree with us are mistaken. The view I defend avoids moral imperialism because it is symmetrical: My view not only explains how I can be in a position to criticize the moral judgments of others as mistaken; it also explains how others can be in a position to criticize mine as mistaken. Others have moral blindspots. So do I. Moral blindspots are difficult to identify from the inside. We need other people, often outsiders from other cultures, to help us identify our moral blindspots.

The question to be answered in this chapter is: How is it possible for anyone to attain a standpoint from which to make reliable, though not infallible, universal, rather than wishy-washy, moral judgments? Because it is obvious that all of our judgments are made from our own point of view, and because people get their moral training by learning to fit in with the moral judgments of their own families or communities, to many people it seems obvious that all we could hope to aspire to would be to accurately reflect and perhaps build upon the moral judgments of our families or communities. This seems to me to be a mistake. Even though moral training is culturally conditioned, when successful it makes it possible for us to adopt a universal moral standpoint, from which it is possible to make reliable, though not infallible, particular moral judgments. In order to explain this conception of a universal moral standpoint, I discuss an extended hypothetical example, based in part on the life of Bartolomé de Las Casas. I have taken the liberty of making my own additions and modifications where they help to clarify the relevant philosophical issues. Throughout this chapter I distinguish between the historical Bartolomé de Las Casas and the protagonist of my hypothetical example by referring to the latter as *BLC*. Before I begin my hypothetical example, it will be useful to do some stage setting.

Reconstructing a Potential Justificatory Argument for the Spaniards' Treatment of the American Natives

On the way home from his first trip to the Americas, Columbus wrote to the Spanish court that the natives "are fit to be ordered about and made to work, to sow and do everything else that may be needed" (Sale 1990, 112). On his return to the Americas, he began shipping natives back to Spain to be sold in the slave markets, even before he had received permission to do so. When he did get permission, it was qualified: Queen Isabella wrote that he could capture and sell cannibalistic and idolatrous natives (presumably meaning those who did not worship the God of the Christian Bible) and utilize their services, "paying us the share that belongs to us" (Josephy 1994, 123).[1] As a matter of fact, most, if not all, of the natives with whom Columbus came into contact were not cannibals, and Columbus and his compatriots did not limit slavery to the natives they believed to be cannibalistic.[2] Some practices of some Native American groups—most notably the Aztec rituals of human sacrifice—did involve acts of cannibalism (Todorov

1984, 155). So it would seem that Queen Isabella's "cannibalistic and idola-trous" rationale could potentially have been used to attempt to justify the enslavement of at least some American natives.

I want to use Queen Isabella's reply to Columbus to illustrate both top-down and bottom-up epistemic justifications of moral beliefs, and especially how the bottom-up variety can lead to radical moral discoveries, including the conclusion that even moral norms antecedently regarded as infallible may be mistaken. For most of the European settlers, the discovery of the Americas was the discovery of a new land. For Bartolomé de Las Casas, it turned out to be a profound moral discovery.

The story of Las Casas's moral development has been told as the discov-ery of moral relativism (e.g., Todorov 1984). My goal in this chapter is to explain why it is a mistake to think that Las Casas was an extreme moral relativist. In my interpretation, Las Casas's main discovery was a universal moral standpoint accessible from bottom-up moral reasoning. I do believe his discovery led him to a form of moral relativism, not extreme moral rela-tivism, but cultural relativism about internal norms.

I begin the story by considering how a Spanish conquistador might have relied on Queen Isabella's rationale to justify enslaving a particular Ameri-can native (see example 4–1). At this point, I set aside all questions about the adequacy of the justificatory argument in example 4–1. Initially, my goal is simply to identify its parts and to understand it.

MN3. It is not wrong to enslave cannibalistic and idolatrous peoples.
P3. This native (the one being seized) is cannibalistic and idolatrous.
PMJ3. Therefore, it is not wrong to enslave this native.

Example 4–1. First Reconstruction of Queen Isabella's Justificatory Argument for Enslaving a Particular American Native.

As presented, the justificatory argument in example 4–1 is an example of top-down epistemic justification, because the goal of the argument is to transmit epistemic justification from the premises to the conclusion. A top-down justifying argument can epistemically justify its conclusion only if the premises are epistemically justified. Neither of the premises of the argument in example 4–1 could reasonably be thought to be epistemically justified on its own, so their justification must come from other epistemically justified beliefs. Of course, in the equilibrium model, it is possible that the premises themselves have sources of bottom-up epistemic justification. I will illustrate this shortly. I am particularly interested in the epistemic justification for premise MN3, that it is not wrong to enslave cannibalistic and idolatrous peoples. The *official* defense of MN3 given by the apologists for the Spanish colonists at the time was that the natives were barbarians and thus, according to Aristotle, as interpreted by Aquinas, natural slaves (Pagden 1982, chap. 3).

However, few of the colonists themselves had ever read Aristotle or Aquinas and I doubt that many of them had the official justification in mind during their conquest of the Americas. Reading the Spanish colonists' own descriptions of the American natives suggests a slightly different justification for MN3. Beginning with Columbus, the Spanish explorers continually referred to the natives as or compared them to beasts—that is, to nonhuman animals.[3] Moreover, in their treatment of the American natives, the Spanish colonists provided overwhelming evidence that they did not believe there was anything wrong with treating them in the most brutal manner imaginable. A 1530 judicial report to Charles V on the colonists' treatment of slaves in the Americas stated that they treated them "as dogs."[4] Actually, they treated their dogs better than they treated the natives. Las Casas reports some of the incidents he himself witnessed:

> [The Spaniards] made bets as to who would slit a man in two, or cut off his head at one blow; or they opened up his bowels. They tore the babies from their mother's breast by their feet, and dashed their heads against the rocks. . . . They spitted the bodies of other babes, together with their mothers and all who were before them, on their swords. . . . [They hanged Indians], and by thirteens, in honor and reverence for our Redeemer and the twelve Apostles, they put wood underneath and, with fire, they burned the Indians alive. (Sale 1990, 157)[5]

Las Casas's description fits with other eyewitness descriptions of equally brutal behavior: "Some Christians encounter[ed] an Indian woman, who was carrying in her arms a child at suck; and since the dog they had with them was hungry, they tore the child from the mother's arms and flung it still living to the dog, who proceeded to devour it before the mother's eyes."[6] Of course, it is possible that such acts were committed with no beliefs about their moral justifiability. However, I think it is useful to construct a potential *unofficial* justification to explain why they would have believed themselves to be morally justified in doing anything they wanted to do to the American natives. So, on the unofficial justification, the answer to the question "Why is it not wrong to enslave cannibalistic and idolatrous peoples?" is that cannibalistic and idolatrous peoples are not significantly different from beasts and it is not wrong to do anything one wants to a beast.

This answer naturally raises the further question: Why is it not wrong to do what one wants to a beast? A Spanish colonist might have replied that beasts don't have souls and it is not wrong to do whatever one wants to do to a being without a soul. This answer suggests that the unofficial justification for enslaving the American natives would have been that they do not have souls. I must emphasize that this could only be the unofficial justification. Because the official religious view was that the natives could save their souls by converting to Christianity, it is clear that, on the official view, the natives did have souls. However, I believe that the actual treatment of the American natives by the Spaniards is better explained by this sort of unofficial justification—according to which, from a moral standpoint, the natives were not significantly different from beasts—than by the official justification. Of course, any proposed reconstruction of the Spaniards' own reasons for treating the American natives as they did will involve idealizations and simplifications of the actual psychology of the Spanish explorers. I propose this unofficial justification for its suggestiveness and for its usefulness to me in explaining how a universal moral standpoint is possible.

I think it would have seemed obvious to fifteenth- or sixteenth-century Spanish colonists that it was not wrong to do what one wanted to do to a being without a soul. I believe it would have also seemed obvious to them that a being without a conscience lacked a soul. So, as I reconstruct it, the unofficial justification for enslaving the American natives would have been that they lack a conscience. What would make them think that the American natives lacked a conscience?

To Spanish colonists, cannibalism and idolatry would have seemed so obviously wrong that they would have thought that only a being without a conscience could engage in such practices without recognizing that they were wrong. Some American natives did engage in such practices and did not regard them as wrong. This might have been taken to be conclusive evidence that they lacked a conscience.

From the point of view of the Proof paradigm, there is still a missing piece to the unofficial justification of enslaving the American natives: a justification for believing cannibalism and idolatry to be wrong. The Spanish colonists could have filled in this piece of the puzzle by invoking the Christian Scriptures, a text they regarded as the report of an infallible God.[7]

It is possible to put all of the justificatory steps in what I am calling the unofficial justification for enslaving a particular American native in the form of a deductive argument (see example 4–2).

P13. God exists.

P12. The moral norms in the Christian Scriptures are endorsed by God.

P11. God is infallible.

P10. Therefore, the moral norms in the Christian Scriptures are true.

P9. The Christian Scriptures contain moral norms against cannibalism and idolatry.

MN6. Therefore, cannibalism and idolatry are wrong.

P8. Cannibalism and idolatry are so obviously wrong that only a being without a conscience could fail to see they are wrong.

P7. Cannibalistic and idolatrous peoples do not regard their cannibalism and idolatry to be wrong.

P6. Therefore, cannibalistic and idolatrous peoples do not have a conscience.

P5. Those who do not have a conscience do not have a soul.

P4. Therefore, cannibalistic and idolatrous peoples do not have souls.

MN5. It is not wrong to do anything one wants to a being without a soul.

MN4. Therefore, it is not wrong to do anything one wants to cannibalistic and idolatrous peoples.

MN3. Therefore, it is not wrong to enslave cannibalistic and idolatrous peoples.

P2 This native (the one being seized) is cannibalistic and idolatrous.

PMJ3. Therefore, it is not wrong to enslave this native.

Example 4–2. Reconstruction of an Unofficial Justification for Enslaving an American Native.

Because example 4–2 has the form of a deductive argument, it fits well the Proof paradigm's top-down model of epistemic justification. However, once it is understood this way, it is almost inevitable that it is seen to be a *failed* attempt to satisfy the Proof paradigm. The Proof paradigm would make the justification of the conclusion PMJ1 depend on a proof of the premises that God exists, P13, and that the Christian Scriptures are endorsed by God, P12. Although there were many philosophers in the Enlightenment who claimed to have a proof of God's existence, today few philosophers would accept their proofs.

From within the Proof paradigm, the only other alternative would be to find self-evident moral principles or to find some other proof of moral principles from self-evident premises. Today, few philosophers believe that moral principles are self-evident or susceptible of proof. So within the Proof paradigm, moral skepticism, the view that moral beliefs cannot be epistemically justified, is almost inevitable.

From moral skepticism, it is a short step to denying the existence of a universal moral standpoint. If all moral norms received their justification by being traced back to texts or other authorities regarded to be infallible, then moral disagreements based on clashes in moral authorities would be in principle irresolvable. There would be no single universal moral standpoint, just a multiplicity of irreconcilable moral points of view, each based on a different moral authority. This is a common picture of the nature of moral disagreement.[8]

There is an alternative: Give up the Proof paradigm as the model of epistemic justification for moral beliefs. Giving up the Proof paradigm opens up a new way of understanding a universal moral standpoint. No longer is it a standpoint from which one obtains infallible moral knowledge by deriving it from rationally self-evident premises. Instead, it is a standpoint from which one can make fallible, though reliable, moral judgments about particular cases, both actual and hypothetical. These particular moral judgments provide the main source of epistemic justification for fallible belief in moral principles.

On this alternative view, moral training is not so much learning to apply principles as it is the development of moral sensitivity. This moral sensitivity enables a person to make reliable particular moral judgments. Moral norms gain support to the extent that they help to satisfactorily explain a person's particular moral judgments.

The Hypothetical Example of BLC

I illustrate this possibility by way of a hypothetical story about a hypothetical Spanish colonist, BLC. My hypothetical story is loosely based on the life of the actual Bartolomé de Las Casas. By making my story hypothetical, I can make useful simplifying hypotheses about the structure of justification of BLC's moral views without having to trace them back to the historical Las Casas. The actual Las Casas arrived in the Americas in 1502. Upon his arrival, he actively participated in the conquest of Cuba and was rewarded with a large estate and many slaves. Gradually, he became convinced that the Spaniards' treatment of the American natives was wrong. In 1512 he was ordained a priest, and in 1514 he announced he was giving up his slaves. From then on, he was a tireless advocate for the American natives, a cause to which he devoted his life. By the end of his life, his experiences with the American natives had radically transformed his moral views, perhaps even more radically than he himself realized.

In my hypothetical story of BLC, I suppose that before his arrival in the Americas, there was general agreement among the members of his culture on all of the premises of the argument in example 4–2, and thus general agreement that there were no moral constraints on the treatment of the American natives. It is easy to imagine BLC agreeing with the members of his culture in accepting the full justificatory argument in example 4–2. Could he have been epistemically justified in accepting it? In order to answer that question, I must say something more about BLC's background, including his moral training as a child.

BLC grew up in a country where he and the other children began their moral training even before they had learned a language. Their moral training did not begin with learning moral principles. It began in situations in which something they did was disapproved of and judged to be wrong by the adults around them and in situations in which they observed other children doing things that were disapproved of and judged to be wrong. Often these judgments were accompanied by physical punishment. As a result of years of this sort of training, BLC began making judgments of right and wrong even before he began his formal religious training. In his formal religious training, he was taught moral norms—for example, the norm "Thou shalt not kill." These norms were taught to him as the infallible deliverances of God, and he regarded them as such. Because he was convinced that these norms were infallible, he did not even notice that, from a literal point of view, they had many exceptions. For example, although he regarded "Thou shalt not kill" as an infallible directive from God, his parents and relatives told him many stories of heroic killing.

Why didn't BLC (or the other members of his culture) feel any conflict between the norm against killing and the approval of individual acts of killing? If BLC had interpreted the norms literally, the conflict would have been unignorable. That is not, however, how BLC interpreted his moral norms. Instead, without stopping to think about it, BLC (like almost everyone else) used his particular moral judgments to fix the interpretation of his norms. If his particular moral judgments approved of acts of killing in self-defense, then such acts of self-defense were not interpreted to be within the scope of the norm that prohibited killing. This flexibility in the interpretation of the moral norms was so unconscious and so automatic that BLC and his compatriots were not even aware they were doing it. Thus, when confronted with an actual or hypothetical example of cannibalism, involving the killing and eating of another human, they *believed* that their justification for believing it to be wrong was traceable to what they regarded as the infallible divine injunction against killing. Thus, they regarded the structure of the epistemic justification of their moral beliefs to be top-down, from divinely inspired moral norms to particular judgments. In fact, the structure of epistemic justification had at least a substantial component in the opposite direction. Their strong conviction that cannibalism was wrong made them sure it was covered by their norm against killing. Thus, the epistemic justification of their moral norms had a largely bottom-up structure, because their convictions in particular cases gave content to their moral norms.[9]

BLC grew up in a community in which the nonhuman animals (beasts) were simply regarded as things to be used to serve human purposes. There were no moral limits on the treatment of beasts. Growing up, BLC was exposed to many cases of what might have seemed like mistreatment of beasts, and he himself may have objected to some extreme cases of mistreatment. If so, his judgments were corrected by the adults around him until he stopped regarding beasts as the kind of things that could be mistreated. Later, in his religious training, he was given an explanation for why there were no moral limits on the mistreatment of beasts. People have souls; beasts do not. Moral norms only applied to the treatment of beings with souls, not to the treatment of beings without souls. He was taught that one of the distinguishing characteristics of beings with souls is that they have a conscience; those without souls do not.

Now imagine BLC when he first hears of the discovery of the Americas. He hears that the New World is already inhabited. His first tendency is to think that his moral norms apply to the natives of the New World. Then he is told that the American natives are idolatrous and cannibalistic, that they don't wear clothes, and so on—in short, they violate just about every one of the divinely established moral norms that BLC has been taught. Even more incredible, he is informed, they not only engage in such behaviors, they do not even regard them as wrong.

Remember, at this point, he has no experience of the American natives himself. His impression of them is based on how he imagines them, based on the reports he has received. These descriptions invoke stereotypes of bloodthirsty savages, beasts in human form. Of course, he is not aware that the explorers' reports have triggered his stereotypes. He imagines that these stereotypes reflect what the natives are really like. In fact, he cannot imagine any other possibility.

Once he has imagined the American natives in accordance with his stereotype of a bloodthirsty savage, a beast in human form, he concludes that there are no moral limits on the treatment of the American natives. Could he be epistemically justified in believing it? With no firsthand knowledge of his own, I think he could have been epistemically justified in believing the reports of the first explorers to be reliable. Also, because he had no firsthand knowledge of the natives, I think he could have been epistemically justified in imagining them to fit his stereotype and, thus, in concluding that the American natives must have lacked a conscience. It is more difficult for me to imagine that he could have been epistemically justified in believing there are no moral limits on the treatment of beasts and other beings without a conscience. I am sure many people have held such beliefs. There are such strong self-serving motives for human beings to hold them that I find it hard to disentangle the genuine reasons from the self-serving ones. Nonetheless, I do believe it would be *possible* for someone to be epistemically justified in believing there were no moral limits on the treatment of beasts and other beings without a conscience. So, for expository purposes, I suppose BLC was epistemically justified in believing this, also.

If so, then it seems to me that, before arriving in the New World, BLC could have been epistemically justified in believing that there were no moral limits on the treatment of the American natives by way of an argument at least roughly like the argument in example 4–2. When BLC arrives in the Americas, he no longer has to rely on the reports of others and on his own limited ability to *imagine* what the American natives are like. For the first time, he can experience them himself. His experience will necessarily be limited, even more so because he will never learn any native language. Fortunately, enough natives will learn his language that he will have no lack of native informants. And much of his experience—for example, the anguish of a mother as she sees her child thrown to ravenous dogs—will not require a translator.

What happens when BLC arrives in the Americas? For one thing, he discovers that some of the reports about the natives were false. However, those discoveries turn out to be irrelevant to the bigger change taking place: From his experience with the American natives, BLC discovers a new way of imagining how the reports could be true. Back home in Spain, he could only imagine the reports being true by imagining the natives as stereotypical savage monsters. When he arrives in the Americas, he discovers that the stereotypes are mistaken. Even the natives he believes to be idolatrous and cannibalistic live together in peaceful communities in which agreed-upon customs define the responsibilities of parents to care for their children, the responsibilities of husbands and wives to each other, and the responsibilities of community members to each other. What is referred to as idolatry and cannibalism turn out to be highly ritualized religious rites of sacrifice to their deities. This provides him with an entirely new perspective on the reports he had received about the natives.

The result is not merely more information about the natives, but a new way of understanding his information. BLC finds himself starting to identify with the natives. He gets to know them as individuals, to form relationships with them. He begins to be able to imagine what it is like to be them. I refer to this change as the development of *empathic understanding*. It is important to note that this is not a purely intellectual change.

As I imagine it, the development of empathic understanding in BLC is gradual, at least in the beginning. Initially, BLC might find his compatriots' treatment of the natives disturbing. When he expresses his qualms, his companions attribute his reaction to squeamishness, and they taunt him for his weakness. Perhaps he agrees with them that he is just squeamish and does not yet believe that what they are doing is wrong. The more BLC interacts with the natives, the more he identifies with them, until eventually, he cannot help but see the brutal actions of his compatriots as terribly wrong. This realization has a powerful emotional component, a feeling of horror at what is being done combined with guilt about his own involvement in it.

Inside, BLC is in emotional turmoil. His moral beliefs are in disequilibrium, because his moral norms seem to provide epistemic justification for believing the colonists' treatment of the natives not to be wrong, but his particular moral judgments rebel in response to the obvious wrongness of that treatment. To restore equilibrium, his moral norms must be brought into equilibrium with his particular moral judgments.

Because BLC is himself convinced that judgments of rightness and wrongness can only be epistemically justified by reference to the norms endorsed by the Christian Scriptures, he finds himself drawn to reread the Scriptures. Without consciously realizing it, he is looking for something to make sense of his feelings. One day he reads the following verse: "the bread of the needy is their life, he that defraudeth him thereof is a man of blood."[10] Suddenly, in an epiphany, it seems obvious to him that the scriptural verse is condemning the colonists' treatment of the natives. His inner turmoil is resolved by a new equilibrium between his moral norms and his particular moral judgments. This newfound equilibrium translates into a newfound confidence that his reactions to the treatment of the natives are not mere squeamishness, but a reasonable response to the awfulness of the Spaniards' mistreatment of the natives. As a result, he resolves to devote himself to improving the treatment of the natives.

Because BLC lived at a time when it was taken for granted that epistemic justification had to be top-down, he regards his epiphany as derived from the moral norm that he found in Scripture. On his own way of understanding the transformation, the norm epistemically justifies him in believing that the colonists' brutal treatment of the natives is wrong. The truth is that most of the epistemic justification is going in the other direction, bottom-up. The particular judgments of wrongness introduce disequilibrium into BLC's moral beliefs, which is ultimately resolved by BLC's new understanding of his previously held moral norms.

As I have told the story, BLC *first* makes particular moral judgments about the wrongness of the colonists' behavior, and only *later* does he alter his interpretation of his moral norms to bring them into equilibrium with his particular moral judgments. I should note that, on the equilibrium model of epistemic justification, it is not necessary for one change to *precede* the other. It could have been that the colonists' brutal treatment of the natives made BLC feel uneasy and guilty, but that he could not decide whether the treatment of the natives was really wrong until the moment of epiphany, a moment at which he became convinced that the particular acts were wrong at the same time that his interpretation of his moral norms changed. Even in this case, there is a substantial component of bottom-up epistemic justifi-cation. The change in his particular moral judgments would *not* be due to top-down reasoning from new moral norms. It would be due to the unease and guilt triggered by the particular cases. The simultaneous change in moral norms and particular moral judgments would resolve a disequilib-rium introduced from *below*, that is, by his response to particular cases.

It is useful to return to the hypothetical story of BLC, to illustrate how disequilibrium from below can lead to and epistemically justify changes in moral norms. Indeed, ultimately I will show how disequilibrium from below can lead one to question the most fundamental norms of one's culture, even norms antecedently thought to be infallible.

In my hypothetical story, through contact with the American natives, BLC eventually developed sufficient empathic understanding of them to be upset by the way his compatriots' were treating them, and eventually to conclude that his compatriots' treatment of the natives, including enslaving them, was wrong. As a result, BLC would have disagreed with most of his compatriots by rejecting their particular moral judgments that endorsed en-slaving the natives.

Rejecting those particular moral judgments would introduce a disequilib-rium into BLC's beliefs that would have ramifications upward to his other moral beliefs. I illustrate this sort of resolution of disequilibrium by using example 4–2 to trace out the changes in BLC's moral norms resulting from his giving up PMJ1. Though I trace out the changes in a conscious, step-wise fashion, it is important to realize that in an actual case, the changes are largely unconscious and simultaneous.

Initially, BLC had believed it was not wrong to enslave peoples who are cannibalistic and idolatrous. Although BLC believes that many of the ac-counts of cannibalism by the natives are false, he does accept some of them. In any case, his empathic understanding of the natives convinces him that even if they were cannibalistic and idolatrous, it would still be wrong to enslave them. So BLC resolves the initial disequilibrium by giving up his belief that it is not wrong to enslave cannibalistic and idolatrous peoples.

Giving up that belief generates another source of disequilibrium, because it conflicts with his former belief that cannibalistic and idolatrous peoples lack a conscience. Now he can understand how beings with a conscience could have different religions from the Christian religion and could believe it was right to engage in human sacrifice to the gods of their religions and that the sacrifice could include cannibalism. So he no longer has any dif-ficulty imagining how cannibalistic and idolatrous peoples could have a conscience.

Thus, BLC is able to *restore* equilibrium to his system of beliefs without ever questioning whether cannibalism and idolatry are really wrong and without questioning the scriptural basis for his belief that they are really wrong. Because BLC continues to believe that the Christian Scriptures are an infallible source of moral norms that apply universally, it is correct to classify him as a moral imperialist. Because the historical Bartolomé de Las Casas held these beliefs for most of his life, he too was a moral imperialist for most of his life. Shortly, I discuss how disequilibrium from below led the historical Bartolomé de Las Casas to give up his moral imperialism.

As I have described it, pressure from below leads BLC to give up the moral norm that it is not wrong to do anything one wants to cannibalistic and idolatrous peoples. In the terms introduced in the preceding chapter, this is an *external* norm, because it governs the interactions between members of different cultures. Because the story of BLC concerns only external norms, there is nothing in the story or in my interpretation of it that the advocate of cultural relativism about internal norms need disagree with. Indeed, my discussion of extreme cultural relativism in the previous chapter was intended to explain why the advocate of cultural relativism about internal norms should welcome my interpretation of the story of BLC. Only if it is possible to attain a standpoint from which one can make objective moral judgments of some kind is it possible to hold that the Spanish colonists' brutal treatment of the American natives *really was wrong.*

As I reconstruct it, the advocate of cultural relativism about internal norms and I agree that the brutal treatment of the natives *really was wrong,* and thus that external norms that would justify it, such as MN3, *really are mistaken.* Thus, we are committed to the possibility of an objective moral standpoint. Because the picture of moral objectivity that is part of the Proof paradigm—the picture of ourselves as having direct rational insight into self-evident moral truths—is a hopeless one, it is important to see there is an alternative. The alternative I have proposed is one that locates the source of moral objectivity not in a rational ability to discern self-evident truths, but in a fallible sensitivity we can develop to the moral rightness and wrongness of particular cases. Is it really plausible to think that moral judgments about particular cases reflect a sensitivity to objective rightness and wrongness?

Are Moral Observations Inevitably Parochial Rather than Universal?

When we look at the historical process of changes in moral norms from the point of view of the equilibrium model of justified belief, moral development is in many ways analogous to developments in science. Not even the most fundamental moral principles are self-evident or rationally unquestionable.

They are the result of a process of discovery, justified by their role in explaining particular moral judgments. New particular moral judgments or revisions to previously accepted particular moral judgments can produce effects that reverberate through the structure of one's moral beliefs to produce changes in the most fundamental moral principles.

In order to be able to test and justify belief in scientific theories, we must have some sensitivity to the objective world they purport to describe. For science, the sensitivity is the perceptual sensitivity that enables us to make experimental observations. Scientific theories are then justified by their role in explaining those observations. Similarly, to be able to test and justify belief in moral norms, we must have some sensitivity to an objective moral world. I believe we do have such sensitivity, a kind of moral perception, which enables us to make directly justified particular moral judgments about what we are experiencing. Because of the analogy, it is plausible to think of the directly epistemically justified particular moral judgments as *moral observations.*

Both the ability to make scientific observations and the ability to make moral observations are cultural achievements. Science does not exist outside of culture and neither does morality. Although I believe there are many analogies between the structures of the justification of belief in science and in morality, it is important not to overstate the analogy. Morality is not itself a science. Science attempts to explain purely descriptive experimental observations about the way things are. Moral rules and principles attempt to explain normative judgments about what ought or ought not to be done.

The possibility of objectivity in science depends on the possibility of making reliable experimental observations that, when true, are true from any point of view, even from the point of view of beings with perceptual equipment very different from the perceptual equipment of human beings. Some philosophers doubt the objectivity of science on the grounds that such objectivity in experimental observation is impossible. On my account, the objectivity of normative moral theories depends on the possibility of making reliable moral observations that, when true, are true from any point of view. Many more philosophers doubt the objectivity of morality on the grounds that such objectivity in moral observation is impossible. One of the deepest puzzles in moral philosophy is to explain how, on the basis of culturally specific moral training, we can acquire the ability to make reliable moral observations—that is, how we can become sensitive to objective and universal moral truths about which particular acts and practices are right and which are wrong.[11] This is too big a puzzle for me to solve by myself. All I can do is try to outline some features I think the solution will have.

At the most fundamental phenomenological level, the particular moral judgment of the wrongness of an act typically appears not as an intellectual thought, but as a feeling which is expressed by words such as: "That is wrong; it ought not to be done!" Because, phenomenologically, moral judgment typically appears as more of a feeling than a thought, many philosophers have concluded that moral judgment is merely the expression of a feeling rather than the judgment of something objective. I believe they have made a mistake. Although they are correct about the phenomenology of particular moral judgments, the phenomenology does not rule out the possibility that our moral feelings themselves reflect our sensitivity to universal, objective moral rightness and wrongness.

It is important to recognize that particular moral judgments are *conditional* upon purely descriptive judgments. For example, it makes a difference to the moral evaluation of an act whether, viewed purely descriptively, it really is an intentional beheading or it is a stage trick, intended to give an audience the impression of seeing a beheading though no one is actually harmed. For particular moral judgments to be universal and objective, they cannot be reducible to some purely descriptive judgment plus a nonjudgmental feeling or attitude. The judgment that it is wrong to behead an innocent native merely in order to test the sharpness of one's sword is an irreducibly moral judgment, even though it may manifest itself by a feeling of horror when one thinks about the action.

Although there is a structural analogy between the role of experimental observations in the justification of scientific principles and the role of moral observations in the justification of moral norms, there are also many disanalogies.[12] For example, there is widespread agreement on the experimental observations that a successful scientific theory is expected to explain, but there is substantial disagreement over moral observations. I am not referring to the disagreement over moral norms from culture to culture. This is not a challenge to the universality and objectivity of particular moral judgments, because it is quite possible for two societies to have different norms without any disagreement on particular moral judgments. For example, if society R has the rule to drive on the right side of the road and society L has the rule to drive on the left side of the road, the members of both R and L might agree that in R one should drive on the right side of the road and in L one should drive on the left side of the road.[13]

Consider again the case of Bartolomé de Las Casas, on whom my hypothetical story of BLC was loosely based. If he was able to "see" directly that his compatriots' treatment of the American natives was wrong, why were they not able to see it also? In fact, Las Casas was one of only a few Spaniards in the colonies who objected to the treatment of the natives. They were all able to observe the same behavior. Why were only Las Casas and a few others able to see its wrongness? Why did almost all of the other colonists have a moral blindspot? The explanation has two parts: (1) the role of empathic understanding in moral observation, and (2) the role of socially enforced self-serving beliefs. I take them up individually.

The Role of Empathic Understanding in Moral Observation

In my story of the hypothetical BLC, I suggested that before he had any experience of the American natives, the information that they were cannibalistic and idolatrous triggered stereotypes that led him to imagine them as a kind of beast in more or less human form. His stereotypes of the American natives might not have been called into question until he came to the Americas and interacted with them. The most likely way that his interactions with the natives would have altered his stereotypical representations of them would be if he were able to have imaginative access to what their lives were like, from the inside, to put himself in their shoes, so to speak. I refer to this as *empathic understanding.* Empathic understanding breaks down stereotypes and makes it possible to respond to the humanity of others. It must also be acknowledged that powerful stereotypes often block empathic understanding and thus prevent a recognition of the humanity of others.

I would not know how to explain empathic understanding to someone who lacked it. So I am just going to assume you have it. Because of his empathic understanding, the historical Las Casas came to see that what his countrymen referred to as the "idolatry" of the natives was in fact a distinctive view of the world. What is most remarkable about Las Casas is that in spite of a powerful stereotype of cannibals as savages, and in spite of what he took to be infallible moral norms prohibiting cannibalism, Las Casas developed sufficient empathic understanding of the natives' way of life that even their cannibalism started to make sense to him. I return to this development shortly, because it marks an extremely important transformation in Las Casas.

Attempts at empathic understanding across cultures are always fraught with difficulties and with potential misunderstanding. The Spaniards who traveled with Columbus endured great hardship and risked their lives, all in the hope of finding riches. Men who were so motivated by the hope of great wealth were unlikely to have empathic understanding for those who stood in their way. Even knowing this, it is difficult to imagine how they could have had so little empathy with the natives as to be able, for example, to take young children from their parents and feed them alive to their dogs.

Because empathy is often understood to be a feeling—a kind of vicarious sharing of experience—it is important to emphasize that, on my account, moral observations cannot be explained merely as a conjunction of purely descriptive judgments plus a *feeling* of empathy.[14] The feeling of empathy itself cannot be separated from a judgment about what it is like to be the other person, and that judgment provides the basis for a moral judgment about how the other person ought to be treated. Feeling another's pain does not by itself determine how one should treat the other. In some cases, it is morally appropriate for the other person to feel pain—if, for example, it is the result of a justified act of self-defense or a justified punishment. Empathy is not a substitute for moral judgment, but it is an important component of the sensitivity required to make reliable moral observations.

Even if it required empathy for Las Casas to recognize the wrongness of the Spaniards' treatment of the American natives, my emphasis on empathy may seem to be a mistake or, even worse, a way of discounting the moral judgments of the natives themselves. After all, the American natives did not have to have empathic understanding of the Spaniards to recognize that the Spaniards' treatment of them was wrong.

Consider the case of Guarocuya, a native of Hispaniola. When Guarocuya was a young boy, Spanish colonists brutally killed his father. Guarocuya was taken in and raised by missionaries, who baptized him and changed his name to Enrique. As an adult, Enrique was placed in the service of a Spanish landowner, Valenzuela. Las Casas reports that Valenzuela treated Enrique "as though he were dung" (Josephy 1994, 128). Enrique had no trouble recognizing that the Spaniards' treatment of the natives was wrong. He told them to their faces: "Christians . . . are bad men, tyrants, who want only to usurp the land of others and only know how to spill the blood of those who have never given offense" (Josephy 1994, 129). Enrique did not have to empathize with the Spaniards to reach this conclusion. So why do I stress the importance of empathic understanding in moral judgment?

The answer is that nothing so far in the story of Enrique and Valenzuela indicates the possibility of a universal moral standpoint. From the point of view of Valenzuela and the other colonists, there was nothing wrong in treating Enrique as though he were dung. From the point of view of Enrique, the treatment of him was wrong. If there were nothing more to be said, this sort of case would only seem to show the utter subjectivity of the moral standpoint and the impossibility of attaining a universal moral standpoint. Empathic understanding makes it possible to move beyond one's own personal point of view in the evaluation of an act. Such an evaluation requires that one be able to take into consideration the point of view of each person affected by the act.

Empathic understanding is not meant to be a substitute for talking to the natives and finding out what they think. However, there is a big difference between talking to someone with whom you have an empathic understanding and talking to someone with whom you do not. It requires a fair amount of empathic understanding to fully hear what another person says, because in conversation we communicate much more than simple facts.

Although my primary example of someone who adopted a universal moral standpoint is Bartolomé de Las Casas, it is important to emphasize that the universal moral standpoint is accessible from within any moral tradition. Consider the example of Tecumseh. As a Shawnee youth, Tecumseh grew up in a culture with a tradition of burning alive white prisoners, even women and children. Any warrior who refused to participate would be accused of cowardice, one of the most serious accusations against a Shawnee male. Nonetheless, at age fifteen, Tecumseh disavowed all torture as dishonorable. Even though he was one of the youngest warriors and had no position of authority in the tribe, he was able to persuade those who fought with him to disavow it also (Eckert 1992, 256–261). Like Las Casas, Tecumseh was a moral reformer of his culture. Like Las Casas, Tecumseh had an emotional reaction, a revulsion from acts of torture, based, at least in part, on an empathic understanding of the position of the victims. I would add that the reaction was not merely an emotional one. The feelings were the emotional manifestation of a particular judgment of wrongness—in this case, the wrongness of torturing defenseless prisoners.

One reason I have focused on Las Casas rather than on Enrique is that it would have been harder for someone in Las Casas's position to attain the necessary empathic understanding of the natives than it would have been for Enrique. Las Casas had once been a perpetrator of the wrongs against the American natives, and his friends and compatriots were continuing to perpetrate those wrongs. It is important to understand why it was so much harder for someone in Las Casas's position than someone in Enrique's position to recognize the colonists' wrongs in order to understand why moral observations sometimes seem irreducibly subjective.

Socially Enforced Self-Serving Beliefs

Because of their pursuit of riches, the Spaniards had an obvious interest in believing it was morally permissible to enslave and otherwise mistreat the American natives. Whenever one has a strong interest in performing a certain act or a strong desire to perform it, there is a danger that the interest or desire can influence one to *consciously bias* the evidence and reasons made available to others so they will come to believe (or continue to believe) that performing the relevant act is not morally wrong. Even more insidiously, there is a danger that the interest or desire can *unconsciously bias* one's own evidence and reasons so as to generate *self-serving particular moral judgments* and *self-serving reasons* for believing that the act is not morally wrong. When a justification for a conclusion is self-serving, it is not the case that the conclusion is accepted because the justification is accepted; rather, the causal relation is reversed, and the justification is accepted because it supports the desired conclusion. Las Casas describes this sort of bias in the epigraph to this chapter.

Of the two sorts of biasing, conscious and unconscious, the conscious sort is the easiest to explain (though, of course, not always to detect). When it is in their interests or when it satisfies a strong desire, people sometimes lie or suppress relevant evidence. This is conscious biasing. When the biasing is unconscious, the result is typically self-deception.[15]

How can unconscious bias influence one's particular moral judgments? I see at least four ways, three direct and one indirect:

1. Selectivity of Moral Observations. The simplest way to bias one's moral observations is to be selective about what observations one makes. By unconsciously avoiding situations in which I might make troubling moral observations, I can avoid acquiring particular moral judgments that might cast doubt on my other moral beliefs.

2. Biasing One's Relevant Nonmoral Observations. Although particular moral judgments are not reducible to purely descriptive judgments, they are conditional upon them. For example, if a doctor convinces himself that he is dealing with a hypochondriac, the doctor may be able to discount the patient's complaints and make them seem (to the doctor) to be less morally urgent.

3. Interference with Empathy. It is usually much more difficult to empathize with another person when doing so would lead one to give up something that is the object of a powerful interest or desire. I am sure that the Spanish colonists would have had more empathy for the American natives if they had thought that their own wealth depended on the happiness of the American natives.

4. Rationalization. The first three sorts of influence are pathways by which a bias can prevent an observer from having any idea that something wrong is being done. The fourth pathway makes it possible to explain away apparent wrongness. An act that would typically be regarded as wrong—for example, taking a child from its mother and feeding it to dogs—can be judged not to be wrong if it is supported by a rationalization constructed out of reasons that are self-serving. These other reasons can themselves be the product of any of these four mechanisms. Rationalizations can make acts that otherwise would seem wrong seem to be benign.

I do not claim this is an exhaustive list of the ways that interests and desires can bias one's particular moral judgments. They simply illustrate some of the ways that interests and desires can have a substantial biasing effect on one's particular moral judgments.

There is no simple test for determining when a particular moral judg-ment is biased, but it is possible to recognize particular cases. We easily recognize the phenomenon in the explanation of the Shawnee warrior Chik-sika to his younger brother Tecumseh: "When a white man kills an Indian in a fair fight, it is called honorable, but when an Indian kills a white man in a fair fight, it is called murder. When a white army battles Indians and wins, it is a great victory, but if they lose it is called a massacre" (Eckert 1992, 176). The tendency to interpret whatever the Indians did as wrong and whatever the white settlers did as honorable is a manifestation of the white settlers' unconscious bias, which enabled them to generate self-serving justifications for their treatment of the Indians.

For many of the false claims made about the American natives by Colum-bus and his countrymen—for example, the claim that the natives had no religion and no culture (Todorov 1984, 34–36)—it is hard to tell which ones were conscious lies, aimed at providing others with reasons for believ-ing that the mistreatment of the natives was justified, and which were the result of unconscious bias due to their all-consuming desire for wealth. What seems almost certain is that they were not simply honest mistakes.

The biasing effects of the Spaniards' interests and desires made them blind to the wrongness of what they were doing. The result was a kind of moral blindness. However, if I stop the account here, with the effects of each individual's biases, I omit an important element in the way this moral blindness is sustained. The further element is *social enforcement* of the self-serving moral beliefs.

Though I am no expert on this phenomenon, I had a powerful experience of it on my visits to my grandmother in Kentucky during the 1950s. Ken-tucky was not one of the eleven states of the Confederacy, but in the 1950s, like the former Confederate states, Kentucky had a strict system of racial segregation backed by Jim Crow laws. Not only did Black people have sepa-rate residences, churches, schools, bathrooms, drinking fountains, and so on, but there was also a strict limitation on the jobs they were permitted to perform—mostly subservient and menial labor. There was also among the white population a generally shared self-serving justification for the segrega-tion, which insisted that segregation was good for both races. This self-serving justification was socially enforced by requiring Blacks not only to accept their position but also to express their appreciation for it. This en-forcement took both mild and more sinister forms.

When my grandmother's young Black housekeeper expressed her dream of going to college to become a schoolteacher (even the Black schools needed teachers) she was ridiculed for "putting on airs" and not being satisfied with her station. Because she had no aspirations beyond attending an all-Black college and teaching in an all-Black elementary school, she was not perceived as challenging the segregationist status quo, and the response of my grandmother and her friends was limited to ridicule. I do not mean to underestimate the effectiveness of ridicule on human motivation. However, had the housekeeper ever voiced doubts about the desirability of the segregation system for Blacks or any aspirations to cross the borders defined by it, she would have been put in a different category, one that invoked much more sinister enforcement—the category of an "uppity n——r." To be "uppity" was to fail to be properly appreciative of the "benefits" of being allowed to occupy the subservient positions permitted by the segregation system. It was to fail to have the primary virtue necessary for survival in the Jim Crow system—that is, to "know your place" (code words for being satisfied with and even grateful for your subservient position). Although I had no knowledge of the ways that Blacks who were classified as uppity were punished— that is, no knowledge of the history of lynchings, race riots, and Ku Klux Klan attacks—even as a child I could feel the ominous threat behind the words.[16]

There were two ways that the classification of uppity prevented Black people from raising questions about the justification of the system of segregation.[17] First, the fact that Blacks categorized as uppity would be punished, by the Ku Klux Klan or by other whites, was a great deterrent to any Black person ever expressing the slightest dissatisfaction with the system. Second, to be classified as uppity was to be regarded as failing to appreciate the benefits of the system of segregation for Black people. So any Black person who expressed dissatisfaction with the system of segregation would, by that very expression, show that they did not appreciate the benefits of the system for Black people. Thus, nothing that a Black person said would ever be interpreted by whites as a reason to think there was something wrong with the system of segregation.

So long as opposition from uppity Blacks could be effectively silenced and suppressed, if there were to be a challenge to the system from within, it would have to come from whites. If a white person raised any questions about the system—even to merely try to excuse the behavior of a Black person who was regarded as uppity—it would simply be taken as evidence that the white person was a "n——r lover." Being so classified carried with it at least social ostracism, and sometimes worse, so it was not a label most white people would risk. For example, no businessperson who catered to a white clientele could stay in business with such a label.[18]

So long as social enforcement was effective in silencing Black objections to the system of segregation and was effective in making sure that only the most marginal members of white society might raise any objection to the system of segregation, it was unlikely that there would be a successful challenge to the self-serving justifications for the segregationist society from within.[19] However, even before the beginning of the civil rights movement in the South, a reasonably empathic outsider, such as Gunnar Myrdal, could recognize the injustice of the system of Jim Crow in the South and the use of self-serving justifications by whites in the South to blind themselves to the injustice (Myrdal 1944). This illustrates a general fact about socially enforced self-serving moral beliefs: It is often easier for a suitably empathic outsider to recognize that a given practice or social arrangement is supported by self-serving rationalizations than it is for an insider, at least when the outsider has no personal interest in believing that the practice or social arrangement is morally justifiable and when the outsider is not subject to the social enforcement mechanisms to which insiders are subject. I return to this point shortly.

When a practice or social arrangement is supported by socially enforced self-serving rationalizations, it is difficult for those who benefit from it to be able to make unbiased moral observations. Las Casas provides a striking example of someone who was able to do so. Somehow, his empathy overcame all of the powerful motivations not to see anything wrong with the Spaniards' brutal treatment of the American natives.

One lesson we can draw from this example is that agreement on moral observations should not be expected when some observers have powerful interests or desires biasing them in one direction and others do not. Another lesson we can draw is that not all moral observations are equally trustworthy. An outsider should be skeptical of moral justifications of practices or social arrangements offered by those who benefit from them and should even be skeptical when they are offered by those who seem to be disadvantaged by them, if belief in the appropriateness of the practice or institution is socially enforced. In such a case, an appropriately empathic outside observer may be in a better position than insiders to morally evaluate the practice or social arrangement.

Are All Moral Beliefs Self-Serving?

Recognizing the pervasiveness of self-serving moral beliefs can lead to the even more radical claim that *all* moral beliefs are merely self-serving. There are many different variants of this extreme claim, of which the most influential has been the Marxist view that morality is simply the ruling class's tool for legitimating its power. Such views are too extreme. If they are taken seriously, they undermine the possibility of any epistemically justified moral judgments. Indeed, the judgment that all moral justifications are self-serving can even undermine itself, if it suggests that it itself is merely part of an attempt at a self-serving moral justification; and it can even undermine the moral judgment that self-serving moral beliefs are themselves morally objectionable. The result of such an extreme view is moral skepticism.

The power of interests and desires to motivate self-serving beliefs should not drive us to moral skepticism. It should give us a greater appreciation for such individuals as Bartolomé de Las Casas. Las Casas was a slaveholder himself. In spite of his financial interest in continuing to hold slaves and the powerful social pressures brought to bear on those who opposed the self-serving justifications used to justify slavery, he was able to come to appreciate the wrongness of what he was doing.[20] As a result, after he freed his slaves he spent the rest of his life arguing and working on the natives' behalf.

The biasing effects of interests and desires should also alert us to the difficulties of making reliable moral judgments when the issue is one in which we have a strong interest or one about which we have strong desires. Though it is not impossible to make moral judgments that oppose one's powerful interests or desires, it is much easier to make reliable moral judgments in situations that do not trigger them.

There is no infallible test to determine whether biasing interests and desires have influenced a moral judgment. However, there is a striking and important fact about self-serving moral judgments. Other things being equal, it is often easier for an outside observer, at least one who has no interest in maintaining or opposing the moral judgments in question, to determine whether a person's moral judgment is self-serving than it is for the person herself. The reason is simple. The very interests and desires that motivate a self-serving moral judgment will also serve to oppose coming to believe that it is self-serving. If one comes to the conclusion that one's moral judgment J is self-serving, then J will no longer be able to serve the justificatory role that motivated it in the first place. Thus, someone who is motivated to acquire a self-serving moral belief J will also be motivated not to believe that J is a self-serving belief.[21]

Awareness of the power of interests and desires to bias moral observations and other moral judgments should alert us to strictly scrutinize the moral justifications of a practice offered by those who benefit substantially from it. Queen Isabella's reasons for permitting Columbus to sell the American natives (quoted earlier) are immediately thrown into question when she makes her permission conditional on his "paying us the share that belongs to us" (Josephy 1994, 123).

Because of the power of interests and desires to bias moral judgment, moral observation can never be infallible. In addition, human beings will never achieve on moral observations anything like the consensus that exists on scientific observations. Where a culture's practices are supported by socially enforced self-serving justifications, the result will typically be a widespread moral blindness, a blindness that is unlikely to be detected by the members of the culture who benefit from the practices and, because of the social enforcement, unlikely to be voiced by those who are disadvantaged by the practices.

Other Sources of Unreliability

Although socially enforced self-serving justifications for social practices seem to me to be the most important source of moral blindspots, there are other sources of unreliability in particular moral judgments. Consider, for example, the feeling of revulsion that some people have when they think about sexual relations between mixed-race or same-sex couples. The feeling itself is often interpreted by those who feel it as a response to the wrongness of mixed-race or same-sex sexual relations. If they construct their moral principles and norms bottom-up from their particular moral judgments, wouldn't they inevitably come to accept racist and homophobic norms? Given the strength of their feelings, wouldn't such norms necessarily be justified for them?

The answer to both questions is negative. To see why, recall that my model of moral reasoning is an equilibrium model. On an equilibrium model, it is possible to overturn moral principles or moral norms on the basis of particular moral judgments and it is possible to overturn particular moral judgments on the basis of moral principles or moral norms. I believe that the historical development of human rights principles has made it possible for people with strong emotional reactions to mixed-race or same-sex couples to recognize that their reactions are not reliable moral responses. In this case, the principles justify giving up some of the particular moral judgments. I return to the topic of discrimination based on race or sexual orientation in chapter 6.

If even the most emotionally compelling particular moral judgments can be mistaken, what reason is there to think that any of them are reliable? The answer to that question requires a fuller appreciation of the equilibrium model of epistemic justification. In moral development, we begin by trusting our particular moral judgments, where those that have powerful emotional components are often trusted more than those that do not. Over time we learn that some of our emotional responses are not moral responses at all. This raises the question of whether all of them are simply emotional responses triggered by something other than rightness or wrongness.

This problem seems particularly pressing if one accepts, as I do, an account of human development in terms of processes of genetic and social evolution. It would seem that there would be a complete evolutionary account of the development of human emotional responses that would not make any reference to objective rightness or wrongness.[22] So it would seem that even if there were objectively right and objectively wrong acts, there would be no reason to expect that our particular moral judgments would be able to reliably distinguish them.

What is correct about this objection is that if the processes of genetic and social evolution had made our particular moral judgments completely unreliable, there would be no way we could correct them to make them reliable. But there is another possibility. The difference between objective rightness and wrongness or some approximation of it might be an important distinction for human beings to be sensitive to. This possibility has received some support from evolutionary psychologists who have reported powerful evidence for psychological modules aimed at "cheating" detection (Cosmides and Tooby 1992).

One way of reading this literature would make moral judgments parochial rather than universal. On this reading, our evolutionary history has determined what *we* think cheating is. Other beings with a different evolutionary history would have a different idea of what it is. The alternative I favor is that cheating is universally wrong, and our evolutionary history is simply one way we have come to recognize it to be so.[23]

It is implausible that evolution could have made us infallible about objective rightness and wrongness. However, if our particular moral judgments are reliable enough, equilibrium reasoning can lead us to become more reliable over time, by leading us to formulate principles and norms that can themselves be used to question some of our particular moral judgments.

Determinations of the reliability of our particular moral judgments are themselves a product of equilibrium reasoning. It may seem that such reasoning will inevitably lead us to conclude that our particular moral judgments are reliable, but that is not so. Suppose, for example, the principle that best explained each individual's particular moral judgments was: Everyone should do what most benefits *me*. Each individual's moral judgments would be best explained as veiled attempts to promote her *own* well-being. In such a case, there would be little justification for thinking that human beings were reliable judges of objective rightness and wrongness. A better alternative would be to explain all of their particular moral judgments in terms of self-serving justifications and personal bias.

So in gauging the reliability of our particular moral judgments, it is important to consider what sorts of principles best explain them. When we look, we find such principles as the various versions of the Golden Rule, the utilitarian principle of maximizing overall well-being, and the human rights principles in the UN Universal Declaration of Human Rights. The various versions of the Golden Rule are best understood as a corrective for placing too much weight on one's own well-being. The utilitarian principle specifically excludes giving greater weight to our own well-being or to the well-being of our own social group or our own species. The UN declaration extends human rights to all human beings, so it does not give special consideration to any individual or social group. It has been criticized for giving special consideration to our species, but this criticism fails if human rights are understood not as rights we have because we are biologically human, but rather as rights we have because of typically human capacities we have. Imagine a planet occupied by beings with very much the same cognitive and emotional capacities we have. It would be a mockery of the idea of human rights if human beings one day discovered this planet and enslaved its occupants on the grounds that they were members of a different biological species.[24]

The upshot of this discussion is that in determining the reliability of our particular moral judgments we are not limited to evidence internal to the judgments themselves (e.g., how strongly we feel). Even if our principles largely derive their support from our particular moral judgments, the equilibrium model of moral reasoning explains how the content of those principles can play an important role in determining whether it is reasonable to believe the particular moral judgments to be reliable.

Those enamored with the Proof paradigm will not be satisfied with equilibrium reasoning as a basis for trusting the reliability of our ordinary moral judgments. They will insist on a *proof* of their reliability. I believe this is a misguided goal. It almost always leads to moral skepticism.[25]

Can a Universal Moral Standpoint Avoid Moral Imperialism?

It is essential to my position that we be able to see moral progress over time—progress in making universal particular moral judgments about actual and hypothetical cases and progress in formulating principles to explain the particular moral judgments. I have already given some examples of what I take to be progress in chapter 2 and I will give others in coming chapters. It might be objected that all of my examples simply reveal my own moral imperialism, because my standard of progress is the degree to which others agree with my moral beliefs.

This objection reflects a failure to appreciate what it means to be epistemically modest. On my view, moral progress is a process of correcting our moral mistakes. I believe there is room for much more progress in the future, because I am confident that all of us, myself included, have moral blindspots. Of course, I can't identify any mistakes I am currently making, because if I could, I would correct them. So my evidence of my own mistakes is indirect. When we look to the past, we have no trouble identifying some of the moral blindspots of our ancestors. I have already mentioned that the authors of the Declaration of Independence had moral blindspots concerning the treatment of Blacks and women. Only during my lifetime has there been any considerable awareness of our moral blindspots in our treatment of nonhuman animals.[26] I have no doubt that when our descendants look back at us 200 years from now, they will have no trouble identifying other moral blindspots of which we are now unaware.

Epistemic modesty must be distinguished from moral wishy-washiness. I express my epistemic modesty when I insist that my moral beliefs are fallible and express my belief that I myself have moral blindspots. Moral wishy-washiness is the view that my moral claims only apply to those who agree with me or that all moral beliefs are equally valid.

Moral wishy-washiness would prevent us from asserting that the Spanish colonists' brutal treatment of the American natives really was wrong, because the Spanish colonists, with few exceptions, did not agree it was wrong. To avoid wishy-washiness, it is necessary to explain how a moral claim could apply to someone who disagrees with it and why not all moral judgments are equally reliable. I have emphasized two factors to help explain why they are not all equally reliable. First, reliable moral observation, especially across cultures, requires empathic understanding. Not all moral observers have the same degree of empathic understanding. Second, one's interests or desires can introduce biasing factors that lead to self-serving rationalizations of one's moral judgments. Other things being equal, moral observers without such biases are more likely to make reliable moral judgments than those with such biases. The problem is exacerbated if the self-serving judgments are socially enforced. These are not the only sources of unreliability in moral judgments, but they seem to me to be the most important ones.

Although my view is not wishy-washy, it avoids moral imperialism because of its symmetry: When it comes to reliable moral judgment, no culture or individual has a monopoly on it. And when it comes to self-serving moral belief, no culture or individual has an immunity to it.[27] It is important to emphasize that I am not limiting my discussion to terrestrial cultures. If, someday, extraterrestrials arrive on earth, what would we expect them to think about the Western Europeans' treatment of the American natives? If all moral judgments are parochial, we would not have any idea what to expect. Because the extraterrestrials share no cultural or biological heritage with us, if all moral judgments are parochial, there would be no reason to expect them to share any of our moral judgments. This seems to me to be a mistake. I do not insist that the extraterrestrials would necessarily agree with our moral judgments, only that if they did disagree with us, only one side of the disagreement could be correct.

Could the extraterrestrials, for example, just find it obvious that the Spaniards' ripping native children from their mothers' breasts and throwing them to their dogs for food was not wrong? I don't believe they could. They might well believe it was not wrong. If so, they should recognize the necessity of giving some reason to support their position. Because none of our moral judgments is infallible, we should be prepared to listen to their reasons for disagreeing with us. Not everything they might say would count as an adequate reason. Suppose that, when asked for reasons for thinking it was not wrong for the Spaniards to throw live native children to their dogs, they answered that the native children were a good source of nutrition.

To someone who holds that moral judgments are parochial, not universal, this might simply indicate that the extraterrestrials had their own, unique extraterrestrial concept of wrongness. Again, this seems to me to be a mistake. Concepts of morality cannot vary arbitrarily. Perhaps the extraterrestrials mistakenly believe that the Spaniards lacked the capacity for moral judgment, in which case nothing they did would be wrong; or perhaps they believe that the American natives were incapable of suffering, in which case it would not be so obviously wrong to treat them as the Spaniards treated them. We would need to explore these questions to make sure we were in agreement on the relevant facts. Even after settling the factual issues, it might be that the extraterrestrials themselves lacked the necessary empathic understanding for them to appreciate the wrongness of the Spaniards' treatment of the American natives. They might well lack this empathic understanding if they intended to enslave us, because they might well have developed socially enforced self-serving rationalizations for treating us the way the Western European colonists treated the American natives. Remember, the Spanish explorers came from a culture that accorded central importance to various versions of the Golden Rule, but this did not prevent them from feeding Native American children alive to their dogs. However, even if the extraterrestrials believe that enslaving us is not wrong, that won't make it true.

In moral judgment, there is no substitute for sensitivity to moral rightness and moral wrongness. Anyone in any moral tradition, extraterrestrial as well as terrestrial, can develop it. Those who develop it are able to make reliable, but not infallible, particular moral judgments.

How Las Casas Gave Up Moral Imperialism

So long as Las Casas agreed that cannibalism and idolatry were wrong, he could object to the colonists' mistreatment of the natives, but not to the goal of converting them from their idolatrous, cannibalistic way of life to Christianity. Indeed, for most of his life, Las Casas never questioned the justifiability of that goal, only the means used to achieve it, because for most of his life, Las Casas was a moral imperialist. If Las Casas had remained a moral imperialist to the end of his life, he would still be rightly esteemed an important moral reformer for his devotion to the cause of protecting the American natives. However, near the end of his life, Las Casas made one more change that makes him a particularly appropriate example to illustrate my model of epistemically modest, metaphysically immodest moral judgment. Near the end of his life, Las Casas gave up his moral imperialism.

Although the historical Las Casas never would have accepted the full unofficial justification for enslaving Native Americans given in example 4–2, for most of his life he would have accepted the part of it that takes the Christian Scriptures to be an infallible source of norms against cannibalism and idolatry. So long as he accepted the Christian Scriptures as an infallible source of moral norms, he had to agree that it was wrong for the American natives to engage in cannibalistic and idolatrous religious practices. However, he was not completely content with this conclusion. Over the course of his life, he became more and more disturbed by it until, sometime near the end of his life, he gave it up and came to believe that the natives' traditional religious practices, including human sacrifice, were appropriate for them and that it was *not* wrong for them to engage in their traditional religious practices, even when they were cannibalistic and idolatrous.[28]

It is almost impossible for most of us to imagine how difficult it was intellectually for him to make such a change. It required him to question the most fundamental moral beliefs of his culture, beliefs that he himself antecedently took to be infallible. In addition, Las Casas lived in a time when this sort of questioning could be fatal, because of the Inquisition, and would at least lead others to doubt his sanity. Nonetheless, by the end of his life, Las Casas had abandoned moral imperialism.[29] Did Las Casas become a moral relativist?[30] Not an extreme moral relativist. Extreme moral relativism is wishy-washy. As I explained in the previous chapter, no wishy-washy relativist could consistently hold that the Western Europeans' external norms were mistaken. I believe that when Las Casas, a member of the Spanish culture, recognized the moral appropriateness of the natives' religious practices for the natives themselves, he was making a judgment true from any point of view.

To give up the moral norm that cannibalism and idolatry are wrong would have introduced a disequilibrium into Las Casas's moral beliefs. Although Las Casas attempted to resolve the disequilibrium without admitting to himself that he was radically reinterpreting the Christian Scriptures, in fact he had to give up what was generally regarded as God's first commandment ("Thou shalt not have false gods before me").[31]

Las Casas's final move away from moral imperialism illustrates how moral observations can lead to and epistemically justify changes in one's most fundamental moral beliefs. His unease and guilt about altering the natives' way of life ultimately led him to question what had previously seemed beyond question—whether his own moral authority, the Christian Scriptures, was a source of infallible moral norms that applied to everyone. Although Las Casas may not have even acknowledged to himself the radicalness of his departure from the moral imperialism of his Christian culture, Las Casas had quite clearly given up moral imperialism by the end of his life. This makes him not only an important moral reformer but also an important figure in the history of moral discovery.[32]

Las Casas's Moral Blindspots

I seem to have put Las Casas up on a pedestal as a moral exemplar. Las Casas was not perfect. He was a human being with flaws of his own. Why then would I hold him out as an exemplar? As I have reconstructed it, there were two crucially important steps in Las Casas's moral development: first, when he changed the interpretation of his moral norms to include the American natives; and second, when he concluded that his culture's norms against cannibalism and idolatry should not be applied to the natives. Especially in the first step, the change can be described as a broadening of the range of Las Casas's concept of who counts morally, extending the concept of *us* to include *them*. Some people find this whole idea morally noxious. They find it morally presumptuous of Las Casas even to have a concept of *us* and patronizing to think of him as extending it to the natives.

This objection is based on a mistake. Everyone has a concept of *us*, understood as those who count morally. To avoid insanity, everyone must have a concept of *us* that excludes some things as *not-us*. People who believed that everything, including tables and chairs and other physical objects, had feelings that had to be taken into account in making choices, would go insane, because either they would be constantly worried about the feelings of tables and chairs and other physical objects with no way of telling what they were or they would have recurrent delusional beliefs that they had empathy with tables and chairs and other physical objects.

If human beings had direct rational insight into true moral principles, then the gradual extension of the concept of *us* that we find in human moral development would seem like a painfully slow way to make moral progress. Because human beings have no such direct access to moral principles, there is no other way for human beings to make progress.

A more telling moral criticism of Las Casas is that in his efforts to protect the American natives from slavery, he supported replacing native slaves with Africans.[33] It is true that he later regretted the suggestion and stated his principled opposition to all slavery. However, it is generally agreed that he did not oppose African slavery with the same determination that he opposed enslaving American natives.

It is disturbing to think that Las Casas more strongly opposed enslaving American natives than enslaving African natives, but it should not be too surprising. If moral beliefs were the result of direct rational insight into self-evident moral principles, then one would expect Las Casas to directly see that all slavery is wrong. If, as I believe, moral principles get their justification from one's moral observations, then we should expect variability due to differences in moral observations. Las Casas was an eyewitness to the brutality involved in enslaving the American natives. In addition, he had extensive experience with the American natives that provided the basis for an empathic understanding of their plight. And this same empathic understanding was eventually extended to the Africans. After he learned the facts about the African slave trade, he repented his earlier suggestion to replace Indian slaves with Africans.[34] In fact, Las Casas was one of the first Europeans to denounce the African slave trade (Gutiérrez 1993, 329).

How should we respond to the fact that Las Casas was not morally perfect? If anything like the picture I have presented is correct, we should not expect moral perfection from human beings. I can confidently predict that, with the passage of time, the image of any moral exemplar will become tarnished because, over time, new moral discoveries are made and previously undetected moral blindspots are revealed. How should we respond to these discoveries? If our moral standards are adjusted to fit fallible human beings, we can make moral distinctions and identify moral exemplars without requiring moral perfection. Measured by comparison to the general level of moral sensitivity in the general population at the time he was living, who today would compare with Las Casas?[35]

What Is the Universal Moral Standpoint?

I have used the story of Las Casas's moral development to illustrate what is involved in making particular moral judgments from a universal moral standpoint. What exactly is the moral standpoint? My only way of answering that question is to look at the historical development of moral principles to explain our particular moral judgments and to ask what sort of point of view they represent. Consider first the various versions of the Golden Rule. All of them require us to consider the impact of our actions from the point of view of those who are affected by them. The problem with all versions of the Golden Rule is that they do not give us satisfactory guidance on how to balance our own interests with the interests of others affected by the act. Utilitarianism claims to solve this problem. It tells us to count everyone's well-being the same.

So it is clear that the moral standpoint has something to do with considering everyone's point of view. Harsanyi (1953) and Rawls (1971) have proposed very similar models of this standpoint. Rawls calls his version the *original position.* The original position is a hypothetical construction in which we imagine ourselves choosing behind a *veil of ignorance.* Behind the veil of ignorance, we do not know our sex, race, religion, social class, or any other particular information about ourselves. Though Harsanyi (1953) did not use Rawls's terms, his construction of the moral standpoint was similar to Rawls's. On both accounts, because we don't have any way of identifying ourselves in the original position, we must try to look at things from everyone's point of view.

Both Harsanyi and Rawls thought the agents in the original position should be purely rationally self-interested. As I explain in chapter 7, I do not think the moral standpoint is in any way rationally self-interested. The moral standpoint is a completely different point of view from the personal, rationally self-interested point of view. I regard the original position thought experiment as a heuristic for reasonable people to use to help them get clear on what fairness requires.[36] Reasonable people are not purely rationally self-interested.

Finally, both Harsanyi and Rawls used the original position to attempt to derive the basic principles of justice. One indication that they failed is that they disagreed on which principles would be agreed to in the original position. To make matters worse, many people who do the original position thought experiment find that they do not agree with either Harsanyi or Rawls. Unlike Rawls and Harsanyi, I do not find the original position useful for determining the basic principles of justice. My use of it is more modest: to find rules for resolving disagreements over fairness or equity.

In the original position, reasonable agents facing a problem of fairness or equity try to find a rule to resolve the problem that everyone can agree on. Here is a simple example. A husband and wife have a disagreement over how much housework they each should do, so they sit down to negotiate a fair division of the housework. Both work full time. Both know that, on average, husbands do about one-quarter of the housework and wives do three-quarters of it. A purely rationally self-interested husband who wanted to minimize the amount of housework he did would argue that he should do no more than one-quarter. A rationally self-interested husband who wanted to please his wife might offer a one-third/two-thirds division. To what rule of division would they agree behind the veil of ignorance? Behind the veil of ignorance, they would not know whether they were male or female, so they would look for a rule that would protect both parties. Unless there were unusual circumstances, the two would almost surely agree that the only equitable solution was a rule of evenly dividing the housework.

When I adopt the *personal point of view*, I focus on how best to promote my own projects and goals, regardless of how they affect others. When I take the *moral standpoint*, I attempt to look at my actions from the point of view of everyone who might be affected by them and attempt to find a course of action that no one could reasonably object to (Scanlon 1998).

Because the moral standpoint requires me to look at my actions from the point of view of everyone who might be affected by them, it is easy to see why empathic understanding would be an important part of moral judgment. Also, it is easy to see why self-serving beliefs would be an impediment to it. Empathic understanding is necessary to truly understand other people's concerns. Self-serving beliefs can blind us to the true effects of our acts on others or to their true responses.

Evaluating Both External and Internal Norms from the Moral Standpoint

The main question addressed in this chapter is: How is it possible to morally criticize a culture's external norms? To answer that question, I have suggested that there is a moral standpoint that is different from our own personal point of view. When we adopt the moral standpoint, we can make reliable, though not infallible, universal particular moral judgments. Having identified the moral standpoint, I can now return to the question left hanging at the end of the last chapter. Recall that at that point, the advocate of cultural relativism about internal norms had acknowledged that it is possible for an outsider to morally criticize a culture's external norms, but had denied that an outsider could ever be in a position to morally criticize a culture's internal norms. The question was: Why not?

I postponed answering that question until we had answered the question of how it is possible to criticize the external norms of another culture. My answer to that question has involved an account of moral reasoning and the moral standpoint. The moral standpoint is one from which we are able to make reliable, though not infallible, particular moral judgments that hold universally. Individuals do not attain the moral standpoint without the help of a developed cultural tradition. But it is a point of view that can be attained from within any culture. The moral standpoint requires us to evaluate actions and practices from the point of view of others and to respond to reasonable objections others might make to them. Empathic understanding is an important factor in making moral judgments from the moral standpoint. Self-serving beliefs and self-serving reasons are distorting influences that make it easy to believe that one's actions are morally justified when they are not. When external norms play a role in the oppression of one group by another, they are typically upheld by socially enforced systems of self-serving beliefs. Oppressive norms upheld by socially enforced systems of self-serving beliefs often include norms that require the oppressed to express their gratitude to their oppressors, with harsh punishments for those who do not. In such a system, it is a rare insider who will have the empathic understanding and the strength of character to raise objections to the system of oppression. It is often much easier for an outsider to have the empathic understanding to recognize the oppression and to raise objections to it.

Although the previous paragraph is a summary of my discussion of external norms, it also explains why cultural relativism about internal norms is an intellectually unstable position. Everything I said about oppressive external norms applies equally well to oppressive internal norms. Internal norms can also be oppressive. They can also be upheld by socially enforced self-serving beliefs. For example, the fact that Untouchables in India who object to the way they are treated are subjected to terrorist attacks by members of the upper castes—eerily similar to the Ku Klux Klan attacks in the United States—strongly suggests that the norms are supported by socially enforced self-serving justifications (e.g., Moore 1994). Any justifications offered by those who benefit from these practices should be suspect.

Exactly the same moral standpoint makes it possible to criticize oppressive external norms and oppressive internal norms. In both cases, what is needed is a cultural background that makes possible the development of moral sensitivity and empathic understanding to be able to give consideration to other people's points of view. And, in both cases, because the oppressive norms are typically upheld by socially enforced self-serving beliefs, it is often easier for an outsider to recognize and criticize an oppressive norm than for an insider to do so. In the next chapter, I focus on a family of internal norms that are near cultural universals and show how it is possible for an outsider to adopt the moral standpoint and raise moral objections to them without being a moral imperialist.

Did Las Casas Discover Human Rights?

The story of the moral development of Bartolomé de Las Casas has all of the elements we need to explain the development of human rights principles. It is the story of how empathic understanding enabled a moral imperialist to reach a universal moral standpoint from which he was able initially to criticize the oppressive external norms of his culture and ultimately to give up the morally imperialistic norms of his culture. Did he also discover human rights? This is a difficult question, because the concept of human rights has evolved over hundreds of years. Las Casas certainly did not have the kind of understanding of human rights we have today. How much would his understanding have to resemble ours for him to qualify as having the human rights concept? There is no precise answer to this question.

He certainly thought that there were moral limits on the treatment of the American natives by the European colonists. His objections to European colonization can be seen to be the historical precursors of the statutes defining war crimes and crimes against humanity. They did not become part of international law until the twentieth century. So a strong case can be made for his having discovered some individual human rights.

On the other hand, fifteenth- and sixteenth-century Spain was an absolute monarchy with an established religion, both of which used torture to obtain convictions and inflicted gruesome punishments on those judged to be guilty. Las Casas did not indicate that he thought his own countrymen had rights that were violated by the state and by the church. This is not a moral criticism of Las Casas, for to criticize Las Casas for failing to discover individual human rights would be like criticizing Isaac Newton for failing to discovery relativity theory. It is simply to underscore how difficult it is to apply contemporary political categories to those who lived 500 years ago.

The fact that Las Casas did not object to an absolute monarchy and established religion for Spaniards suggests to me that the best way of understanding his position in our contemporary terms is to think of Las Casas not as the discoverer of individual human rights, but as one of the first exponents of some sort of right of groups to live according to their own internal norms. Call this a *group right to religious and cultural freedom.* This seems to me to be the guiding idea behind cultural relativism about internal norms, so Las Casas may have been one of the first advocates of cultural relativism about internal norms.[37]

Notice that the existence of a *group* right to religious freedom would not imply that *individuals* had rights to religious freedom. On the contrary, where a culture was dominated by a single religion that endorsed persecution of apostates and heretics, respect for a group right of religious freedom for that culture would entail permitting the religious leaders of that culture to deny individual rights to religious freedom by persecuting apostates and heretics. The fact that Las Casas did not object to his own culture's treating apostates and heretics in just this way indicates to me that he is better understood as an advocate of group rights than as an advocate of individual rights. So even though he took positions that we would expect an advocate of individual human rights to take, including opposition to forced conversions, torture, and slavery, I think it is anachronistic to classify Las Casas as an advocate of individual human rights.

Even if he did not discover individual human rights himself, Las Casas provided the model for how to discover them. The same process by which he came to endorse a group right to religious and cultural freedom is one that eventually leads to a recognition of an individual right to religious freedom and to a recognition of the other important human rights. That is the story that I tell, in microcosm, in the next chapter.

Conclusion

From within the Proof paradigm, moral universality depends on the possibility of proving at least some moral truths. From within the Proof paradigm, if there are no proofs of moral truths, then all there can be is a multiplicity of points of view, none of which can claim validity beyond those who accept its authority.

Giving up the Proof paradigm opens up a new way of understanding a universal moral standpoint. No longer is it a point of view from which one obtains infallible moral knowledge by deriving that knowledge from rationally self-evident premises. Instead, it is a point of view from which, in favorable circumstances, one can make reliable, though not infallible, judgments about particular cases, both actual and hypothetical. These judgments are universal because, when true, they are true from any point of view. The universality is not in the *form* of the claim—for example, that killing or even torture is always wrong—but in the *understanding* of the claim, for example, that a particular instance of killing or torture is wrong from any point of view.

Universality does not imply universal agreement. When there are powerful interests involved, it may be difficult to make reliable particular moral judgments. The example of Bartolomé de Las Casas shows how an individual can be justified in making particular moral judgments that conflict with the opinions of his moral authorities and with the opinions of a large majority of the members of his community.

To say that particular moral judgments are universal is just to say that when two disputants disagree on a particular moral judgment, at least one of them is mistaken. To attain a universal moral standpoint on a particular issue requires moral training (to develop a sensitivity to right and wrong), empathic understanding, and a lack of bias (from one's interests and desires) on the particular issue.

Anyone from any moral tradition can attain this universal moral standpoint, even Lee Kwan Yew. It is ironic that Lee has criticized the West for trying to impose its own parochial cultural values on societies with different, Asian values. As I explain in chapter 8, it seems to me that Lee's defense of his rule is better understood as an appeal to universal principles of moral justification. In addition, I believe that Lee can make a strong case that proponents of human rights sometimes have self-serving reasons for seeking to impose them on other cultures. If even Lee's defense of his own rule is best understood as an appeal to universal standards of moral justification and his criticism of the West is best understood as an appeal to universal standards of self-serving justification, it is hard to see what reason he would have to be a cultural relativist.

5

THE DEVELOPMENT OF WOMEN'S
RIGHTS AS A MICROCOSM
OF THE DEVELOPMENT
OF HUMAN RIGHTS

If they really be capable of acting like rational creatures, let
them not be treated like slaves.

> —Mary Wollstonecraft

I should like to hear somebody openly enunciating the doctrine
 (it is already implied in much that is written on the subject)—
"It is necessary to society that women should marry and produce
children. They will not do so unless they are compelled.
Therefore, it is necessary to compel them." The merits of the
case would then be clearly defined. It would be exactly that of
the slave-holders of South Carolina and Louisiana.

> —John Stuart Mill

We were neither alive nor dead.

> —Parveen Hashafi's description of life under
> the Taliban in Afghanistan

In the preceding chapter, I used the history of Bartolomé de Las Casas to
illustrate the first step toward the recognition of universal human rights,
the recognition of some kind of group right to religious and cultural freedom. This is an important first step, because it marks a path between moral
imperialism and moral wishy-washiness. This is the path that ultimately
leads to the recognition of individual human rights.

The recognition of individual human rights requires a standpoint from
which to criticize not only a culture's external norms, but also its internal
norms. Cultural relativism about internal norms denies that this is possible.
In this chapter, I illustrate how it is possible. Rather than try to review the
entire history of the development of individual human rights, I focus on the
development of women's rights as a microcosm of the entire history.

Movements for basic human rights usually develop in reaction to oppressive social practices. The oppressive practices have many common features.

First, there is a privileged group and an oppressed group. Second, in the culture, established internal or external norms deny opportunities to members of the oppressed group. Typically, the members of the oppressed group are limited to subservient roles. Third, the privileged group justifies its dominance with an ideology that purports to explain why the members of the oppressed group are not fit to have the same opportunities as those in the privileged group. Usually, the members of the oppressed group are regarded as morally or intellectually defective. Fourth, the members of the privileged group regard themselves as better judges of what is good for members of the oppressed group than the oppressed themselves. This makes it possible for the privileged to justify their oppression paternalistically, as being good for the oppressed. Basic human rights emerge when members of the oppressed group are able to develop and exercise their own judgment, to speak in their own voices, and to articulate their own aspirations.

This pattern has been repeated many times in the development of basic human rights: the rights of the commoners against the aristocracy; the rights of colonized peoples against their colonizers; the rights of Black people in the United States, South Africa, and other countries with legally established segregation; the rights of Untouchables in Hindu society; and the rights of women in patriarchal societies. In each case, the oppressors have described those whom they oppress as "children." Paternalism is appropriate for dealing with children. But children are expected to grow up. These groups were prevented from growing up. Typically, they were denied the opportunity for an education; in many cases, it was against the law even to teach them to read and write.

In each case, the members of the oppressed group were effectively silenced by an ideology that denied that they were capable of good judgment and by a legal and social system aimed at preventing them from developing it. Basic human rights represent the radical idea that all human adults with normal cognitive, emotional, and behavioral capacities should be able to develop and exercise their own judgment about what kind of life is appropriate for them and how best to pursue it. In this sense, it is appropriate to describe the history of basic human rights as the history of the development of a certain kind of respect: respect for individual judgment. Basic human rights are the necessary guarantees for people to be able to develop and exercise their own judgment.

A Near Cultural Universal: The Oppression of Women

One reason for focusing on the development of women's rights as a model for the development of basic human rights generally is that, historically, almost every culture has had internal norms that discriminate against women. Because almost every culture has had such norms, this example will illustrate how it is possible to criticize a culture's internal norms without inviting invidious distinctions between different cultures. In addition, a good case can be made that the development of women's rights is the most important development in the history of human rights.

If human beings had direct insight into moral truths, the development of basic human rights would not have taken millennia. Women's rights are a particularly good example of the bottom-up development of basic human rights, because even the pioneers of rights for men often had a moral blindspot that prevented them from seeing that those rights should extend to women.

Jean Jacques Rousseau was the inspiration for the French Declaration of the Rights of Man in 1789, but neither he nor the revolutionary government extended those rights to women. Immanuel Kant extended some rights to women, but not the right to vote. In 1792, in *A Vindication of the Rights of Woman*, Mary Wollstonecraft wrote a plea to the advocates of rights for men not to deny them to women. Her main target was Rousseau, because of his prominence in the movement for universal rights and because of his assumption that a woman's highest aspiration would and should be to please her husband. When she wrote the book, she realized that her hopes would seem like "Utopian dreams" ([1792], 72). They were still utopian when John Stuart Mill published *The Subjection of Women* in 1869. At that time, in most of the Western world, legal control of all property and children was the husband's alone. Everywhere, women were excluded from higher education and from most professions. In no country did they have the right to vote in national elections.

The first country to grant women the right to vote was New Zealand in 1893. In Switzerland, women did not obtain the right to vote until 1971. So it would be a mistake to think that the West has a tradition of respect for women's rights. Like almost every religious and cultural tradition, the West has a history of discrimination against and mistreatment of women.

Although the process is not yet complete even in the West, since the turn of the twentieth century, women's autonomy has greatly expanded. Is this ongoing transformation in the status of women merely a local, Western phenomenon or does it represent something more universal? To answer that question, it is useful to begin with a related question. When viewed historically, why have internal norms that greatly restrict the educational, employment, and other social opportunities of women (to which I refer as *patriarchal norms*) been so widespread? To use the term introduced in chapter 1, why has there been a historical overlapping consensus in favor of patriarchal norms? The discrimination has been so severe that when Brownmiller investigated legal and social remedies for rape in a variety of traditional cultures, she came to the conclusion that in almost all traditional cultures the status of women was that of chattel (1975, 7).

Today it is fairly well understood why societies in which women were treated as men's property would be evolutionarily stable. To say they are evolutionarily stable is not to say that they are inevitable, but only that groups that develop them will tend to perpetuate themselves in the processes of biological and social evolution.[1] There is a large literature on this topic in evolutionary psychology. In an article aptly titled "The Man Who Mistook His Wife for a Chattel," Wilson and Daly (1992) provide an overview of this literature and an interpretation of it. According to them, sexual proprietariness makes it evolutionarily advantageous for men to make "major parental investments in their putative offspring despite the problem of uncertain paternity" (298).

One way to make male investment in offspring evolutionarily stable is to make it highly probable that the man is investing in his own offspring. As a result, a great variety of different institutional arrangements can be stable, if they enable a man to effectively restrict sexual access to the women in whose children he invests. Monopolization of sexual access to women tends to favor institutions that limit almost every aspect of the woman's existence, especially during her reproductive years. The many cultures that strictly segregate the sexes and cloister women are social solutions to this problem that seem to have evolved independently. This evolutionary point of view helps to explain the remarkable independent convergence of many different cultures in the Far East, Europe, Africa, and the Americas in defining adultery on the basis of the woman's marital status, not the man's (310).

Evolutionary psychologists look for evolutionary explanations of psychological attitudes (e.g., jealousy) as well as behavior. Those attitudes can include attitudes of endorsing or disapproving of certain behaviors. Thus, for example, evolutionary psychologists would want to explain not only the attitude and behavior of the jealous husband who kills his wife's lover, but also the attitudes of the other members of society who excuse the killing or otherwise resist classifying it as murder. It is a short step from this approach to an approach that regards a culture's norms themselves as subject to selection pressures from biological and social evolution. Although I do not believe that evolutionary pressures alone determine a culture's normative beliefs, it is almost surely true that a culture cannot be stable if it believes itself to be illegitimate according to its own norms. Thus, in human evolution, there will be selection pressure for cultural norms and other background beliefs that endorse the culture's own institutions. Because of these selection pressures, the fact that a culture's institutions are endorsed by the culture's understanding of its own norms should not settle the question of whether they are morally justifiable. Evolutionary pressures will pretty much guarantee that a culture's institutions satisfy its understanding of its norms, regardless of whether those institutions are morally justifiable.

Cultural Justifications
of Patriarchal Institutions

There is a large variety of different combinations of patriarchal institutions and normative justifications of them that could be evolutionarily stable. All of them will assign to women roles that severely limit their opportunities for extramarital sex, which they typically do by limiting lots of other opportunities as well.

No patriarchal culture has ever attempted to justify its limitations on women in evolutionary terms, for the obvious reason that cultures developed their normative understanding of themselves long before the processes of biological and social evolution were discovered. Although each culture has developed a normative world view that justifies its own institutions, the type of justification offered is remarkably uniform across cultures. Patriarchal cultures typically hold that men and women have essences that have been defined by a creator or by nature itself, and that their essences fit precisely the roles that their society assigns to them. It is easy to see how such a justification would tend to make patriarchal institutions stable. So long as it is generally accepted, no one would even suggest making a change to those institutions.

The problem for such justifications is that they often seem to be self-serving: When a justification for an institution is self-serving, it is not the case that the institution exists because the justification is accepted. Rather, the causal relation is reversed: The justification is accepted because it supports the existing institutions. For example, patriarchal institutions are often justified as being good for women. To determine whether the justifications are self-serving, we would have to determine whether those who offer the justifications are genuinely open to considering whether the patriarchal institutions are good for women, or whether their conviction that they are good for women is motivated by their desire to be able to justify the patriarchal institutions. There is no simple test for whether or not a justification is self-serving, but there are important clues:

1. Mandatory Limits on Education. Any attempt to justify mandatory limits on education is by its nature suspect. Education makes people aware of alternative possibilities and gives them the tools to formulate and pursue alternative life plans. At the turn of the twentieth century, it was generally accepted in the West that women were not suited for most professions open

to men and that what was appropriate for a woman's education was different from what was appropriate for a man's education. Few women obtained
bachelor's degrees and those who did generally majored in women's subjects—for example, home economics. We now realize that there was no
objective basis for those limitations. In the United States today, 58 percent
of those who graduate from college are women and the percentage is rising
(S. Thomson 2003, A3). Currently, 45 percent of medical school graduates
in the United States are women (McCullough, 2003). They will soon constitute a majority.

So any justification for mandatory limits on education is likely to be self-
serving. In the case of limits on women, the evidence is even more incrimi-
nating. As I mentioned above, Wollstonecraft criticized Rousseau on the
education of women. Rousseau thought that a girl's entire education should
be aimed at making her pleasing to men (Rousseau [1762], 365). He was
contemptuous of women who aspired to literary, artistic, or scientific
achievements (409).

What are we to say when a man claims to morally justify limiting the
education of women to what will make them pleasing to men? It is not
logically impossible that the happiest life for a woman would be to become
whatever men find most pleasing. However, it would be incredible to think
that men could be relied upon to impartially evaluate the pros and cons of
limiting women's education in this way. Institutions and practices based on
paternalist justifications of this kind might be evolutionarily stable. That
only shows something I have been at pains to illustrate: that institutions
and practices supported by self-serving justifications can be evolutionarily
stable, without being morally justifiable.

2. Mandatory Exclusions from Certain Occupations. Traditional cultures
typically have legal or socially enforced norms that exclude women from
certain occupations. Often, the justification offered is that such occupations
are not suitable for them. There might have been a time when it was reasonable to think that male authorities could make reliable judgments about
which occupations are suitable for women. Those judgments have been mistaken so often that it is no longer reasonable to trust them. In addition,
when the reasons offered are scrutinized, they turn out to be strongly self-
serving. For example, it is often claimed that women are too emotional to
be trusted in positions of authority. But it is typically men, not women,
whose emotions make them willing to shoot a driver who cuts them off in
traffic or who delays them extra seconds at a stop sign. It is typically men,
not women, whose emotions make them willing to kill others whom they
believe to have "disrespected" them. I am not claiming there is no explanation of why evolution would have selected for men having such violent
emotional reactions, but only that it is hard to see how an impartial ob-

server could believe that the world would be a worse place if women were in positions of power and men were excluded from them. Such beliefs about women are almost invariably self-serving. Similar objections can be raised to the mandatory exclusion of women from almost all professions.

3. Women's Own Endorsement of Patriarchal Institutions. Because men's attempts to justify patriarchal institutions are almost invariably self-serving, they often look to evidence from the women who live under those institutions to justify them. This evidence can take two forms: first, the testimony of women endorsing the institutions; and second, their voluntary participation in the institutions. The value of both kinds of evidence is much diminished when the discrimination against women includes mandatory limits on education, because limits on education make it harder for women to obtain the information and the intellectual skills they would need to make cogent criticisms of existing institutions. An even more important issue to be considered in evaluating the evidence is whether there are methods of social enforcement that assure that the evidence from women will be mostly favorable. I discuss each form of evidence separately.

a. Women's testimony. In the previous chapter, I discussed how the norms of racial segregation in the southern United States were supported by socially enforced norms that required Black people to express gratitude for their positions. Thus, southern whites had lots of "evidence" that Blacks themselves favored the system of racial segregation. The social enforcement of patriarchal norms is equally pervasive. Social enforcement can take many forms. Norms that prevent women from owning property or that exclude them from paid employment assure they will be dependent on men for their livelihood. This kind of dependence becomes coercive if expressing dissatisfaction with their position is a risk to their economic status. In such a case, it is to be expected that not much dissatisfaction will be expressed.

Economic dependence is not the only mechanism of coercive enforcement of patriarchal norms. There are many more blatant forms of coercion. In patriarchal cultures, violence against women is usually condoned and it is almost always widespread. This is not violence between strangers; it is violence perpetrated by intimate partners or relatives. The UN Population Fund reports: "Around the world, at least one in every three women has been beaten, coerced into sex, or abused in some other way—most often by someone she knows, including her husband or another male family member" (UN Population Fund 2000, chap. 3). In the United States, 25 percent of women have been raped or physically assaulted by an intimate partner (Tjaden and Thoennes 1998, 7). Because violence against women is no longer officially condoned in the United States, this percentage is higher in many other countries. The UNPF reports the following percentages of women who have been physically assaulted by a male partner: 40 percent in the six states of India that were surveyed, 45 percent in Ethiopia, and 47 percent in Bangladesh (2003, chap. 3). The UNPF reports that in cases of domestic violence, the offenses that triggered the violence typically fell into the following categories: "not obeying the husband, talking back, refusing sex, not having food ready on time, failing to care for the children or home, questioning the man about money or girlfriends or going somewhere without his permission" (chap. 3). It is difficult to hold that women's testimony provides moral support for patriarchal institutions, when they can be beaten for not obeying their husbands or for talking back to them.

The violence against women reported by the UNPF included "rape, genital mutilation and sexual assault; forced pregnancy, sterilization or abortion; forced use or non-use of contraceptives; 'honour' crimes; sexual trafficking; and dowry-related violence" (2003, chap. 3). The report estimates that there are 5,000 "honor killings" per year and the number is increasing.[2] It listed the following countries where they have been reported: Bangladesh, Brazil, Ecuador, Egypt, India, Israel, Italy, Jordan, Morocco, Pakistan, Sweden, Turkey, Uganda, and the United Kingdom (chap. 3). The harm to women caused by honor killings extends far beyond the harm to those who are actually killed. The purpose of honor killings is to terrorize women generally into accepting the limited role that their patriarchal society defines for them. It is hard to imagine anything more cruel than being put to death by your own mother for the "dishonor" of having been raped by your brothers (Nelson 2003).

A logistical problem that no country, including the United States, has solved is that strategies aimed at deterring violence against women by intimate partners often only deter reports of such violence, not the violence itself. Most men who assault their female partners are not likely to treat them kindly if they are punished for it.

In many parts of the world, the issue is not seen as one of deterring violence against women, but of deterring complaints about it. In many countries, women who have tried to organize public opposition to violence against women have been harassed and in some cases threatened with death. For example, the UNPF estimates that at least 1,000 honor killings took place in Pakistan in 1999 (2000, chap. 3). Asma Jahangir, a lawyer who has worked to stop honor killings and other violence against women in Pakistan, has been denounced by Pakistani religious leaders. She has been threatened with death many times. She was fortunate that she and her son were not at home in 1995 when five gunmen broke into her house intending to kill them both (McGirk 2003).

In many parts of the world, sanctions against "uppity" women are at least as severe as the Ku Klux Klan's sanctions against "uppity" Blacks in the southern United States in the first half of the twentieth century. Throughout the Islamic world, advocates of women's rights are routinely threatened with death.[3] When those who question a culture's norms are threatened with death, it is not surprising that little questioning takes place. Under such circumstances, even if women endorse the patriarchal norms they live under, such endorsement cannot be used to morally justify them.

b. Voluntary participation. Death threats and physical violence are paradigmatic methods of social enforcement. Another kind of social enforcement of norms is much more subtle. This kind of social enforcement can motivate the oppressed to voluntarily participate in their oppression. So voluntary participation is not always evidence that a norm is morally justifiable.

To illustrate this more subtle kind of social enforcement, consider the practice of foot binding in China or the practice of female genital cutting. In chapter 1, I reviewed Waldron's (1999) three ways to argue for universal human rights. One of the three was to focus on shocking practices such as foot binding and female genital cutting, which have been endorsed by the norms of some cultures, to undermine the claim that no culture's norms can be morally criticized. Because I am going to discuss foot binding and female genital cutting, there will be some temptation to think that I am following Waldron's recipe. That would be a mistake. Instead, I want to use the examples for a different purpose. I do not want to use them to argue for universal human rights against foot binding and female genital cutting. The case for such rights is so strong there is nothing I can add to it. What I want to do is to show how understanding the way that foot binding and female genital cutting norms can be self-enforcing opens up the possibility for seeing many other norms as self-enforcing also. Here is Chang's description of her grandmother's foot binding:

> My grandmother's feet had been bound when she was two years old. Her mother, who herself had bound feet, first wound a piece of white cloth about 20 feet long around her feet, bending all the toes except the big toe inward and under the sole. Then she placed a large stone on top to crush the arch. My grandmother screamed in agony and begged her to stop. Her mother had to stick a cloth into her mouth to gag her. My grandmother passed out repeatedly from the pain.
>
> The process lasted several years. Even after the bones had been broken, the feet had to be bound day and night in thick cloth because the moment they were released they would try to recover. For years my grandmother lived in relentless, excruciating pain. When she pleaded with her mother to untie the bindings, her mother would weep and tell her that unbound feet would ruin her entire life, and that she was doing it for her own future happiness. (1991, 24)

It is difficult to imagine such prolonged, severe pain. The details of infibulation are equally gruesome. Infibulation typically takes place when a girl is between four and eight years old. The procedure involves removal of the clitoris and both labia. Then both sides of the vulva are sewn together. When the wound heals, the skin grows together, leaving a small opening the size of a pinhole to allow the passage of urine and menstrual blood. After marriage, the woman must be cut open to make intercourse and childbirth possible. Infibulation is thought to comprise 15 percent of the estimated 2 million cases of female genital cutting each year.

What is most striking about these practices is not that foot binding was once widespread in China or that infibulation still exists and is widespread, but that in villages in which they are practiced, mothers typically force their daughters to undergo them. Part of the reason may be that they have socially enforced false beliefs about the practice. The Bambara of Mali believe that contact with the clitoris can be fatal to a man; some groups in Nigeria believe that contact with the clitoris during birth can be fatal to a newborn (G. Mackie 1996, 1009). In some cases, women are led to believe that what are in fact side effects of the procedure (e.g., infection, bleeding, difficulty in urinating) are due to something else (e.g., their own lack of courage in the procedure). This sort of misinformation contributes to making these practices evolutionarily stable, but they are not necessary for the social enforcement of the practice, as is illustrated by the fact that foot binding was socially enforced for hundreds of years without any such mistaken beliefs about its effects. As Chang reports, a mother who could not bring herself to inflict the torture of foot binding on her daughter would later be blamed by her daughter for her weakness, because she "had to endure the contempt of her husband's family and the disapproval of society" (1991, 24). In a society that practices infibulation, a woman who has not undergone the procedure will be regarded as "unclean" and will be ostracized by the village, so a woman will also blame her mother if she has not forced her to undergo the procedure (Melching 2000).

Because mothers either perform the procedure or arrange for it to be performed on their daughters and because, when they become adults, their daughters are grateful that they underwent the procedure, the participation of the women in the procedure seems voluntary. Their voluntary participation is not a reason to conclude that the procedure is not oppressive, but only that there are mechanisms of social enforcement other than direct threats.

In villages in which the procedure is generally practiced, those who do not undergo the procedure are regarded as of lower value and, in the extreme case, unmarriageable. In a society in which women are excluded from gainful employment, this is a severe sanction. Even if they are not excluded from gainful employment, to be denied the opportunity to marry and have a family and to be regarded as a pariah would greatly diminish the desirability of their lives.

Because the bad consequences of failing to undergo the procedure are entirely conventional, I refer to these cases as cases of *enforcement by convention*.[4] When there is enforcement by convention, each individual has a strong motivation to comply with the practice, if others are expected to comply. It is hard to overestimate the power of this sort of motivation. For example, the importance of preserving family "honor" has motivated women to kill their own daughters when they are raped and become pregnant (Nelson, 2003). Because the definition of family honor is conventional and the punishment for loss of honor is lower social status for the family, including lower marriage prospects for the other children, this is another example of enforcement by convention.

When there is enforcement by convention, the motivation to comply with the practice depends on the expectation that others will comply. Would it still make sense for a mother to force her daughter to undergo the procedure of foot binding or infibulation if no other mothers were going to do so? The answer seems to be no.

What would happen if no mother forced her daughter to undergo the procedure? It is almost certain that the standards of marriageability would be altered so that women who had not undergone the procedure would suffer no loss of marriageability and the social norms would be altered so that women who had not undergone the procedure would no longer be regarded as pariahs. The conventions would change in ways that would remove all or most of the motivation to force one's daughter to undergo the procedure. It is reasonable to think that this change in conventions would make all women better off, because they would not have to undergo such a painful and dangerous procedure and suffer all of the serious side effects in order to be marriageable and to avoid being ostracized.

Foot binding and infibulation are examples of cases in which enforcement by convention can place women in a collective action problem called an *n-person assurance game*.[5] Given that everyone else is expected to conform to the practice, the reasonable thing for each individual to do is to conform to the practice. However, from a collective point of view, it would be better to change the conventions and eliminate the practice. No single individual can change the conventions, but the group acting as a whole can. G. Mackie points out that foot binding existed in China for hundreds of years and survived even during periods when those who practiced it were subject to severe penalties. But it disappeared in one generation, largely as a result of the formation of "natural foot societies," which made group commitments not to bind their daughters' feet and not to allow their sons to marry women whose feet had been bound (1996, 1011).

This history may well be repeated in the elimination of female genital cutting. Female genital cutting has also existed for hundreds of years and has survived even in places where it is illegal. However, there is an organization, Tostan, that has been effective in eliminating it by voluntary, communal declarations to stop it. I discuss how Tostan has achieved this result shortly.

Does Evolution Morally Justify Patriarchal Institutions?

I have presented many reasons for thinking that the cultural justifications given for patriarchal institutions are self-serving. What is often presented as a divinely ordained division of social roles is in fact the result of a process of selection that favored social institutions that made determinations of paternity reliable. Is there an evolutionary justification of patriarchal institutions? Consider this proposed evolutionary justification: Patriarchal institutions solve the problem of making male parental investment in their offspring evolutionarily stable. Societies in which males are motivated to make parental investments in their offspring have a selective advantage over those in which they do not. It is good for a society to have institutions that give it a selective advantage of this kind. Therefore, patriarchal institutions are morally justified.

I should make it clear that nothing I have said would support this sort of attempt to morally justify patriarchal institutions. Even supposing it is good for a society to be evolutionarily stable, it is almost never the case that there is only one potential evolutionarily stable outcome. There are usually many, some of which may be morally preferable to others. If it is agreed that discrimination against women is harmful to them and its only justification is to solve the problem of motivating males to make parental investments in their offspring, there is now an obvious alternative that does not require discrimination and that makes determinations of paternity more reliable than any system of segregation or discrimination. Simply use DNA tests to determine paternity. The discriminatory institutions would be expendable.

Of course, it can always be asserted that the patriarchal institutions play other roles in making the society evolutionarily stable. The general point remains. So long as evolutionary stability is the test, there will typically be many different ways to achieve it. There should be no presumption that only one kind of social arrangement could do so or that the arrangement that actually evolved is morally preferable to the alternatives.

How Patriarchal Institutions Harm Women

Once it is recognized that a culture with patriarchal institutions will almost surely have developed socially enforced self-serving justifications for them, the question of whether they are justified cannot be settled simply by citing the culture's own answer. The question requires an independent investigation. Amartya Sen undertook that investigation. In 1990, he published the surprising result: By his calculation, more than 100 million women were "missing" due to the excess mortality of women in Asia and North Africa (Sen 1990). Subsequent authors have produced different estimates, but there is general agreement that the number of missing women is at least 60 million (UN Population Fund 2000, chap. 3).[6]

India and China, the two countries in the world with the largest populations, are also the two countries with the most missing women. In India, the child sex ratio (of girls to boys) declined from 976 per 1,000 to 945 per 1,000 in the thirty years from 1961 to 1991. In the following ten years, the rate of decline increased as the ratio declined from 945 to 927 per 1,000 (UN Population Fund 2003).

China adopted its one-child policy in 1979. At the time, the ratio of male to female births was close to the norm of 105 boys to 100 girls. By 1990, the ratio had increased to 111.3 to 100. In 2002, the ratio had risen to 116.9 to 100—and to 135 to 100 in Hainan province (Gittings 2002).

In both India and China, the change in the ratio of boys to girls is primarily due to selective abortion. Infanticide also plays a role. Aborting female fetuses and killing female infants are the most direct means of effecting a preference for males over females. However, indirect effects are also important. For example, one cross-cultural manifestation of patriarchal institutions is the practice of feeding men and boys first, while the women and girls wait to eat what they leave behind (Goodwin 1994, 44). Another manifestation is the disparity in medical care for boys and girls (Sen 1999, 194). Differences in the distribution of food and health care mirror the differences in the perceived value of males and females in patriarchal societies. These differences in turn generate differences in survival that show up in Sen's report of missing women.[7]

These statistics represent real differences in the life prospects of women and men. However, the most important differences are not captured by statistics of this kind. The most important differences are the differences in what a life is like from the inside. To find out about that, we must penetrate below the statistics to the reality underlying them.

Patriarchal institutions make men more valuable than women. Some of the difference in value between men and women is economic—for example, when men are permitted to work at remunerative occupations and women are not or when a wife lives with her husband's family, giving her own family little or no return on the resources they invested in her while she was growing up. Some of the difference in value is social—for example, where the family name is transmitted through the male offspring. The difference in value leads to differences in the investment of family resources; at its extreme, the refusal to invest familial resources in female offspring leads to selective abortion or infanticide.

The difference in the perceived value of men and women in patriarchal societies has effects that color every facet of a woman's life. For an Orthodox Jewish wife, it means having a husband who prays each day to thank God for not having made him a woman. (Orthodox Jewish wives do not pray to thank God for not having made them men.) For a conservative Hindu wife, it means being expected to treat your husband as almost god-like. (Her husband does not have nearly so exalted an opinion of her.) In traditional Christian religions, wives are enjoined to obey their husbands. (Is there any tradition in which husbands are enjoined to obey their wives?) These practices help to capture what it is like to live as a woman in a society with patriarchal institutions, but even they do not adequately convey what her life is like. Consider the following description of Islamic life in Pakistan, summarized from Goodwin (1994, 43–46). Most of the practices have correlates in other religious traditions:

The birth of a boy is a time for celebration; the birth of a girl is a time for mourning. When asked how many children he has, a man will answer with the number of his sons. Girls don't count.[8] The wife is held responsible for the sex of the child. If a wife does not produce a son, her husband will probably take a second wife or divorce her.

An unmarried girl is referred to by her family with a phrase that means "another's wealth," because a girl will leave her parents to join her husband's family when she marries. In the family, girls get less food and less medical care than boys, though they do twice as much work. Even the youngest boy is given priority over all of the women and girls.

Girls are not allowed to play outside and they are much less likely than boys to go to school. Girls are taught that they "should be like water, unresisting. It takes on the shape of the container into which it is poured but has no shape of its own" (quoted in Goodwin 1994, 45). This is a recipe for being invisible. A report on the status of women in Pakistan in 1985 concluded: "The average woman is born into near slavery, leads a life of drudgery, and dies invariably in oblivion" (quoted in Goodwin 1994, 440).

In almost every patriarchal society, the amount of violence against women is much greater than an outsider would ever imagine, because of socially enforced silence on the subject. In defending violence against women, one Jordanian commentator argued that beating does not hurt a woman's dignity, because women have no dignity (Goodwin 1994, 264). In many parts of the Islamic world, wife beating is regarded as a God-given right and those who, like Taslima Nasrin, draw attention to it and to other inequities between the sexes are threatened with death and even may have a bounty put on their heads (Weaver 1994). When Western women (e.g., Goodwin 1994 and Seierstad 2003) have lifted the veil on violence against women in the Islamic world, they have been criticized as outsiders who do not respect other cultures.[9] The fact is that they are giving a voice to women who risk death if they dare to tell the truth.

What *Do* Women Want?

Patriarchal institutions are often defended with paternalistic claims that define what is good for women in terms of their reproductive role. I discuss paternalistic opposition to human rights more fully in the next chapter. There was a time when women were so silenced that it was possible for men to believe in good faith that they really did know what was good for women. However, as women have begun to find their own voices, that conviction has been exposed as mere conceit. When Freud famously asked "What do women want?" he expressed the exasperation of patriarchal paternalists everywhere. It did not occur to him that women might need the physical, intellectual, and emotional space to figure it out for themselves. Providing that space is the guiding idea of basic human rights.

In this chapter, I have explored only some of the motives that men in patriarchal societies have for thinking they know what is best for women. What about the belief itself? It would be possible to provide endless examples of mistaken male beliefs about what women want or what is good for them. At the turn of the twentieth century, it was generally believed that women did not want a college education and that they were not suited for intellectual pursuits. In the United States today, women comprise 58 percent of college graduates and the percentage is rising. Fifty years ago, it was generally believed that women did not want to participate in athletics and that, because of their delicate constitutions, it was not good for them to do so. Girls weren't supposed to sweat (Kelley 2002). Since the early 1960s, participation in sports by girls and women has skyrocketed. In the twenty-eight years from 1971 to 1997, the number of girls participating in high school athletics in the United States increased eightfold. Is this good for women? They seem to think so. In addition to the obvious health benefits, girls who participate in sports are much less likely to use drugs or to have an unwanted pregnancy and much more likely to graduate from high school.

Still today, most women on the planet are born into a role that provides little scope for individual autonomy. That is changing. For the first time in history, large numbers of women are being encouraged to develop their own life plans, rather than to fit into an assigned plan. The first step was for women to rebel against their assigned life plans. This has taken place on a large scale only in the past fifty years. The second step was for women to adopt new life plans. Inevitably, the first attempts were often modeled on the life plans of men. But many women have found the male models to be unsatisfactory. The next step, which is already under way, is for women to develop their own distinctive life plans that better reflect their own distinctive orientations toward life.

The development of rights for women has initiated a process, still in its initial stages, of women themselves discovering what they want and what is good for them. It is now generally recognized that the process of discovery has benefited both men and women. Providing educational opportunities for women (measured by literacy rates) is one of the most effective ways to improve the health of all children, boys and girls (Sen 1999, 195). Providing educational and employment opportunities to women is the most effective way to control population growth, more effective than China's coercive one-child policy (217–221).[10] Statistically, increases in the female-male ratio are correlated with reductions in violent crime (200).

What about the costs? In the early twentieth century in the United States, divorces were rare and limited mostly to the wealthy. In the United States today nearly 50 percent of first marriages are expected to end in divorce. This is not good for children. However, I think it is a mistake to see this as social decay. It represents the disorder that almost always occurs when a coercive social arrangement is dismantled. In the United States, two-thirds of divorces are initiated by women.

Although there will always be happily married heterosexual couples, it seems clear that many countries are moving toward a less rigid model of what is often called the *family* but is better thought of as the *household*. Undoubtedly, there will continue to be husband-wife, two-parent households. Though such a model is still socially enforced in most countries, there is now the possibility for new models to be tried. And new models are being tried. Even in husband-wife, two-parent households, there is much more sharing of child rearing and housework than there was fifty years ago. No one knows what new kinds of households will exist 100 years from now.

Viewing Patriarchal Institutions from behind the Veil of Ignorance

In chapter 4, I suggested that there is a moral standpoint from which a culture's external norms can be morally criticized. The same moral standpoint that makes it possible to criticize a culture's external norms also makes it possible to criticize a culture's internal norms. The Harsanyi-Rawls idea of the original position behind the veil of ignorance helps to orient us to the moral standpoint. Behind the veil of ignorance, we look out on our society without knowing any of our identifying characteristics, including whether we are male or female, although we can have general information about human beings, human history, and the variety of different social arrangements that have existed.

When we look at traditional patriarchal societies from this point of view, the inequities between men and women are highlighted. Behind the veil of ignorance, where you do not know your gender, would you be content to think that some people might be born into a gender that made their births a cause for celebration and that you might be born into a gender that would make your birth a cause for mourning? Would you be content to think that some people might be born into genders that made them full legal persons and that you might be born into a gender that would make you the legal equivalent of chattel? Would you be content to be consigned to a life that you yourself would describe as being "neither alive nor dead"? Would you be content to think that, if you married, your husband could beat you with impunity, divorce you at will, or take other wives if he wished? From the original position, behind the veil of ignorance, the unfairness of the division between men and women of the benefits and costs of social cooperation in traditional patriarchal cultures is striking.

I can think of only one way that it could be reasonable to agree to such an unfair division of the benefits of social cooperation—if it could be shown that no other alternative would be better for women. This sort of self-serving claim is easily made by men defending a patriarchal society, when their real motivation is the fear that any alternative will be worse for *men*. Behind the veil of ignorance, it would be evident that there are many ways of improving the lot of women.

The original position thought experiment can be performed by anyone in any culture capable of empathic understanding. The defenders of patriarchal cultures would almost surely refuse to give it any weight. Instead, they would probably appeal to their religious authority as moral support for the status quo. Such an appeal could not be made behind the veil of ignorance, because, from behind the veil of ignorance, a person would not know his religion or even if he had one. Behind the veil of ignorance, no appeal to a religious or moral authority will be acceptable, because there will be no agreement on who the relevant authorities are.

At this point, all of the familiar relativist objections reappear. For example, how can I advocate the original position reasoning over reliance on a religious authority without being a moral imperialist? The presumption of these objections is that there is no acceptable middle ground between moral wishy-washiness and moral imperialism. The burden of the first four chapters of this book was to define just such a middle ground. It is a middle ground where all moral opinions should be listened to, but where all moral opinions are not equally valid. When moral opinions are based on self-serving reasons, their validity is compromised. We know that defenders of a husband's right to beat his wife have claimed that women are born without dignity. Anyone who would make such a claim has a moral blindspot. However, it is also evidence of a moral blindspot to believe that the opinion that women are born without dignity is as valid as the contrary opinion.

Self-Reinforcing Paternalism and Human Rights

In this chapter, I have reviewed one important period in the historical process of the expansion of basic human rights: the extension of basic human rights to women. One of the most important steps in the process is overcoming the paternalistic presumption that autonomy is not good for women or the presumption that they do not want it. This kind of paternalism is much more objectionable than garden variety paternalism, for example, requiring that drivers wear seat belts, because it is so much harder to overcome. If you are denied an education on the grounds that education will not do you any good, your very lack of education will make it much more difficult for you to recognize that an education would be good for you. I refer to this sort of paternalism as *self-reinforcing*, because these sorts of paternalistic policies (e.g., denial of an education) have the effect of making their targets *need* paternalistic protection. They prevent people from being able to develop and exercise their own good judgment.

In the next chapter, I discuss more fully how the development of basic rights has often involved overcoming this sort of self-reinforcing paternalism. Each step in the expansion of the circle of those who have successfully overcome self-reinforcing paternalism is an important one, but I am inclined to think that the expansion to include women is the most important of all or, at least, the most important so far. In terms of sheer numbers, it is the largest expansion ever. However, there is another reason. To understand it, consider each expansion of the circle as an expansion of the universe of human possibilities. The extension of the circle to include women represents a qualitative expansion in the range of human possibilities because, in some respects, women really do want different things from men. This expansion of the universe of human possibilities benefits both men and women because, just as women can learn new values from men, men can learn new values from women. For example, in a patriarchal culture, child rearing is typically regarded as the work of women, which makes it unmanly. As a result, patriarchal norms often cut men off from one of the most challenging and rewarding of human activities. When women achieve equality with men, opportunities to work outside the home open up new possibilities for women; opportunities to participate in child rearing open up new possibilities for men.

The opportunity to participate in child rearing is part of an even more important change that equality for women makes possible: an increase in the possibilities for empathic understanding. In chapter 4, I described the role of empathic understanding in moral judgment. In patriarchal cultures, empathic understanding is often depreciated as "womanly." As I mentioned in chapter 4, when the young Shawnee warrior Tecumseh objected to the torture of prisoners, he was accused of being a coward, one of the worst insults that could be leveled at a Shawnee warrior. What did Red Horse, who leveled the charge, actually say to Tecumseh? As Eckert reconstructs it, Red Horse called Tecumseh a "woman" (1992, 258–259). Sad to say, a man from almost any culture would immediately recognize that using *woman* as an epithet means "coward." Tecumseh's "womanliness" represents an important possibility for both men and women: to combine courage with empathic understanding.

In every country in Europe and North America, the great majority of violent crimes are committed by males (UN Economic Commission for Europe 2003). In the entire known history of the world, there has probably not been any time when there were no groups engaged in violent hostilities toward one another.[11] These are manifestations of the fact that in a patriarchal society, the destructive manly emotions of anger, revenge, and the desire for power have higher status than the womanly emotions of empathy and compassion. If moral development depends on empathic understanding, elevating the status of women, itself a moral improvement, may be the impetus for much more development.

From Microcosm to Macrocosm: Autonomy and Human Rights

Sometimes human rights are presented as protections against things so obviously bad that no one could reasonably disagree about their badness. Torture, rape, and murder are obvious examples. Human rights guarantees do play this role. But there is nothing distinctively human about such rights. Many animals deserve the same protections. Distinctively human rights play a different role. They provide the necessary background conditions to enable a person to develop her own conception of a good life and to form, evaluate, and pursue a life plan. This is part of what it is to be *autonomous.* The best way of understanding *human* rights is that they are the rights that make possible the development and exercise of individual autonomy.

What exactly is autonomy? Many different answers have been given to this question. In the psychology of child development, two-year-olds are said to develop autonomy. That is not the kind of autonomy I am talking about, though it may be an essential step in becoming autonomous in the sense I am talking about.

Kant thought that autonomy was a metaphysical property in virtue of which we could make choices free of causal determination and that respecting rights was the appropriate way to treat beings with this metaphysical status. Unlike Kant, I do not think that autonomy requires any special metaphysical status.

In the next chapter I will say more precisely what autonomy is; however, one common misunderstanding of autonomy should be addressed here. Often an autonomous agent is thought of as necessarily selfish or as necessarily individualistic or as necessarily competitive. This is a misunderstanding, because to be autonomous is not to *be* a particular way (i.e., to be selfish or individualistic or competitive); it is instead a *way* of being (i.e., a way of being selfish or unselfish, competitive or cooperative, and so on).

The development of human rights is a two-pronged development. The first step involves working out an answer to the question: Who should be guaranteed basic human rights? Answering this question has been a centuries-long process of expanding the class of beings believed to be capable of forming, evaluating, and pursuing life plans. The second step involves working out an answer to the question: What rights should be guaranteed to all those capable of autonomy? Answering this question has been a centuries-long process of understanding the conditions necessary to be able to form, evaluate, and pursue life plans.

In this chapter, I have used the example of women's rights to illustrate why it has taken so long to work out an answer to the first question. Many of the original champions of human rights thought these rights should extend only to white, male property owners. Only gradually did it become accepted that they should extend to other white males, and then to men of other races, and then to women.

Why has the process been so slow? Human beings have no direct rational insight into moral truth. Also, expanding the universe of rights-holders invariably reduces the universe of the exploited and oppressed. Exploiters and oppressors typically have socially enforced self-serving justifications for not granting rights to those they exploit or oppress.

Basic human rights are the rights necessary for the development and exercise of autonomy. Which rights are basic in this sense? This is the second question that a theory of human rights must answer. I do not believe that human beings have direct rational insight into the answer to this question either. The answer to it has emerged in a historical process that has unfolded over centuries. In the next two chapters, I review some of the crucial developments in that process and use them to develop a list of basic human rights that should be universal.

How to Advocate Universal Human Rights without Being a Moral Imperialist

In the introduction, I promised a defense of universal human rights that avoids moral imperialism. Have I delivered on that promise? In this chapter, I have made many claims about what is good for women and what is not good for them. For example, I have claimed that foot binding and infibulation are not good for women, even if they themselves believe otherwise. This sounds morally imperialistic. I need to explain why it is not.

Recall that one can be a moral imperialist in two ways: first, by claiming to be infallible on moral matters, and thus insisting that anyone who disagrees must be mistaken. I am not this kind of moral imperialist, because I acknowledge that all of my claims are fallible. The second way to be a moral imperialist is to be a moral paternalist. A moral paternalist imposes his idea of what is right on those who disagree for their own good. It is not morally paternalistic to intervene to protect a potential victim from torture, rape, or murder, if the victim wants the protection. However, it is morally imperialistic to use coercion to force women to give up foot binding or female genital cutting if they don't want to give it up.

In this chapter, I have explained why those practices are bad for women. I did not mean to imply that because they are bad for women, I think outsiders should use coercion to stop the practices. As I already mentioned, legal prohibitions on both foot binding and female genital cutting have not been effective. However, there is a nonpaternalistic approach to ending the practices that has been effective.

Foot binding in China ended in a two-step process.[12] The first step was education. Part of the education was simply finding out that there are places where women do not undergo the procedure. Another part of the education was finding out the true benefits and harms of the practice. After the educational step, the next step was a group decision to end the practice. A group decision was necessary, because the practice involved enforcement by convention. When a practice involves enforcement by convention, each individual will be motivated to do whatever she expects the rest of the group to do.

The Epistemically Modest Advocacy of Human Rights: Tostan

The same two-step process can end female genital cutting. Tostan, a nongovernmental organization in Senegal, is showing the way.[13] Tostan is not an anti–female genital cutting organization. It is an educational organization. When invited by a village to do so, it organizes educational workshops for women. There are only two required topics or modules: human rights and group problem solving. The module on human rights uses existing human rights documents to teach women about their rights. The module on group problem solving gives them the skills to work together to solve what they perceive to be problems. These modules represent an epistemically modest view of human rights, because they empower the women to make their own judgments about how to improve life in their villages and to work together to make those improvements. After completing those two modules, the women themselves decide which other topics or modules they want to study. Sanitation and health care are popular modules. They generally lead to proposals for changes in village sanitation and health care.

In villages where female genital cutting is practiced, the Tostan training on human rights and health care empowers women to question the practice. The practice does not end until the men and women of the village (or of several intermarrying villages) come together to make a joint declaration to end it. The first village in the Tostan program to end female genital cutting did so in 1997. In the fall of 2003, 202 villages came together to make a joint declaration ending the practice, bringing the total number of villages that had done so to 1,140 (20 percent of the total number of villages in Senegal that had engaged in the practice).

None of those 1,140 villages is in Matam, a northern region of Senegal, because of fierce opposition to the cessation of female genital cutting from religious leaders in the region. However, in spite of the opposition of religious leaders, on October 22, 2003, thirteen villages in the Matam region jointly declared an end to female genital cutting and forced marriage. Now the prospects are good for ending female genital cutting in all of Senegal within a few years. Epistemically modest advocacy of human rights sometimes takes time to produce change. But when the change occurs, it can happen fast.

Although Tostan gets most of its publicity for ending female genital cutting, it is important to realize that Tostan's goal is not the narrow one of ending female genital cutting. The true goal is to educate women and men to understand themselves as bearers of human rights, to enable them to exercise their judgment on how to improve their lives, and to empower them to make those improvements. Tostan's programs have led to many changes other than the elimination of female genital cutting, including improved sanitation and health care, ending caste discrimination, promoting vaccinations and family planning, and joint declarations to eliminate violence against women and forced marriage. Tostan has provided a model for bottom-up social change based on human rights.

Because Tostan does not substitute its own judgment for the villagers' judgments about what changes are desirable, Tostan avoids one kind of paternalism. What about its educational modules? Isn't it paternalistic for Tostan to decide what modules the villages should study first, and isn't it paternalistic for Tostan to determine the content of the other modules also? For example, in requiring the villagers to study a module on human rights, isn't Tostan deciding for them what education they should have? Isn't this paternalistic? Suppose a religious leader objects to Tostan's educating women about human rights. He says that women's education should be limited to what they need to know to perform their natural roles of wife and mother. How can Tostan respond without being morally paternalistic?

From a logical point of view, the answer to this question is the same as my answer to the question of how the advocate of human rights can avoid moral relativism (moral wishy-washiness) without being a moral imperialist. The moral standpoint is not a neutral standpoint from which all moral opinions are equally valid. It is a point of view from which we can reliably though not infallibly make important moral distinctions, including the distinction between education and indoctrination. There is an objective difference between education and indoctrination. It might seem that to make such a distinction it would be necessary to have a definition of the key terms. However, there are almost never adequate definitions of important moral and philosophical terms. We can say that an important difference between typical cases of education and indoctrination is that indoctrination typically involves the forcible suppression of dissent and education typically encourages the consideration of different views, but these are neither necessary nor sufficient conditions. For one thing, there is a social component to the distinction. Embedded in a society with freedom of expression and of the press and where there is free discussion of a variety of viewpoints, a class that aimed to impart an orthodoxy (e.g., accepted chemical theory) might well be educational. Embedded in a society in which there is no freedom of expression or freedom of the press, a class that made a show of encouraging consideration of different viewpoints might qualify as indoctrination.

It is a mistake to think that we need a definition of education in order to promote it. On the contrary, one sign that education has been successful is that each succeeding generation is able to improve on the preceding generation's understanding of what education is.

Education must also be distinguished from brainwashing. If Tostan brainwashed women into accepting human rights norms, then it would be morally paternalistic. However, it is not paternalistic to provide information and training and then to allow the villagers themselves to judge what information to accept and how to employ the skills they have acquired. Another sign of Tostan's epistemic modesty is that the content of the educational modules themselves is not determined purely top-down. The content of the modules has evolved over time, in response to suggestions for improving them made by the villagers themselves. This is what epistemically modest education looks like.

What Basic Human Rights Protect

Although human rights advocates often become energized by the goal of eliminating such awful practices as foot binding and infibulation, for an epistemically modest advocate of basic human rights, the goal should not be simply to eliminate such practices. The real goal should be to enable the victims of these practices to make their own judgments about their advantages and disadvantages and to empower them to act so as to give effect to those judgments. The epistemically modest advocate is guided by a picture of a certain kind of process, rather than by a particular outcome. Although it is reasonable to expect that any reasonably informed group of autonomous women would never voluntarily endorse foot binding or infibulation, for epistemically modest advocates of basic human rights, what is morally significant is what women themselves endorse, even if it is not what they think women should endorse.

Tamir (1996) tries to make this point by imagining a situation in which it would be reasonable for women to endorse infibulation. Her example is unpersuasive, because infibulation is so harmful that in any imaginable circumstances, there will always be a more reasonable alternative.[14] A better example would be Islamic veiling, or *al-hijab*. The extreme form of this requirement is that women cover themselves completely from head to foot in the chador.

Epistemically modest advocates of basic human rights object to the use of coercion to enforce veiling. They may also think that it is bad for women

to be bound by such extreme norms of female modesty. But the epistemically modest advocate must allow that some autonomous women might
choose to exercise their rights by voluntarily adopting the practice of veiling. They might, for example, come to the conclusion that unveiled women
are inevitably judged on the basis of their appearance rather than on their
character or the quality of their thought. Thus, they might adopt veiling to
avoid being judged on the basis of their appearance. It is even imaginable
that the advocates of the practice might be so successful in persuading other
women of its benefits that ultimately all or almost all women might choose
to be veiled. I myself do not believe that most women would autonomously
choose to be veiled. I could be mistaken. An epistemically modest advocate
of basic human rights holds that what is morally important is that women
be able to make their own choices, regardless of what they actually decide
to do.

Can an epistemically modest advocate of basic human rights endorse any
kind of government coercion in favor of human rights? There is one kind of
coercion that can easily be justified: the coercion required to prevent one
person from violating the rights of another when the victim wants the protection, for example, the use of coercion to protect women against rape and
other violence. In the next chapter, I discuss another category of justified
government coercion.

The Verdict on Cultural Relativism
about Internal Norms

Though more attractive than extreme cultural relativism, cultural relativism about internal norms has the same kind of defect: It is too wishy-washy.
If cultural relativism about internal norms were true, it would not be possible to morally criticize patriarchal norms. Because almost all cultures have
internal norms that oppress women, the example of women's rights shows
how it is possible to criticize the internal norms of almost all cultures.

I should emphasize that criticisms of the internal norms of a culture as
oppressive to women need not imply that anyone is to blame for those
norms or for the oppression. One can believe that a culture's norms reflect
moral blindness without thinking that those who uphold the norms are
morally responsible for their moral blindness. However, there is no implication the other way either. Sometimes the defenders of oppressive norms do
seem to be morally blameworthy. Many whites who joined the Ku Klux
Klan to terrorize Blacks crossed the line of moral culpability. Some of those
who defend patriarchal norms by calling for the death of those who oppose
them also cross the line, for example, those who called for the deaths of

Asma Jahangir in Pakistan, Taslima Nasrin in Bangladesh, Toujan Faisal in Jordan, and Shirin Ebadi in Iran.

Though cultural relativism about internal norms is too extreme in its insistence that an outsider can never be in a position to make moral criticisms of the internal norms of another culture, there is an important fact that it draws to our attention: Outsiders should not place much stock in their initial impressions of the internal norms of another culture. In order to be in a position to make reliable moral observations about another culture, one must be willing to make the effort to empathically understand the roles occupied by the members of the other culture. For an outsider to understand the significance of another culture's practices to its members is not an easy thing to do. It is much too pessimistic to think it is impossible.

There is one more thing to be said on behalf of cultural relativism about internal norms. Even if cultural relativism about internal norms is mistaken about the possibility of being in a position to criticize the internal norms of another culture, it can serve as a caution to think carefully about actions justified by those criticisms. Even if a culture has internal norms that legitimate a hierarchy of power, status, and privilege supported by socially enforced self-serving justifications, it does not follow that it is morally permissible to forcibly intervene in that culture to eliminate the hierarchy. Even if, as a moral principle, cultural relativism about internal norms itself is too extreme, in a world in which countries are all too eager to justify military conquest and other forcible intervention in the affairs of other countries, cultural relativism about internal norms serves a useful function if it at least raises the question of whether such interventions are morally justifiable.

Conclusion

Though it is possible for an outsider to morally criticize internal practices such as foot binding and female genital cutting, it is a mistake to think that the guiding idea behind human rights is the elimination of such evils. The guiding idea behind human rights is to enable all people to develop and exercise autonomy, to become the authors of their own lives. Human rights should be universal, because all human beings with normal cognitive, emotional, and behavioral capacities have the ability to become autonomous. In order to identify the basic human rights that should be universal, it is necessary to investigate the conditions necessary for autonomy, which I undertake in the next two chapters.

6

AUTONOMY RIGHTS

Without democracy, you have no understanding of what is
happening down below; the situation will be unclear; you will be
unable to collect sufficient opinions from all sides; there can be
no communication between top and bottom; top-level organs of
leadership will depend on one-sided and incorrect material to
decide issues.

—Mao Zedong

In the previous chapter I used the example of women's rights as a microcosm for the development of basic human rights. Women's rights illustrate
a recurrent theme in the development of basic human rights: the rebellion
of an oppressed group against limits on their autonomy, enforced by oppressors who claim to know what is good for them.

The basic human rights are the rights necessary for the development and
exercise of autonomy. Why should these basic human rights be guaranteed?
There are two kinds of answer to this question. The first kind of answer is
the simplest: Beings capable of autonomy should be permitted to develop
and exercise it. This answer is *nonconsequentialist*, because it does not appeal
to any good consequences of people's developing and exercising their autonomy. To the nonconsequentialist, autonomy is so important that it does not
have to lead to good consequences in order to be justified. Most philosophical defenders of human rights are nonconsequentialists.[1]

I think the nonconsequentialists are right to insist that autonomy has
value independent of the goodness of the consequences it produces. However, a second kind of justification for basic human rights is also important.
This kind of justification is *consequentialist*, because it justifies them on the
basis of their contribution to (appropriately distributed) well-being.[2] The
connection between human autonomy and human well-being is not direct.
In this chapter and the next, I trace some of the indirect connections. My
goal is to construct the framework for a justification of the basic human
rights necessary for the development and exercise of autonomy based on
their contribution to (appropriately distributed) human well-being.

Though most of my attention in the next two chapters is focused on the
consequentialist account of basic human rights, my goal is not to supplant

the nonconsequentialist account, but to supplement it. There are two main ways the consequentialist account can supplement the nonconsequentialist account of basic human rights:

1. The consequentialist account can help to explain how basic human rights were discovered. I doubt that human rights would ever have been discovered if non–rights-respecting autocracies had done a good job of promoting human well-being. I do not believe liberation movements arise from a philosophical appreciation of the nonconsequential value of autonomy. They develop in response to oppression and exploitation, where the interests of the oppressed and exploited are sacrificed to the interests of the oppressors and exploiters. Ending oppression and exploitation promotes well-being by promoting autonomy.

2. The consequentialist account can help to undermine the most influential justifications offered for *not* respecting basic human rights, because they are based on claims about how to best promote well-being. In this chapter and the next, I consider the two most important consequentialist justifications for autocracies: self-reinforcing paternalist justifications and social contract justifications. Throughout most of human history it has seemed obvious to most educated people that one or both of those justifications is successful. It took thousands of years to discover that neither sort of justification succeeds. In large part, the historical discovery of basic human rights is the result of the discovery of the failure of self-reinforcing paternalist and social contract justifications of autocracy.

The Reliable Feedback Problem and the Appropriate Responsiveness Problem

Both the consequentialist and nonconsequentialist agree that governments should be just. However, they disagree about what justice requires. To the consequentialist, justice is to be understood in terms of the promotion of (appropriately distributed) well-being; to the nonconsequentialist, justice cannot be fully analyzed in such terms. Though they disagree about what justice is, they can agree that to promote justice a government needs to obtain reliable feedback on the justice (or injustice) of its policies and to be appropriately responsive to the feedback it receives—for example, by continuing and expanding policies that promote justice and by discontinuing or overhauling policies that do not. Call these two problems the *reliable feedback* and the *appropriate responsiveness* problems.

For the consequentialist about justice, the reliable feedback problem becomes the problem of the government's obtaining reliable feedback about how successful its policies have been in promoting the well-being of its citizens. This is the *consequentialist version* of the reliable feedback problem. The appropriate responsiveness problem becomes the problem of responding to that feedback to better promote the (appropriately distributed) well-being of its citizens—for example, by continuing or expanding those policies that have successfully promoted its citizens' (appropriately distributed) well-being and by discontinuing or overhauling those that have not. This is the *consequentialist version* of the appropriate responsiveness problem. These two problems play an important role in the consequentialist account of basic human rights that I develop in this chapter and the next.

The Discreet Charm of Autocracy

The clearest evidence that basic human rights norms are not self-evident is the large number of philosophers and other intellectuals who have provided moral support for autocrats. Part of the explanation is due to selection. In most autocracies, opinions opposing the autocrat are ruthlessly suppressed. This is a powerful selection mechanism for expressions of support. However, this sort of selection cannot explain the large number of philosophers and intellectuals living in democracies who have supported autocracy. The list begins with Socrates and Plato and includes countless philosophers and intellectuals who supported twentieth-century Marxist dictatorships, as well as those who supported twentieth-century fascist dictatorships.[3] Why are autocracies so attractive to philosophers and other intellectuals?

I think I can illustrate at least one of the reasons. Suppose you discovered a ring that gave whoever wore it dictatorial powers. Putting on this ring would give you the power to enact any laws you desired to enact. Would you use the ring?

If you live in a democracy with a free press, you are undoubtedly aware of lots of problems and conflicts in your country. (One way of knowing you are living in a country *without* a free press is if the news only reports how well things are going.) What gets people's attention is conflict and problems, so the press reports on them when it is free to do so. Also, unless you are exceptionally modest, you know how to solve some of the conflicts and problems you have read about. Why not put on the ring for a day? During your day, you will be free to implement any solutions to existing problems and conflicts you favor, and your solutions will be maintained after you relinquish power. What would you do in your day as dictator?

When you think of all you could do in one day, it is natural to ask: Why remove the ring after only one day? No matter how many problems and conflicts you could resolve in one day, there would always be more in the future. Why not extend your dictatorship indefinitely so you will be able to deal with them as they arise? In a nutshell, I think it is this kind of reasoning that has led so many philosophers and other intellectuals living in democracies to favor dictatorships. Looking at all of the problems and conflicts that exist in any democracy, it is hard to believe that, over the long term, a democracy is better at identifying them and resolving them than any dictatorship, especially one with you (or me) as the dictator. Thus, it is understandable that most people would be tempted to put on the ring and wear it for life.

Consequentialist Justifications of Autocracy

Although I believe that those philosophers who provide moral support to autocrats are mistaken, I want to take seriously the idea that consequentialist considerations could, in theory, justify the use of governmental coercion. For the next three chapters, I am going to assume for the sake of argument that there is a consequentialist principle that justifies a policy of coercion when it is reasonable to believe that the policy is good for the targets of the coercion and the costs and benefits of the policy are appropriately distributed. In Talbott (forthcoming) I attempt to formulate the principle more precisely. For my present purposes, this rough characterization suffices.

It is important to understand that merely *believing* that a policy of coercion is good for those it targets is not enough to justify the policy under the consequentialist principle. It is necessary to be *epistemically justified* in believing it to be good for them. The consequentialist account of basic human rights that I am developing makes guarantees of basic human rights necessary for a government to be epistemically justified in believing that its coercive policies promote the (appropriately distributed) well-being of its citizens.

Recall that I asked you to imagine being a dictator. As a dictator, you could enact laws and use the threat of prison to compel your citizens to comply. The consequentialist principle holds that you could be morally justified in doing so, if it were reasonable to believe that your citizens would benefit from the enactment and enforcement of your laws and that the benefits and costs would be appropriately distributed. To some people, this seems obviously right; to others, it seems obviously wrong. I won't try to settle the issue here. In this chapter I ask: Suppose there were such a principle, would it in fact justify an autocracy? Apologists for autocrats often claim that it would, but would it?

Historically, two powerful consequentialist justifications have been given for autocracy. First, there are the *paternalist* justifications, exemplified by Plato's defense of the rule by the philosopher-autocrat in the *Republic*. Second, there are *social contract* justifications, exemplified by Hobbes's defense of absolute sovereigns in *Leviathan*. I discuss the Platonic rationale in this chapter and the Hobbesian in the next.

Self-Reinforcing Paternalist Defenses of Autocracy

A law is paternalistic when it is enacted to promote the good of those targeted by the law by *overruling* their own judgment about what is good for them. A law is an instance of *self-reinforcing paternalism* when one of its effects is to prevent its targets from being able to make their own judgments about what is good for them, on the grounds that it is better for them not to make their own judgments about what is good for them.

At least until the eighteenth century, even in the West, the overwhelming majority of educated commentators would have agreed that ordinary people are not reliable judges of what is good for them. They would have agreed that the best way to promote the good of ordinary people was to establish someone in authority to tell them what was good for them and to force them to do it. Arguments of this kind for autocracy seem to be culturally universal. The *locus classicus* in philosophy of a self-reinforcing paternalist argument for autocracy is Plato's *Republic*,[4] but many religious traditions have provided similar rationales for autocracy, typically on the grounds that the ruler is a god, or the ruler receives orders directly from a god, who knows what is best for everyone.

Although Aristotle disagreed with Plato on the ideal form of government for Greek men, he found self-reinforcing paternalist arguments quite congenial to justify the enslavement of non-Greeks and the subordination of Greek women.[5] Given the strong tradition of such arguments in Western philosophy and Western religions, it is somewhat parochial for Lee Kwan Yew and other defenders of Asian values to claim that a paternalist conception of government is a distinctively Asian or Eastern value. Perhaps Asians developed paternalist justifications for autocracy before Westerners did, but paternalist justification of autocracy is itself universal.

It is no accident that both Plato and Aristotle thought of political rulers as shepherds of men, for it seems uncontroversial that shepherds can be justified in forcing their flocks to do something for their own good.[6] In the same way, parents' treatment of their children sometimes involves forcing them against their will to do something for their own good, and the treatment of human adults with serious brain injuries may also require this kind of intervention. The Plato of the *Republic* thought that most normally functioning adults also needed someone to look out for their good and to force them, if necessary, to do things for their own good. The system of government he advocated for his *Republic* has become the paradigm of a self-reinforcing paternalist autocracy: absolute rule by the philosopher-autocrat.[7] In Plato's *Republic*, there would be no respect for autonomy or basic human rights. The philosopher-autocrat would be justified on paternalist grounds in interfering in every aspect of his subject's lives.[8] Plato's ideal was a *beehive society*.[9]

In order for his justification of the beehive society to be successful, Plato had to solve two problems: (1) the *benevolent information* problem, which is to explain how a philosopher-autocrat can make reliable judgments about what is good for everyone in society, judgments that are more reliable than people's own judgments about what is good for them; and (2) the *benevolent motivation* problem, which is to explain how a philosopher-autocrat who has acquired the requisite benevolent information would be motivated to use that information to promote the good of everyone in the society, rather than pursue his own individual good.

Plato's solution to the benevolent information problem was quite simple. The model of mathematical knowledge (which I have called the *Proof paradigm*) convinced him that a philosopher-autocrat would be able to acquire infallible knowledge of what is good for people just as the mathematician can acquire infallible knowledge of arithmetic or geometry, without having to rely on experience or on common opinion.[10]

To solve the benevolent motivation problem, Plato tried to design his beehive society so that the individual interests of the philosopher-autocrat would precisely coincide with the interests of the citizens. This was as utopian as Marx's idea that in the dictatorship of the proletariat, the interests of the dictators would be the same as the interests of ordinary workers. Neither Plato nor Marx included any safeguards to protect the ruled when, as inevitably they would, the interests of the rulers did not coincide with the interests of the ruled. The history of Marxist dictatorships provides an antidote to all such utopian solutions to the problem of benevolent motivation.

Some Historical Evidence on the Problem of Benevolent Motivation in an Autocracy

No other social movement in history claimed to have a more benevolent motivation than the communist movement. Nonetheless, the communists were unable to devise a system that would reliably produce rulers motivated to do what was good for their people.[11] In each case there was an initial period of high hopes and glowing reports of success. Eventually, rumors of awful events would emerge, which were always met with official denials and accusations that the rumors were malicious lies. Ultimately, often years or decades later, the facts would be disclosed. Often the truth was more awful than any rumors had suggested.

Because Stalin, Mao, and the other communist leaders were absolute autocrats, no one will ever know the full extent of the crimes committed against their own peoples. We do know that Stalin intentionally killed between 3 and 10 million people, most from starvation, as part of his forced collectivization of agriculture in 1932–1934 (Tucker 1990, 195). Overall, it is estimated that, under Stalin, 20 million died from famine, labor camps, and execution (Glover 1999, 237).

In China, during Mao's Great Leap Forward from 1958 to 1962, it is estimated that 30 million Chinese starved to death. In the Cultural Revolution in 1966–1968, millions suffered severe persecution. In Cambodia between 1975 and 1979, Pol Pot and the Khmer Rouge killed 2 million Cambodians, approximately one-fourth of the population, in a ruthless attempt to return Cambodia to an agrarian society (Glover 1999, 309). It is estimated that 2 to 3 million people, 10 percent of the population, starved in famines in North Korea in the 1990s under Kim Il Sung and his son Kim Jong Il (BBC News 1998).

Communist dictatorships always start out with high hopes for improving the lives of their people. Why have the results been so disappointing? Part of the explanation is that Stalin, Mao, Pol Pot, and Kim Il Sung were ruthless leaders. This illustrates the benevolent motivation problem. However, there is another difficult problem for autocrats to solve.

Some Historical Evidence on the Benevolent Information Problem in an Autocracy

Because the benevolent motivation problem is such a seemingly intractable problem, much less attention has been paid to the problem of benevolent information. The benevolent information problem is a serious problem, because even when autocrats are motivated to do what is good for their people, the difficulty of solving the benevolent information problem will often thwart their good intentions. In addition, some of the most important human rights are best understood as solutions to the benevolent information problem, so it is important to say something more about it.

Even if an autocrat wanted to promote the good of his subjects, it would be difficult to obtain the necessary information to enable him to do so effectively. In an autocracy, there is a strong tendency for the truth to be suppressed in favor of whatever subordinates believe their superiors want to hear. In its more benign form, this is the tendency of hierarchies to generate yes men, who tell their superiors what they think they want to hear. In its more sinister form, it is the tendency of autocracy to use death, imprisonment, or exile to suppress negative information and to use promotions and prizes to reward positive information, regardless of the truth.

A striking example of the problem was provided by T. D. Lysenko's influence over genetics and agriculture under Stalin and even beyond.[12] Lysenko championed Lamarckian genetic theory (which held that acquired characteristics could be inherited) over Mendelian genetic theory (which denied that acquired characteristics could be inherited) even though there was no scientific evidence supporting the Lamarckian theory. Although all scientific evidence supported the Mendelian theory, Stalin opposed it for ideological reasons. Stalin favored Lysenko's Lamarckian theory because of what he took to be its political implication: It allowed for revolutionary rather than merely evolutionary biological change. Lysenko's appointment as head of the Lenin Academy of Agricultural Science and later as director of the Institute of Genetics of the Soviet Academy of Sciences enabled him to purge any scientist who advocated Mendelian genetics and to implement his Lamarckian theories in Soviet agriculture. Scientists who raised objections were discharged from their scientific positions and sent to forced-labor camps.

Lysenko's theories led to agricultural disasters. For example, he claimed to have a new method of growing winter wheat in Siberia. In one region of Siberia, tens of thousands of acres of winter wheat were planted with Lysenko's method. The harvest yielded less seed than was used to produce it.[13] His suggestion for summer plantings of sugar beets in Central Asia was implemented several times on tens of thousands of acres. Each time, the shoots withered in the hot sun and died (Medvedev 1969, 165–166). Of course, these failures were not reported publicly at the time. We can only speculate about how much knowledge of these failures reached Lysenko's superiors in the government.

Even more remarkable, when Lysenko announced it was possible for one species to produce offspring of a completely different species, almost immediately the Soviet journal *Agrobiologiya* began to publish scientific reports of such transformations, including transformations of "wheat into rye and vice versa, barley into oats, peas into vetch, vetch into lentils, cabbage into Swedes, firs into pines, hazelnuts into hornbeams, alders into birches, sunflowers into strangleweed" (Medvedev 1969, 170). Of course, such transformations are biologically impossible.

Although Lysenko's policies produced disastrous effects, his subordinates knew better than to report the disasters. Only positive results were reported, as illustrated by the reports of impossible transformations of species. By suppressing negative results and rewarding positive results, Lysenko was able to rule over Soviet biology and agriculture for more than twenty years. Even after Stalin's death, Lysenko remained an important advisor on agriculture to Khrushchev, and his views became orthodoxy in China under Mao.[14]

Another example of the benevolent information problem comes from the communist government of China. As I have already mentioned, it is estimated that during the Great Leap Forward from 1958 to 1962, approximately 30 million Chinese starved because of mismanagement of agriculture (Chang 1991, 234). At the time of the Great Leap Forward, not only was there no information of famine in the Chinese press, the largest Chinese newspaper, the People's Daily, was reporting record harvests and running contests for ideas on how to use the projected agricultural surplus. The problem was not merely that information about the famine did not appear in the public press. Even the information available to the central government greatly underestimated the severity of the shortages, simply because officials who made reasonable projections of future yields were punished for insufficient revolutionary zeal. In such a climate, no one could really know the severity of the problem (Chang 1991, 224–226). It was on the basis of this experience that Mao came to his own appreciation of the benevolent information problem, expressed in the epigraph to this chapter.

I should mention that dictators are not unusual in wanting to suppress sources of negative information. Such a desire seems to be a universal characteristic of governments and other hierarchical organizations. For this reason, even in democratic societies, if a government has the ability to suppress unfavorable information, they will almost always believe that a potential problem is less serious than it really is.

Here is an example closer to home. In 2001 and 2002, Houston high schools reported a "miracle" that attracted the attention of the president and the secretary of education, who pointed to it as a model. Many high schools had less than 1 percent dropout rates, including some with zero dropouts, even in high schools with large poor and minority populations (Winerip 2003, A19). In the rest of the country, urban high schools were reporting dropout rates of 20–40 percent.

How did Houston achieve the "miracle"? The superintendent hired principals on one-year contracts that allowed dismissal without cause. Principals soon learned that if their reports did not satisfy the superintendent, they would be fired. The result was a selection process for principals willing to report what the superintendent wanted to hear. When one assistant principal tipped off a newspaper reporter to the scam, the resulting news article led to a state audit that found thousands of dropouts who had been misclassified. If the superintendent had controlled the newspaper, that report never would have been published and Houston would probably still be touted as a miracle school district.[15]

What distinguishes dictatorships from governments that respect basic human rights is not the desire to suppress negative information, but the power to do it. If they have the power, they will use it.

Correcting Plato's Mistakes

For Plato's defense of his beehive society to be successful, he had to solve the benevolent motivation and the benevolent information problems. His proposed solution to the benevolent motivation problem was hopelessly utopian. His proposed solution to the benevolent information problem was based on the Proof paradigm.

If Plato had been correct, it should have been possible for philosophers to begin from a rationally unquestionable definition of the good to prove theorems about what is good for human beings—on the model of the Pythagorean theorem—to which all rational beings would assent. Instead, the history of philosophy is full of conflict over how to define the good (or well-being or happiness) and especially over what is or is not good for human beings. I believe this conflict is evidence that our justification for our beliefs about what is good for human beings has a largely bottom-up rather than top-down structure. In any case, the extent of disagreement among philosophers about what is good makes it clear that Plato was mistaken in thinking that philosophers would have some special access to this sort of knowledge.

If knowledge does not progress by rational insight into the truth and by proof, how does it progress? Based on historical evidence, John Stuart Mill proposed that it progresses by a social process of free give-and-take of opinions, which is now referred to as the *free market of ideas* (Mill [1859], chap. 2). Although Mill was not the first to have the idea of a free market of ideas, I believe he was the first to use it as a model for understanding knowledge and epistemically justified belief.[16]

Extending the free market of ideas to the question about what kind of life is good for a human being led Mill to make a surprising proposal. He suggested answering that question by providing the framework for a free market of ideas on what is good for human beings and the framework for experiments in living, where people were free (within certain limits) to form their own life plans and try them out. If they were not satisfied, they could revise their plans and try something else. Thus, Mill's alternative to the Proof paradigm led naturally to his proposal that the best kind of society for human beings was not a beehive society, but what I refer to as an *experimental society*. The main contrast between a beehive society and an experimental society is this: In a beehive society, most people do not form and evaluate their own life plans; they have a life plan imposed on them by those in authority. In an experimental society, individuals are guaranteed rights that enable them to develop and effectively exercise their own judgment about what sort of life is worth pursuing and how best to pursue it. Then they are given the freedom to conduct "experiments in living" (Mill [1859], 65).

Mill realized that in order for an experimental society to be better for people than a beehive society, normal adults would have to be reliable judges of what is good for them. I believe Mill was the first to announce the discovery that, when given the necessary education and training, all normal adult human beings are capable of becoming reliable judges about what is good for them. He claimed that when people are free to exercise their judgment against a background that protects the free market of ideas (including rights to freedom of expression, freedom of association, and freedom of the press and other media), their judgments about what is good for them are generally reliable and generally more reliable than their government's judgments about what is good for them (Mill [1859], 95). Call this the *claim of first-person authority*. When it was first announced by Mill nearly 150 years ago, it was met with widespread skepticism. It is far from universally accepted today.

If the claim of first-person authority is true, it is not self-evident. It is a surprising discovery. In historical time, only relatively recently has it been discovered that all normal human beings can learn to read and write. The idea that they might be reliable judges of what is good for them has taken even longer to gain acceptance. Although much evidence can be cited in support of the claim of first-person authority and there are general reasons based on human psychology for expecting it to be true, it is much better to think of it as a hypothesis to be tested than as a proposition that has been conclusively established. It has been and is being tested in many ways. The most important tests of it are the ongoing attempts to design experimental societies that promote the well-being of their citizens by guaranteeing their basic human rights. These tests have yielded some important results, which I discuss in the next chapter.

Some Support for the Claim of First-Person Authority

Plato considered the claim of first-person authority and dismissed it as ridiculous (*Republic*, 493d1–494a5). With the advantage of our greater historical evidence, it does not seem so ridiculous. In this section, I consider reasons that make it seem at least plausible. In evaluating the claim of first-person authority, it is important to recognize that it is only plausible if the society guarantees the rights necessary for the free market of ideas (including the rights to freedom of expression, freedom of association, and freedom of the press and other media).

What reasons are there to think that the claim of first-person authority might be true? I see four main reasons: (1) first-person concern; (2) first-person access; (3) first-person bias; and (4) the value of choice. I discuss them separately.

First-person concern is the fact that most people care about their own good more than other people do. Because how well my life goes matters more to me than it does to other people, I will be more motivated not to make mistakes about it.

First-person access to one's own good begins with one's own access to one's own pleasures and pains. On a hedonistic account, the only thing that is good is pleasure (or positive consciousness) and the only thing that is bad is pain (or negative consciousness). Even nonhedonists can acknowledge that pleasure is often good and pain bad.

Although it is often assumed that people are by nature hedonists, I think this is a mistake. Most people do not live their lives to maximize the sum of pleasure over pain.[17] Psychological research indicates that even large changes in life prospects (e.g., winning a lottery) typically produce only transient effects on one's hedonic state (Brickman, Coates, and Janoff-Bulman 1978). If people were hedonists, this research would undermine almost all motivation.

Instead, I think it supports Millgram's (1997) suggestion that pleasure and displeasure function as *indicators* of what is important or what matters and of how well we are doing in living a life that matters. On Millgram's nonhedonistic view also, each person's access to her own pleasures and pains gives her a unique form of access to how well her life is going.

There is another consideration supporting first-person access. In many circumstances, a person's plans and intentions, resulting from the exercise of her judgment of what is good for her, determine whether or not something that happens to her is good for her. I refer to this as the *constitutive element* in judgments of the good.[18] To explain how there can be a constitutive element in judgments of the good, I need to say something more about what I refer to as the *faculty of judgment*.

The faculty of judgment is a faculty used, among other things, for judging one's own good, including how well one's life is going. It requires that one be able to conceive of one's life as a whole, to formulate and evaluate plans, including overall plans for one's life, to pursue one's plans, and to be able to reevaluate one's plans in the light of future experience. I refer to these abilities as the *ability to form, evaluate, and pursue plans*, including plans for an entire life. When one adopts a plan—especially a life plan—one typically judges it to be a good plan to pursue, at least, the best of the available alternatives. The constitutive element in judgments of one's own good is due to the fact that adopting the plan typically changes one's good. Adopting such a plan can make things that further the plan good. For example, for someone who plans to cut back his hours at work in order to spend more time with his children, being notified that his job has been cut back from full time to part time may be good or at least not nearly as bad as it would be for someone who has accumulated substantial debt and who had planned to work extra to pay it off.

Because one's good is in part constituted by the exercise of one's judgment, anyone who has the faculty of judgment has a unique kind of first-person access to her own good—she is the one who *makes* the plans that in part determine her good. Someone who has the capacity for judgment but is prevented from developing it is ipso facto denied the possibility of constitutive goods of this kind. When beings with such capacities are not able to develop them, their possible goods are greatly diminished.

First-person bias is a negative consideration. The first two considerations are positive considerations that explain why my judgments about what is good for me are generally more reliable than other people's judgments about what is good for me. There are two ways in which first-person bias negatively affects the reliability of our judgment about the good of others. First, we tend to evaluate the good of others using the same framework we use in evaluating our own good. Those who like to read may have difficulty imagining that some people do not. Those who don't like to read will tend to underestimate the value of libraries to those who do. Second, because we generally care more about our own good than about the good of others, it is my impression that most people tend to underestimate the negative effects and to overestimate the positive effects of their actions on the good of others. This kind of partiality is one of the reasons that an impartial judge or jury is needed to determine the amount of monetary damages in civil actions.

The value of choice is the final reason. Mill famously argued that autonomy was essential to human well-being ([1859], chap. 3). This threatens to make the claim of first-person authority trivially true, as it would be if nothing would count as good for a person unless it were autonomously chosen by her. I do not believe that autonomy is essential to human well-being. Indeed, in chapter 9 I give an example of how it could be inimical to it.

Nonetheless, having important consequences depend on one's own choice is itself an important component of the good for most people. Suppose that whenever you wanted something, it would magically appear or occur. You want to be president of the United States—it's done! Most people would quickly tire of these magical powers and want to be rid of them, because the powers would make it impossible to accomplish anything on their own.

If you were clever, you could specify your desire more precisely—for example, to win the presidency in a difficult political contest. You might very well obtain lots of satisfaction from engaging in and winning the competition. Even then, however, there would be something lacking that is valued by many people: It would not be your efforts that brought about the result. It would be your magical powers. Many people would gladly rid themselves of such magical powers—or, at least, significantly curtail them—so that their choices would matter.

By the *value of choice* I refer to the component of well-being that is added by having a good outcome depend on one's own choices. I believe that the value of choice is a significant component in the good of most people. It is important not to overemphasize the value of choice, however. Although choosing often has value, it sometimes has disvalue. For most people, it would be bad to have one of their two children murdered, but it would be worse to have to choose which of them is to be murdered (though doing so might be necessary to prevent both from being killed).

In my defense of the claim of first-person authority, I do not place any significant weight on the value of choice, because it looks too much like a fudge factor introduced to guarantee the truth of the claim of first-person authority. I believe the claim of first-person authority can be adequately supported by the first three considerations alone.

For the claim of first-person authority to be true, how reliable must people's judgments be of what is good for them? At a minimum, they would have to be more reliable than the judgments of government officials. This would set the bar fairly low even if the judgments of government officials were always made in good faith. In fact, government officials are strongly inclined to believe that whatever is good for them is good for their citizens, and they are prone to construct self-serving justifications for that conclusion. Earlier in this chapter, I reviewed some of the disastrous effects of the paternalist policies of twentieth-century communist dictatorships. The reliability of noncommunist paternalist governments is not significantly better. In the previous chapter, I reviewed discredited paternalist beliefs toward women, for example, that women don't have the talent or desire for higher education or that they do not have the ability or interest in participating in athletics. I could just as easily have cited the paternalist beliefs of sixteenth-century European colonists toward the American natives, the paternalist beliefs of the English in the eighteenth and nineteenth centuries toward the Irish, the paternalist beliefs of nineteenth- and twentieth-century white southerners toward Blacks, and so on. The list is seemingly endless. In each case, there is a strong element of self-serving justification for the paternalist beliefs. And in each case, opening up educational and career opportunities to these targets of paternalist policies has shown that the paternalist beliefs were only self-serving justifications for keeping the oppressed peoples in subservient positions. Paternalists do not have a good track record of reliability.

Doubts about the Claim
of First-Person Authority

If the claim of first-person authority is true, why do people make so many mistakes about what is good for them? For example, if people are so good at judging what is good for them, why do almost half of all marriages in the United States end in divorce?

The claim of first-person authority is not a claim that people have clairvoyant powers to see the future. No one is very good at predicting the future. The claim of first-person authority is a more modest claim. It can be illustrated with an example. Suppose that in the beehive society, all of the big decisions in people's lives are made by a government agency empowered with promoting their good. The agency determines how much education you qualify for and what kind, your career, and your spouse. In the experimental society, people are expected to make these big decisions for themselves. Although I believe that individuals in the experimental society would make big decisions that would better promote their own good than the government agency in the beehive society would, my defense of the claim of first-person authority does not depend on this.

The claim of first-person authority comes into play when we acknowledge that, in both societies, it will be important for there to be a way to correct mistakes. In the experimental society, if someone decides that she chose the wrong career, she can plan a career change, perhaps by going back to school and getting more education. Call these adjustments *life course corrections*. How are life course corrections to be made in the beehive society? The most plausible defenses of the beehive society are those, like Plato's, that guarantee infallibility or near infallibility to the rulers, because then it is not necessary to figure out how to make life course corrections.

Of course, if people in the experimental society never learned from their mistakes and just continued to repeat them over and over, life course corrections in the experimental society would not improve anyone's life. So one important ground for the claim of first-person authority is that, given certain basic rights, people tend to learn from their mistakes and make life course corrections that make their lives better. The minimal requirement for allowing people to make their own life course corrections is that they do a better job than a government agency would. This seems to me to be almost surely true, but it is important to reiterate that it is not because it is self-evidently true. Instead, it is a claim that is being tested in autonomy-promoting societies. If it is not true, we will almost surely find out.

The Consequentialist Version
of the Reliable Feedback Problem

The claim of first-person authority is: When normal, adult human beings are free to exercise their judgment against a background that protects the free market of ideas, their judgments about what is good for them are generally reliable and are generally more reliable than their government's judgments about what is good for them. If the claim of first-person authority is true, then any government that hopes to solve the benevolent information problem must be able to obtain reliable feedback from its citizens about how successful its policies have been in promoting their good. This is the consequentialist version of the reliable feedback problem. If the claim of first-person authority is true, the benevolent information problem is transformed into the reliable feedback problem.

If you were a benevolent dictator who accepted the claim of first-person authority and truly wanted to solve the reliable feedback problem, what would you do? You would have to guarantee the rights that would enable your citizens to develop their ability to make reliable judgments about what is good for them and rights that establish the background conditions for their being able to effectively exercise that ability. In other words, you would have to guarantee two important kinds of basic human rights, which I call *development-of-judgment* and *exercise-of-judgment* rights.

Development-of-judgment rights guarantee that a child has what is necessary to become an adult with the ability to reliably form, evaluate, and pursue a life plan, under favorable background conditions. When people have this ability and the background conditions are favorable, I will say they have *good judgment.* Development-of-judgment rights are the rights necessary to develop and exercise good judgment when the background conditions are favorable. Exercise-of-judgment rights guarantee what is necessary for those background conditions to be favorable.

Development-of-Judgment Rights

Development-of-judgment rights are the basic rights necessary for normal physical, cognitive, emotional, and behavioral development. They include two of the rights identified by Shue (1980) as basic: the rights to security and subsistence.[19] I understand *security rights* quite broadly to include protection against the intentional infliction of a variety of harms by others—for example, not to be killed, tortured, physically assaulted, mutilated, disabled, raped, shackled, imprisoned, physically forced to do something against one's will, or to be subjected to the psychological control of another (e.g., by brainwashing or hypnosis). The list is meant to be representative, not exhaustive. In addition to protection against the harms themselves, there would also be protection against threats of such harms.[20] Finally, security rights would include the various procedural rights that fall under due process and the rule of law, because arbitrary government action would be a great threat to individual security. I follow Shue in understanding *subsistence rights* broadly to include "unpolluted air, unpolluted water, adequate food, adequate clothing, adequate shelter, and minimal preventive public health care" (Shue 1980, 23).

What I am calling development-of-judgment rights would go beyond Shue's basic rights in two ways. First, normal child development requires more than physical security and physical subsistence. It requires normal cognitive, emotional, and behavioral development.[21] Second, to develop good judgment requires an education appropriate to one's society. No society could survive if it did not develop good judgment in some of its members. So every society has some system of education. If development-of-judgment rights were universal, all children would receive an education appropriate to their societies.

An almost surefire way of helping children develop into adults who have good judgment is to relate to them in a way that communicates the message that as adults they will be expected to exercise their own judgment—for example, to treat them in a way that communicates the message that they are entitled to their own opinions and to have their opinions respected by others. In any culture, some children will receive this message. The idea that all people are entitled to their own opinions and to have their opinions respected by others is truly revolutionary. Unfortunately, there are still large parts of the world where many children—especially girls—do not receive this message.

Exercise-of-Judgment Rights

Development-of-judgment rights assure the physical, cognitive, and emotional development necessary to develop good judgment. To actually exercise good judgment requires physical security and subsistence or the opportunity to earn subsistence. So again, both of Shue's rights qualify as basic. But something more is required if a person's judgments are to be reliable. For example, in North Korea in the 1990s, all sources of information were controlled by the government. The media parroted whatever the government wanted the citizenry to believe. Of course, the citizens of North Korea had not been educated to be able to exercise good judgment. Even if they had been, because all of the sources of information were biased (and all in the same direction), even someone with good judgment might have been unable to identify the biases and correct for them. It should come as no surprise to find out that North Korean citizens believed their leader, Kim Jong Il, was their protector and savior from a hostile world trying to destroy them. Given that belief, it was almost impossible for citizens of North Korea to reliably evaluate the benefits and harms to them resulting from Kim Jong Il's policies.

So something more than security and subsistence is necessary for the exercise of good judgment. What else is required? One way to answer that question is to look at how autocracies prevent their citizens who have good judgment from being able to use it to make reliable judgments about the government's policies. They do so by blocking Mill's free market of ideas— by limiting freedom of the press, freedom of expression, and freedom of association. Only if there is freedom to voice and publish complaints about and disagreements with the government's policies can citizens be in a position to reliably evaluate those policies. So these standard civil rights should be included with rights to security and subsistence in the exercise-of-judgment category of basic human rights.

If you, as benevolent dictator, guaranteed your citizens all of the rights included under the development-of-judgment rights and the exercise-of-judgment rights, you would have solved most of the reliable feedback problem. It might seem that a complete solution would require a democratic political system, but this is not quite right. All you would really need would be reliable polling information. For example, you could poll your citizens each year to find out which policies they thought were good for them and which ones they thought were not. In a real autocracy, it would be difficult to get reliable information of this kind. First, because pollsters would not want to incur your wrath by reporting that your citizens were unhappy with some or all of your policies, they would design poll questions intended to produce positive responses. Second, because your citizens would fear reprisals, they would often give dishonest answers rather than admitting they were unhappy with your policies. So this solution to the reliable feedback problem for autocracies is highly hypothetical. Its theoretical importance is in showing how basic human rights would be a necessary part of any solution.

The Consequentialist Version of the Appropriate Responsiveness Problem

If you were able to solve the reliable feedback problem, you would have reliable information that you could use to judge which of your policies were benefiting your citizens and which were not. How would you use that information?

Because you are a benevolent autocrat, I assume you would respond appropriately, typically by continuing the policies that were generally benefiting your citizens and replacing or overhauling the policies that were not. The problem of designing a government that will respond appropriately to feedback of this kind is the consequentialist version of what I have referred to as the *appropriate responsiveness* problem. If it were easy to find a benevolent autocrat, it would be easy to solve the appropriate responsiveness problem. Because it is not, if you were a benevolent autocrat, you yourself would be worried about what would happen to your citizens after your death. If you were a truly benevolent autocrat, you would not rest content in enacting laws that received positive feedback from your citizens while you were alive. You would also want to establish a form of government that could be relied upon to be appropriately responsive to reliable feedback even if the government officials' motivations were not always or solely benevolent. This is the problem I take up in the next chapter.

From Good Judgment to Autonomy

In this chapter I have approached the connection between human rights and autonomy by asking what rights a government would have to guarantee to be able to justify its policies as promoting the good of its citizens, on the assumption that the claim of first-person authority is true. The answer is that a government would have to solve the consequentialist versions of the reliable feedback problem and the appropriate responsiveness problem. To solve the reliable feedback problem, the government would have to guarantee the rights necessary for the development and exercise of good judgment.

What is the relation between good judgment and autonomy? An autonomous person not only has good judgment, she also uses it to shape her life. You might have the best judgment in the world, but if you were locked in a small cell against your will you would lack autonomy, because your judgment would not have much scope to shape your life.

The consequentialist account of the importance of good judgment also supports an account of the importance of autonomy. If each person's judgments about what is good for her are generally reliable, then, other things being equal, a good way of promoting well-being is to allow people to make their own decisions, at least on matters primarily affecting their own well-being. Thus, the consequentialist account supports not only the development and exercise of good judgment, but also the development and exercise of some degree of autonomy.

I need a term for the second element, in addition to good judgment, that makes a person autonomous. I will call it *self-determination*. When autonomy is understood as the combination of good judgment and self-determination, then certain presumptions about autonomy must be discarded.[22] For example, it is possible to be autonomous without being individualistic. People with good judgment could conclude that it would be good for them to join a religious order that requires obedience to superiors. Their choosing to join such an order would be an act of self-determination that would qualify as autonomous on my account. Of course, to retain their autonomy, they would have to join a religious order that did not impair their judgment (e.g., by indoctrination or brainwashing) and that maintained the background conditions for reliable judgment (e.g., freedom of expression, freedom of the press, and so on).[23]

If autonomy is good judgment combined with self-determination, it is easy to see how a government that solves the reliable feedback problem and the appropriate responsiveness problem will tend to provide its citizens with substantial scope for self-determination. Most people with good judgment generally believe that their lives will go better if they have a reasonable degree of self-determination. So, except perhaps in times of national emergency, a government that enabled its citizens to develop and exercise good judgment but severely limited their self-determination would generate substantial negative feedback on its policies limiting self-determination, the appropriate response to which would be to change those policies to enhance self-determination. I believe this is the reason that autocrats do not encourage the development and exercise of good judgment in their subjects. Autocrats favor indoctrination and brainwashing, and they suppress free expression and a free press because they realize that if their subjects develop good judgment, they will favor more autonomy and less autocracy. Only autocrats who intend to transform their autocracy into a democracy (e.g., Juan Carlos of Spain) would ever favor guaranteeing their citizens the rights necessary for the development and exercise of good judgment.

Autocrats have endless self-serving justifications for indoctrinating rather than educating and for restricting freedom of expression and freedom of the press. Their real motivation is evident. It is more difficult to govern if citizens make negative judgments about the government, even if there is no feedback mechanism for their judgments to influence the government. From the point of view of an autocrat, an ounce of prevention is worth a pound of cure: It is better to prevent negative judgments than to have to suppress them.

What Is the Relation between Autonomy and Basic Human Rights?

The nonconsequentialist holds that there is a direct relation between autonomy and basic human rights. Respecting basic human rights is the appropriate way to treat a being capable of autonomy.[24]

In this chapter, I have suggested an alternative consequentialist account of the relation. On this alternative account, the link between basic human rights and autonomy is indirect. The first step in understanding the link is to think of a government as having to justify its policies as being good for its citizens. If the claim of first-person authority is true, then to be able to provide this sort of consequentialist justification of its policies, a government would have to guarantee the rights necessary for its citizens to develop and exercise good judgment. These are the development-of-judgment rights and exercise-of-judgment rights. The same reasoning that supports development-of-judgment and exercise-of-judgment rights also supports some sphere of self-determination, at least in choices primarily affecting the person making the choice. In a society that solved the reliable feedback problem and the appropriate responsiveness problem, the sphere of self-determination would be substantial, because citizens who developed good judgment would tend to favor policies that enhanced self-determination.

I myself feel the attraction of both the consequentialist and the nonconsequentialist accounts of the connection between autonomy and basic human rights. In this book, there is no need to choose between them. We can have both. I focus more on the consequentialist account of the connection, because it is less obvious.

What's So Good about Autonomy?

It is easy to see how guaranteeing development-of-judgment rights and exercise-of-judgment rights would promote autonomy. For the consequentialist advocate of basic human rights, the challenge has always been to explain how autonomy promotes well-being. By and large, consequentialists have attempted to answer this question by trying to show that autonomy is an important ingredient of personal well-being. This argument takes two forms: (1) the strong form exemplified by Mill, who argued that autonomy was essential to human well-being ([1859], chap. 3); and (2) the weaker form exemplified by Raz, who argues that institutions in Western societies are so designed that the development and exercise of autonomy are practically, if not logically, necessary for living a happy life under them (1986, chap. 14).

Unlike Mill, I do not believe that autonomy is essential to well-being. It is possible to have a valuable life without autonomy. Like Raz, I believe that, other things being equal, in liberal societies, autonomous lives are usually happier than nonautonomous lives. However, unlike Raz, I do not limit my account of the relation between autonomy and well-being to liberal societies. Unlike both Mill and Raz, I believe that the link between autonomy and well-being has a political dimension.

In the first instance, the link is between well-being and good judgment. In order for a government to be able to effectively promote the well-being of its citizens, it must obtain reliable feedback from them on how well its policies promote this and be appropriately responsive to the feedback. For its citizens to provide this kind of feedback, they must develop and exercise good judgment. So, on the consequentialist account, the main link between autonomy and well-being is a political link between good judgment (an essential part of autonomy) and well-being.

My account does follow Mill's in one respect. Both Mill and I hold that it is the potential for improvements in well-being that makes autonomy so important. If, as Plato believed, by the use of pure reason, it were possible to draw up a blueprint for an ideal government for human beings guaranteed to maximize each person's level of well-being, then it would not be necessary for a government to obtain feedback from its citizens on how well its policies were promoting their good. Once a government had been set up according to the blueprint, no improvement in well-being would be possible.

The reliable feedback problem and the appropriate responsiveness problem are only problems for societies that have the capacity to improve, which is to say they are problems for all human societies. Once it is recognized that they are problems for all human societies, it can be seen that there is a consequentialist justification for basic human rights to be universal.

What's so good about autonomy? The answer has two parts, corresponding to the two components of autonomy, good judgment and self-determination: (1) good judgment plays an important role in enabling governments to reliably improve human well-being; and (2) when people have good judgment, one way of promoting their well-being is to provide them with a sphere of self-determination in which they can exercise their judgment to promote their own good.

What's So Bad about Paternalism?

In the previous chapter and in this one, I have given lots of examples of harmful policies that have been justified on paternalist grounds. Not all paternalism is bad. If a two-year-old wants to run out into a busy street, it is appropriate for his parents to restrain him for his own good. Here I limit the discussion to adults with normal cognitive, emotional, and behavioral development. Is it ever justifiable to coerce them on paternalist grounds?

It seems to me that we are involved in a long-term historical experiment to find the answer to that question. The first step is the discovery that self-reinforcing paternalism cannot be justified toward normal adult human beings. The next step is the development of a guaranteed sphere of self-determination, free of paternalistic interference.[25] Since the 1960s, the U.S. Supreme Court has been engaged in defining such a sphere. Through liberal and conservative Courts, the scope of the right to self-determination has gradually expanded, even though no such right appears in the U.S. Constitution.

This right first appeared in *Griswold v. Connecticut* as the right to "privacy."[26] In *Griswold* the Court struck down a prohibition on the sale of contraceptive devices. Over the years, the Court has expanded this right to define an area of individual autonomy in which people are free to act on their own judgment without having it overruled by the government's judgment of what is good for them. The court has characterized this sphere as "involving the most intimate and personal choices a person may make in a lifetime, choices central to personal dignity and autonomy."[27] Most recently, in *Lawrence v. Texas*, the right has been correctly classified not as a privacy right, but as a liberty right, and the sphere has been defined to include "personal decisions relating to marriage, procreation, contraception, family relationships, child rearing, and education."[28]

This definition of a sphere of liberty protected from paternalist interference suggests the possibility of placing all paternalist laws on a continuum, from those that compromise autonomy the most to those that compromise it the least. The laws that most compromise autonomy would be the laws that substantially affect the choices on the *Lawrence* Court's list. At the other end of the continuum would be the laws that only marginally compromise autonomy (e.g., laws requiring seatbelt use). A continuum of this kind could be used to track the development of the right to autonomy. The expectation would be that the right would expand over time to cover the laws that most compromise autonomy before expanding to cover those that compromise it less. It would even be possible to try to project the endpoint of the process. Will the process lead to a right to freedom from all paternalistic interference or will it stop somewhere short of the end of the continuum?[29]

An even more pressing question is this: Will the Court accept the implication of its own inclusion of marriage on the list of choices within the protected sphere? If so, it would strike down prohibitions against same-sex marriage. Recognizing that laws prohibiting same-sex marriage significantly compromise individual autonomy makes it possible to set aside irrelevancies that have sometimes obscured the true issue. For example, many defenders of rights for gays and lesbians, including the right to same-sex marriage, base their argument on the claim that sexual orientation is genetically determined. But whether or not sexual orientation is genetically determined is no more relevant to the issue of whether same-sex marriage should be legal than whether or not a terminal illness is genetically determined is relevant to the issue of whether a patient with the illness should be free to terminate life support. Both cases involve the ability to make important personal choices. No one would ever suggest that only patients with genetically determined terminal illnesses should be able to terminate life support, and that patients with terminal illnesses resulting from their own choices (e.g., lung cancer in a cigarette smoker) should not. Similarly, the freedom to choose a same-sex marriage partner should be protected as an important exercise of autonomy, regardless of whether or not the preference for a partner of the same sex is genetically determined.

The main nonpaternalistic reason offered for prohibiting same-sex marriage is to protect children. The claim is that gay and lesbian marriages should not be permitted, because marriage includes adoption rights and it would be harmful to a child to grow up in a family with two parents of the same sex. This rationale is undermined by a report of the Committee on Psychosocial Aspects of Child and Family Health of the American Academy of Pediatrics, which concludes: "A growing body of scientific literature demonstrates that children who grow up with 1 or 2 gay and/or lesbian parents fare as well in emotional, cognitive, social, and sexual functioning as do children whose parents are heterosexual" (Perrin and Committee 2002). So the only reasons left are paternalistic ones.

Objections to gay and lesbian marriages are reminiscent of objections to mixed-race marriages. In 1967, the idea of racially mixed marriages evoked the same sort of visceral reaction in some whites that the idea of same-sex marriages evokes in some heterosexuals today. In *Loving v. Virginia*, the U.S. Supreme Court refused to allow visceral reactions to block mixed-race marriages.[30] It should also refuse to allow visceral reactions to block same-sex marriages. A right to marry that includes a right to same-sex marriage is part of a right to develop and exercise one's autonomy, which should be universal.

What Are the Basic Human Rights That Should Be Universal?

In this chapter, I have identified nonconsequentialist and consequentialist rationales for a list of basic human rights. These are the rights that guarantee protection against self-reinforcing paternalism (development-of-judgment rights and exercise-of-judgment rights) and rights against paternalistic interference with the most fundamental personal choices (rights to a guaranteed sphere of autonomy). Here is a summary of the rights so far identified as basic:

1. a right to physical security
2. a right to physical subsistence (understood as a right to an opportunity to earn subsistence for those who are able to do so)
3. children's rights to what is necessary for normal physical, cognitive, emotional, and behavioral development
4. a right to an education
5. a right to freedom of the press
6. a right to freedom of thought and expression
7. a right to freedom of association
8. a right to a sphere of personal autonomy free from paternalistic interference

These eight rights constitute the social basis for autonomy. They are a reminder that autonomy itself is a social achievement. Of the eight items on the list, five of them (numbers 1, 5, 6, 7, and 8) are typically identified as classical liberal rights. The rights that go beyond the classical liberal rights are (2) a right to physical subsistence; (3) children's rights to what is necessary for normal physical, cognitive, emotional, and behavioral developments; and (4) a right to an education. Some commentators (e.g., Cranston 1967) have objected to classifying as human rights any that go beyond the classical liberal rights. I consider this objection in chapter 8, after I have made some additions to the list in the next chapter.

There are consequentialist and nonconsequentialist rationales for the items included on the list. The nonconsequentialist rationale is simple and direct: Self-reinforcing paternalism and paternalist laws that interfere with the most fundamental personal choices fail to adequately respect individual autonomy. The rights on the list are the rights that are necessary to adequately respect individual autonomy.

The consequentialist rationale is indirect. It depends on the claim of first-person authority. If the claim of first-person authority is true, a government must guarantee the basic human rights in order to be justified in believing that its policies promote the (appropriately distributed) well-being of its citizens.

Conclusion

In this chapter I have proposed a consequentialist rationale for eight basic human rights. The consequentialist rationale as developed so far is incomplete. Even if these basic human rights would enable a government to solve the reliable feedback problem, it would still be necessary that there be some way for feedback to improve the government's policies. Thus, the advocate of the consequentialist rationale must show how a government that guarantees basic human rights could solve the appropriate responsiveness problem. How ironic it would be if the very rights that made it possible to solve the reliable feedback problem made it impossible to solve the appropriate responsiveness problem. This is essentially Hobbes's argument for autocracy, which I take up in the next chapter.

In this chapter, I have used the stunning failures of some well-known paternalist autocrats to explain the importance of basic human rights in promoting well-being. As I reconstruct it, basic human rights are an important part of the discovery of how to design a government so it will promote the appropriately distributed well-being of its citizens. Maybe this is the wrong lesson to learn from the past failures of paternalist governments. Maybe what we should learn is how better to design a paternalist government so it will promote the well-being of its citizens. This is the lesson that Lee Kwan Yew would have us learn. I discuss Lee's challenge to human rights in chapter 8.

7

POLITICAL RIGHTS

He generally, indeed, neither intends to promote the public interest, nor knows how much he is promoting it. . . . He intends only his own gain, and he is in this, as in many other cases, led by an invisible hand to promote an end which was no part of his intention. Nor is it always the worse for the society that it was no part of it. By pursuing his own interest he frequently promotes that of the society more effectually than when he really intends to promote it.

—Adam Smith

If men were angels, no government would be necessary.

—*Federalist*, No. 51

The problem of organizing a state, however hard it may seem, can be solved even for a race of devils, if only they are intelligent. The problem is: "Given a multitude of rational beings requiring universal laws for their preservation, but each of whom is secretly inclined to exempt himself from them, to establish a constitution in such a way that, although their private intentions conflict, they check each other, with the result that their public conduct is the same as if they had no such intentions."

—Immanuel Kant

In the previous chapter I discussed the consequentialist and nonconsequentialist rationales for a package of eight basic human rights. As yet, there are no political rights in the package. In this chapter, I add them.

Three Rationales for Democratic Rights

It may seem obvious that democratic rights should be added to the package. Advocates of democratic rights usually try to justify them in one of three ways: by appeal to (1) autonomy, (2) procedure, or (3) results. I discuss each of them briefly and then explain why I favor the third.

1. Autonomy. This kind of account explains the importance of democratic rights in terms of their contribution to personal autonomy. Connecting democratic rights directly with autonomy would give them exactly the same justification as the other rights in the package of basic human rights. The problem with this sort of account is, while the exercise of democratic rights does make some contribution to individual autonomy, the amount of the contribution is often vanishingly small. In a typical national election in the United States, my vote is 1/50,000,000 of the votes necessary for election; in a typical local election in Seattle, my vote is 1/50,000 of the vote necessary for election. Suppose I told you that from now on, decisions about how to live your life would be made by the vote of a group made up of you and 99,999 other people, with each person's vote of equal weight.[1] Would the fact that you had a vote in your life's decisions give you a sense of personal autonomy?[2] Though it is important that each person have an equal voice in democratic elections, it is hard to see how such a small amount of influence over the outcome could be seen as more than a marginal contribution to the autonomy of any individual voter.

2. Procedure. This kind of account would explain the importance of democratic rights in procedural terms. The procedural defense holds that a procedure in which each person affected has an equal voice in determining the outcome legitimates the outcome. Procedural defenses of democratic rights gain support from considerations of the following kind. Suppose everyone agrees that it is necessary to build a sewage treatment plant somewhere. If the decision on where to build it is made democratically, the result has a moral legitimacy it would lack if the decision were made by a single powerful individual who wanted it located as far away from his house as possible.

Can procedural considerations alone justify an outcome? What if a large majority votes to enslave a small minority? No democratic procedure could justify such a result.

Perhaps the explanation of this objection is itself procedural: The problem is that the minority did not *agree* to be bound by the results of the democratic process. However, this procedural explanation is incorrect. Suppose each member of the minority group had signed a written agreement to be so bound. Perhaps at the time they entered into the agreement, there was no prospect of a majority oppressing a minority. Sometime after they signed the agreement, a majority coalition formed and voted to enslave them. Would they be morally bound by their prior agreement to cooperate in their own enslavement? A strict proceduralist would answer yes. That is why I am not a proceduralist.

3. Results. Democratic rights are important. It is important that all people have an equal voice in the selection of their government, even if having an equal voice does not necessarily justify what the government does. It is important that all people exercise their voice in the selection of their

government, even if exercising their voice contributes only marginally to their autonomy. This is because democratic rights make an important difference to what the government does. This focus on results can take two forms. For a consequentialist, the focus would be on promoting (appropriately distributed) well-being; for a nonconsequentialist, the focus would be on promoting substantively just results. Both of these approaches to the justification of democratic rights are *results-oriented.* I begin by focusing on the consequentialist account. I return to the nonconsequentialist account later in this chapter.

I will refer to a government that guarantees the eight basic human rights and the relevant political rights (to be specified more fully below) as a *rights-respecting democracy.* In the previous chapter, I defined a package of basic human rights to assure that citizens are able to make reliable judgments about their own good, but I did not completely solve the reliable feedback or appropriate responsiveness problems. It may seem obvious that a rights-respecting democracy would be able to solve both problems. There are two directions from which this conclusion can be questioned, one optimistic and one pessimistic. I begin with the optimistic one.

A World of Angels

Imagine a world without any government where everyone is an autonomous being guaranteed the development-of-judgment rights and exercise-of-judgment rights. Call this the *state of nature.* What need would such beings have for government at all? Couldn't they just all exercise their autonomy in mutually supporting ways and dispense with government altogether?

In the epigraph to this chapter, the author of *Federalist* No. 51 tries to imagine beings who would need no government, and concludes that they would have to be angels, not human beings.[3] What is an angel? Think of *angels* as beings who always make decisions from the moral standpoint and whose moral judgments are infallible. Thus, in making any decision, angels would always consider the potential effects of their choices from behind the veil of ignorance and would always act in ways that could be justified from every point of view. If we understand *angel* in this way, then it is easy to see why they would be contrasted with human beings. Angels would never intentionally kill, maim, lie, cheat, or steal. So it is easy to see why someone might think that angels would not need any government at all.

For reasons that I take up shortly, I do not think this is quite correct. Even so, an angelic government would be very different from a government of human beings. Angels would never enact a law unless it could be justified from every point of view behind the veil of ignorance. Once a law was enacted, angels would not have to be threatened with punishment to motivate them to comply with it. They would always voluntarily comply with laws that could be justified behind the veil of ignorance.

Human beings are not angels. It would be hopelessly optimistic to think that a political system that would be good for angels would also be good for human beings. The importance of avoiding overoptimism suggests the following strategy: Define *devils* as beings who always act in their own rational self-interest and never adopt the moral standpoint. Then ask: What form of government would be best for devils? This was the strategy that led Hobbes to his too-pessimistic conclusion about the prospects for a rights-respecting democracy.

A World of Devils

Hobbes begins his account with a description of autonomous devils in the state of nature. Hobbes thought this would be hell on earth, a war of all against all. It would be a world with no industry, no agriculture, no justice, "no arts; no letters; no society; and, which is worst of all, continual fear and danger of violent death; and the life of man, solitary, poor, nasty, brutish, and short" ([1651], 107).

Hobbes believed that only an absolute ruler would be able to prevent this disaster, and thus that autonomous individuals would gladly trade their autonomy for a common yoke, secured by an absolute ruler or group of rulers. Although Hobbes's conclusion was too pessimistic, there is an important lesson to be learned from his thought experiment. Hobbes has identified a new kind of consequentialist justification, a *social contract* justification. It is important to understand social contract justification, even if Hobbes is mistaken to think that it justifies autocracy. I illustrate it with some examples.

The Internal Security Problem

One problem that arises in a state of nature is the problem of protecting oneself against being killed or seriously harmed by others who live nearby. Call this the *internal security* problem, to contrast it with the problem of being invaded and conquered by outsiders. It is helpful to use a simple model to understand the problem. Suppose you threaten to punish me for killing you. If the threat is solely yours, I refer to it as *individual deterrence*. Individual deterrence is unlikely to be effective against me if I believe that I can kill you, because you won't be able to punish me after you are dead.

One solution to this problem for individual deterrence that would be favored by evolution would be for you and the members of your extended family to threaten to punish anyone who kills you or any other member of your family. Call this *kin deterrence*.[4] Kin deterrence seems to be close to a cultural universal. Kin deterrence does represent a more effective deterrent to murder than individual deterrence, but it also creates a new kind of problem. Because families have a potentially unlimited future, kin deterrence can generate potentially endless cycles of killing, illustrated in literature by the Montagues and Capulets, and in the real world by the example of the Hatfields and McCoys.

The Hatfield-McCoy feud ended in the nineteenth century, but kin deterrence did not. Here is a current example. In Albania, the code of revenge known as Kanun requires that a killing of a family member be avenged by killing a male relative of the killer. These cycles of revenge go on for years, during which male family members are in constant fear for their lives (Dhimgjoka 2002).

Suppose you had the power to stop these potentially endless cycles of revenge killings. It is easy to see how it might well be in the interests of everyone in both families to have you intervene and announce that you will punish anyone who engages in violence, including those who engage in retaliatory violence. The fact that your intervention would make everyone better off does not imply that everyone would agree to it. At any particular time, at least one family (and perhaps both) will feel aggrieved, because they will feel that they have suffered an unpunished wrong. They might not be willing to agree to your intervention until after they have settled the score. Of course, if you wait until after they feel the score has been settled, the other family will feel aggrieved. No matter when you intervene, at least one side will feel aggrieved. Nonetheless, if you do intervene and end the cycle of violence, it might not take long for everyone on both sides to recognize that your intervention had made them better off.

This illustrates a potential consequentialist justification of your intervention. It is not a paternalistic justification. In a paternalistic justification, the targets of the intervention are forced to do what they typically judge to be bad for them. For example, when the state of Connecticut outlawed contraception, it was not under the illusion that those who wanted to use a method of contraception would think that they personally were better off being prevented from doing so. In the example of revenge killings, even though it requires compulsion to stop the cycle, each individual involved may well agree that ending the cycle would be better for them personally than having it continue.

It is important to see that the inability of the families themselves to end the cycle of violence need not be due to any irrationality on their part. In the absence of an external power to guarantee security, a family's existence might depend on the willingness of each member of a family to do his part in the practice of kin deterrence. The point is not that the individuals involved are irrational, but that there is a great potential for improving everyone's well-being. Hobbes thought that the only workable solution to this sort of internal security problem was the Leviathan, an autocracy ruled by an absolute sovereign.

Where a system of coercion (in this case, coercion to stop the cycles of retaliatory violence) makes those who are coerced better off in their own estimation than they would be without the coercion, the coercion is not paternalistic, because it does not *overrule* their own judgment about what is good for them; it *gives effect* to their own judgment. Situations of this kind in which coercion can make everyone involved better off in their own estimation are referred to as *collective action problems*.[5] In chapter 5, I discussed one kind of collective action problem, an n-person assurance game, illustrated by the practices of foot binding and infibulation. To solve an n-person assurance game does not require a sovereign or other source of external enforcement. All that it requires is a change in conventions. The kind of collective action problems illustrated by cycles of retaliatory violence are more difficult to solve. Solutions to them usually require laws backed up with sanctions.

The Need for External Enforcement

For a law to be effective in solving the internal security problem, it must be backed up with some kind of external enforcement. The reason is simple. Without external enforcement, compliance would quickly break down. To see why, consider another example of the same kind of collective action problem: traffic regulation. Imagine what driving would be like if there were no traffic regulations at all, no speed limits, no stop lights, no stop or yield signs. Traffic would be much more congested and there would be many more accidents. All drivers would be much worse off.

It is in theory possible for all traffic regulations to be enforced by convention in a community in which everyone knows everyone else and everyone keeps track of everyone else's driving. However, in any large city, enforcement by convention could never work.[6] To see why not, consider the example of freeway on-ramp metering, which forces commuters to stop long enough on freeway on-ramps to prevent freeway slowdowns due to merging traffic. Suppose all people want to minimize their own commute time. It is possible to imagine a situation in which a system of on-ramp metering would reduce everyone's commute times if they would all comply with it. Suppose the metering system were not externally enforced. Each driver entering a freeway would have to decide whether or not to stop at the meter signal until it changed to green. In that situation, all drivers would know that, regardless of what the other drivers do, their own commute times would be less if they were to ignore the signal. As a matter of fact, if there were a line of cars stopped at an on-ramp metering signal, a driver could save even more time by driving around all of them and entering directly onto the freeway.

Imagine that you are sitting patiently in line waiting your turn at the on-ramp metering signal. A car comes up behind you. Instead of stopping and waiting in line, it swerves around your car and the other cars in line and enters the freeway. You would probably be angry with that driver. Then imagine it happens again. How many drivers would have to ignore the signal before you and the others waiting at the signal would feel like suckers? Very quickly, almost everyone would be ignoring the signal.

Ignoring the signal is not irrational from the personal point of view. The first person to drive around the line of cars waiting at the metering signal definitely is reducing her commute time, as is each successive driver who ignores the signal. The problem is that everyone who ignores the signal is lengthening many *other* people's commute time, so when everyone ignores the signal, everyone's commute time is substantially longer than it would be if everyone complied with it. In the anonymity of a city, it is unrealistic to suppose there could be conventional enforcement of on-ramp metering. External enforcement is required.

A similar account applies to the internal security problem. The internal security problem and the freeway metering problem are examples of n-person prisoners' dilemmas. Unlike the n-person assurance games discussed in chapter 5, a solution to an n-person prisoners' dilemma often requires external enforcement.

Social Contract Justification

Hobbes discovered a new kind of nonpaternalistic, consequentialist justification for coercion, which I refer to as a *social contract* justification. To have a social contract justification, a policy of coercion must make everyone (or almost everyone) better off in their own estimation and the benefits (and costs) of the policy must be appropriately distributed. This kind of justification is consequentialist. Often social contract justification is explained in nonconsequentialist terms, in terms of agreement. It is important to realize that on both the consequentialist and the nonconsequentialist account, a social contract justification of a policy does not require that everyone actually agree to the policy (e.g., by signing a contract). The social contract is a hypothetical one. Those affected by the policy *could* have agreed if they were willing to negotiate in good faith and if they were willing to accept a reasonable compromise.

To appreciate the potential scope of social contract justifications of coercive policies, it is useful to have in mind some examples of n-person prisoners' dilemmas. Hobbes showed that a criminal justice system with laws against murder, assault, and so on can be a solution to an n-person prisoners' dilemma.[7] I have also mentioned traffic laws. Other potential solutions to n-person prisoners' dilemmas include property and contract law, truth-in-labeling laws, truth-in-advertising laws, product safety laws, including laws requiring the testing of drugs and other potentially hazardous products, the system of tort law (i.e., the law of civil liability for personal injury), licensing laws, antipollution laws, zoning laws, building codes, occupational safety laws, securities laws, antitrust laws, and the collection of taxes to pay for scientific research, streets and highways, mass transit, sewers and utilities, and parks and other protected areas, as well as the collection of taxes to pay for external enforcement of all of these collective action problems. What all these examples have in common is that if everyone abides by them, everyone (or almost everyone) is better off in his own estimation than if no one does, but each individual would be personally better off if he could make an exception of himself without being detected.

Hobbes's social contract argument against a rights-respecting democracy is simple: Only an absolute autocrat can solve these collective action problems for his subjects.[8] Thus, life under an autocrat would be better for human beings than any alternative. Autonomous individuals would agree to give up their autonomy for the security and other benefits provided by an autocrat.

Although Hobbes thought that autocrats should be benevolent and promote the well-being of their subjects, his argument did not require that they be benevolent in order for their subjects to be bound to obey them ([1651], 145). He thought that the alternatives were so bad that even the rule of a nonbenevolent autocrat could be given a social contract justification.

Why was Hobbes so sure that there was no better alternative than autocracy? I think there were two reasons: first, because he could not imagine how a political and social system could avoid chaos unless it was organized in a top-down fashion, with an absolute ruler or ruling body at the top. Hobbes was writing during the period of civil war and disorder of the interregnum in England from 1649 to 1660, so he was vividly aware of the disadvantages of a breakdown in legal authority. I suspect this experience reinforced in Hobbes an intuition that is still widely shared today: that if a process is not *directed by* an intelligent agent, the process will be random and chaotic. It is the same intuition that makes it seem obvious to many people that the order in the universe *requires* that it have an intelligent designer.

The second reason that Hobbes could not imagine how an alternative to an absolute ruler could be stable is that he formulated a worst-case scenario: a government that would work for devils, defined as purely self-interested individuals who would kill, maim, lie, cheat, and steal if it would benefit them and they could do so with impunity.

Hobbes was writing in the seventeenth century, before the appearance of an idea that would enable Kant, as quoted in one of the epigraphs to this chapter, to claim that even a society of devils would evolve into a rights-respecting democracy. Before evaluating Kant's claim, we need to understand the idea behind it.

Invisible Hand Processes

Hobbes wrote *Leviathan* in 1651. More than a hundred years later, in 1776, Adam Smith introduced a revolutionary idea into economics and the other sciences. This was the idea of the "invisible hand" process, referred to in one of the epigraphs to this chapter. The idea is that a competitive market economy can promote everyone's well-being, even if all individuals in the economy pursue only their own individual well-being. Smith reinforced this idea in another famous passage: "It is not from the benevolence of the butcher, the brewer, or the baker that we expect our dinner, but from their regard to their own interest" (A. Smith [1776], I.2.2).

An *invisible hand* process is a process that tends toward a certain outcome, even if no one involved in the process intends that outcome (cf. Nozick 1974, 18–22). Although introduced by Smith to explain competitive markets, the idea of an invisible hand process applies much more broadly. For example, one important application of the idea of an invisible hand process is in evolutionary theory, where it is possible to explain the behavior of many organisms in terms of the propagation of genes even if the organisms know nothing about genes and have no intention of propagating them.[9]

Smith introduced the idea of an invisible hand process in his discussion of competitive markets. He wanted to explain how the result of individuals seeking to increase their own individual wealth could be an increase in overall or national wealth. Smith himself did not believe that human beings are purely self-interested and he would not have thought it would be better if they were. He limited his claim about the value of self-interest to economic transactions in a competitive market economy.

Others after him were not so circumspect. In another epigraph to this chapter, Kant seems to suggest that the evolution of society itself is an invisible hand process by which even intelligent devils (i.e., purely self-interested beings, with no moral motivation at all) would develop a form of government in which they would respect each other's rights. In the nineteenth century, Marx thought of history as an invisible hand process that would inevitably lead to universal liberation, the withering away of the state, and a socialist utopia, even if no one involved in the process had any motivation other than to promote their own interests and the interests of their class.

Why There Is No Invisible Hand Explanation of Rights-Respecting Democracy (or Any Other Kind of Government That Guarantees Human Rights)

In the tradition of Kant and Marx, in the twentieth century, some neoclassical economists realized that if there were to be a complete explanation of competitive markets as an invisible hand process, something would have to be added to Smith's account. Hobbes had pointed out that rational individuals would not make investments unless they could be assured that they would be able to profit from them. This shows that economic activity requires enforcement of property rights. Similarly, rational individuals would not enter into contracts unless they were assured that the other parties would not breach them. This shows that economic activity requires legal enforcement of contracts. So to show that competitive markets qualified as an invisible hand process, it was necessary to explain how a society of rationally self-interested individuals could form a government that would enforce property rights and contract rights and, unlike so many autocrats, would not confiscate the wealth of its citizens. The establishment and maintenance of such a government involves numerous collective action problems. The economist James Buchanan set out to show how even devils could solve all of them. He devoted the major part of his career to this project.

Initially, Buchanan and Tullock thought the problem could be solved in the same way that markets solved other consumer problems, but they took for granted the definition and enforcement of human and property rights (1962, 46). They overlooked the fact that the enforcement of such rights is itself part of the problem that they set out to solve. Subsequently, Buchanan realized that the lack of explanation of initial rights was a gap in the derivation (1975, 8). Thirteen years later, he attempted to fill the gap; again he was unsuccessful (1975, 26–28).[10] Ten years later, Brennan and Buchanan (1985) tried again. Although they began with a model of the individual as *homo economicus* (chap. 4), by the end of the book they had given up that model in favor of a model of individuals motivated by norms (chap. 9).

Buchanan won the Nobel Prize in economics for his efforts, even though he never did show how rationally self-interested individuals could establish and sustain a government that respected individual rights and enforced contracts. It seems to me he was doomed to fail. Although in theory it is possible that a society of rationally self-interested individuals might establish and sustain such a government, the actual impediments are so great that it is a practical impossibility.[11]

Buchanan focused on the effort that would be needed to form such a government. In practice, a rationally self-interested individual would not contribute to that effort, because contributing itself is a collective action problem. Even if everyone would be better off if all contributed than if none did, each individual's contribution is too unlikely to make the difference between success and failure for contributing to be rational for a self-interested individual. A similar argument shows that even if a democratic government were established, if the population were sufficiently large, rationally self-interested individuals would not take the time to inform themselves on the candidates and would not take the time to vote.[12] Even worse, no matter what kind of government was established, it would almost surely not respect individual rights. For example, if the government were a majoritarian democracy, a majority could use its electoral power to oppress a minority. If they were all rationally self-interested, the majority would have no qualms about doing so.

There is more. Even if by chance a rights-respecting democracy were established, it would only be expected to last as long as no one was able to put together a coalition that could seize power. However, there are many different ways that rationally self-interested individuals could form successful coalitions. For example, if the military leaders were rationally self-interested, it would probably not be difficult for them to come up with a power-sharing agreement that they could implement with a coup d'etat.

Thus, more than 300 years after Hobbes introduced the thought experiment, a strong case can be made that the only stable form of government for a society of devils would be an oppressive form of autocracy, and there is some question about whether even that form of government would be stable. If this is right, then Kant was wrong and Hobbes was right, at least about devils. However, applied to human beings, Hobbes's conclusion is too pessimistic, because most human beings are not devils. The person who has done the most important work to show that they are not devils is Amartya Sen.[13] Reviewing some of Sen's work will help us to appreciate how human rights help human beings to solve problems that devils would not be able to solve.

The Role of Basic Human Rights and Moral Judgment in the Elimination of Famines

Sen won the Nobel Prize for important work in many different areas of economics. Some of his most important work is on the economic importance of basic human rights and on the importance of moral motivation in empirical economics. For example, his research has radically transformed the understanding of famines. Before Sen, famines were generally thought of as natural disasters. Sen has shown that they are more political than natural phenomena. Even though droughts and other disasters occur in democratic and nondemocratic countries, famines do not occur in countries with a free press and a democratic government with an active opposition (1999, chap. 7).

Why not? What is the difference between countries where famines occur and countries where they do not? In the previous chapter, I discussed Stalin's intentional starvation of between 3 and 10 million agricultural workers in the early 1930s. Not only was there no mention of it in the Soviet press, but also Walter Duranty, the *New York Times* columnist who won the 1932 Pulitzer Prize for his reporting from Russia, denied that there was a famine and ridiculed reports of it that appeared in other Western publications (Stuttaford 2003). And when Mao's Great Leap Forward led to the largest mass starvation in history, there was no report of it in the Chinese press. Edgar Snow traveled to China and returned to report that he had not seen anyone starving.[14] If the government has the power to suppress bad news, it will do so. As a result, countries without a free press usually do not report famines.

A free press by itself will not end famines. As Sen points out, government officials do not die in famines. So although a free press is necessary for news of an impending famine to become public, it is not enough to prevent famine. In addition, the government officials must be motivated to do something about the potential famine. In a democracy with an active opposition, the motivation comes from the threat of being voted out of office. Thus, Sen's research on famines has shown an important and far from self-evident connection between basic human rights and human well-being.

There is one more link in the chain. Why would a democratically elected government feel threatened by a famine? In a famine, usually only a small percentage of the total population starves, and dead people can't vote. The main threat to the government is usually not from the starving; it is from those who are not starving. Most people will oppose a government that allows people to starve, even if they themselves are not at risk of starvation. And even if a country is very poor, when a famine is imminent, other countries and outside relief agencies will offer relief, which is itself an indication that people in other countries are willing to pay taxes or make voluntary donations to prevent the starvation of complete strangers thousands of miles away.

Sen found that many people are willing to incur a small cost in order to keep other people whom they don't know from starving. Rationally self-interested agents would not be willing to incur those costs. Thus, empirical evidence on the elimination of famines provides powerful evidence that many people are not purely rationally self-interested. Moral judgment from the moral standpoint can make an important difference in politics.

Although many economists would classify moral reasoning as a kind of irrational emotional response or as some other kind of irrationality (e.g., Frank 1988), it is important to realize that there is another way of understanding it. The moral standpoint involves a recognizable form of moral reasoning. It is as much governed by reasons as the rational self-interested point of view. However, different kinds of reasons are involved: moral reasons rather than self-interested ones.

Psychological Evidence on Fairness: The Ultimatum Game and Its Relatives

Sen has found evidence of the influence of moral judgment on behavior in famines and in other dramatic examples, but the influence of moral judgment on behavior is a pervasive phenomenon. Daniel Kahneman and Vernon Smith shared the Nobel Prize in economics for work showing that people do not always act in accordance with the requirements of rational self-interest. They are two of a large number of psychologists doing work of this kind. Many of the experimental results can be explained by the fact that people do not always realize what rational self-interest requires of them. The most important results cannot be explained so simply, because the experimental subjects continue to engage in the relevant behavior even when they realize that it violates the requirements of rational self-interest. It is useful to review some evidence from experiments of this kind.

The Sequential Ultimatum Game

In this game, subjects are assigned one of two roles: Proposer or Respondent (or, alternately, to both). In a typical experiment, the two players are to divide $10 as follows: Proposer offers a division of the $10 to Respondent. Divisions can be made in 50-cent increments from $10 to $0. If Respondent accepts the offer, they each get what Proposer offered. If Respondent rejects it, they each get nothing.

Assume that both players prefer more money to less and they rank the possible outcomes on the basis of how much money they receive. Assume also that they have no prospect of future interactions. Then, there is a unique solution to this problem for rationally self-interested agents: Proposer makes the lowball offer of a $9.50/50-cent division and Respondent accepts it. Why would a rationally self-interested Respondent accept such a meager offer? Because the choice is between receiving 50 cents and receiving nothing, and 50 cents is better than nothing.

Variations on this experiment have been performed on many different populations in many different countries (e.g., Roth et al. 1991). In almost all of the experiments, the most frequent offer is an even split, and in all experiments, some lowball offers are rejected.[15] There are many potential explanations of these results. A common one is that many of the subjects are responding to norms of fairness. This is the one I focus on.

What are norms of fairness? Skyrms proposes an evolutionary explanation (1996, chap. 2). In the next chapter I evaluate his proposal. One proposal Skyrms does not seriously consider is that at least some of the subjects are analyzing the situation from the moral standpoint. This is not to say that they explicitly think about the original position behind the veil of ignorance, but rather they are sensitive to the considerations that become explicit in original position reasoning.

Let's analyze Proposer's choice from the original position. From behind the veil of ignorance, Proposer would not know whether he was Proposer or Respondent. Proposer would therefore propose a division that would be acceptable to either player. Notice there is a complete symmetry between the two players. From the personal point of view, Proposer would most prefer the $10/$0 division; Respondent would most prefer the $0/$10 division. Anything that can be said in support of an unequal division favoring Proposer (e.g., the division $9.50/50 cents) can also be said of the opposite division favoring Respondent (e.g., the division 50 cents/$9.50). The only division neither player could reasonably object to is the even division. Thus, in the original position behind the veil of ignorance, reasonable players would agree to offering an even division.

Now let's analyze Respondent's choice from the original position. Respondent realizes that if Proposer adopts the moral point of view, she will offer an even division. The same considerations that favor making that offer favor accepting it. What if Proposer offers a different split? The original position does not provide a definitive answer to the question of what Respondent should do. Suppose Proposer makes the rationally self-interested offer of a $9.50/50 cents division. Because at a relatively small cost to herself (50 cents), Respondent can impose a relatively large cost on Proposer ($9.50), the importance of not rewarding Proposer for an unreasonable demand makes it plausible to think that Respondent should reject the offer. There is no clear line marking the minimum offer that Respondent should accept. Respondent could reject all offers giving her less than an even split, but I don't see how the moral standpoint would require Respondent to do so. I don't believe there is a definitive answer to the question of how great a loss Respondent should be willing to bear to prevent Proposer from profiting from an unfair offer. However, it seems reasonable that there are some offers that Respondent should reject.

In the sequential ultimatum game, adopting the moral standpoint would lead Proposer to offer an even division. But the results of the sequential ultimatum game do not definitively support the conclusion that Proposer's motivation is moral. Even a rationally self-interested Proposer would offer an even division if Proposer thought Respondent was "irrational" and would veto any offer worse than an even division. It is Respondent's willingness to incur at least a small cost to punish unfairness that is the most important finding of these experiments. A further experiment is necessary to clarify Proposer's motivation.

The Dictator Game

In order to eliminate Proposer's fear of Respondent's veto, Kahneman, Knetsch, and Thaler (1986) simplified the game. In this variation of the game, Proposer was given the choice of how to divide $20 with another subject. There were two alternatives: to divide it $18/$2 or to divide it $10/$10. Respondent had no veto power over the division. Clearly a rationally self-interested subject would choose the $18/$2 option. Nonetheless, 76 percent of the experimental subjects offered an even $10/$10 division. It is easy to see how the original position analysis would lead to this result.

Punishing Unfairness in the Dictator Game

Kahneman, Knetsch, and Thaler (1986) added a further twist to the dictator game. Call those subjects who offered an even $10/$10 division in the first part of the experiment E's (for "even"), and call those who offered $18/$2 in the first part of the experiment U's (for "uneven"). In the second part of the experiment, subjects were given a choice between dividing $10 evenly

($5/$5) with an E or dividing $12 evenly ($6/$6) with a U. The second part of the experiment was performed on two different groups. The percentage of subjects who chose to divide the smaller amount with an E was 74 percent in one group and 81 percent in the other. Thus, a large percentage of subjects were willing to forgo an additional $1 for themselves to reward an E with $5 and to deprive a U of an additional $6. As before, the evidence shows that most subjects are willing to incur a small loss to reward fairness and to punish unfairness. But this experiment also shows that many Proposers are willing to voluntarily take less for themselves in order to make a fair division with Respondent.

Camerer and Thaler (1995) refer to these results as *anomalies* of economics. Again, it is important to distinguish between the anomalies that result from the subjects' failure to recognize the requirements of rational self-interest and those that persist even when the subjects know they are not acting in accordance with rational self-interest. Many subjects who know rational self-interest dictates offering an unequal division will still offer an even division in the sequential ultimatum game and the dictator game, and many will punish U's in the Kahneman, Knetsch, and Thaler extension of the dictator game. What about you? What would you do?

Strength in Numbers

Even if the results of the ultimatum game and other similar experiments show that human beings are not devils—that is, that they are not purely self-interested—it might seem that the assumption that they are devils would be a useful idealization. If self-interest is a much more powerful motivator than fairness, perhaps its effects would generally swamp any effects of fairness. This response gains support from the fact that the dollar amounts in the ultimatum game experiments are so small. Perhaps if the amounts were larger, self-interested motives would become more powerful and would overpower tendencies toward fairness.

Hoffman, McCabe, and V. Smith (1996) tested this claim. They found very little difference between the proportions offered by Proposer when the total amount was $10 and when the total amount was $100. They also found that Respondent was still willing to reject lowball offers when the total amount was $100: three of the four $90/$10 offers and two of the five $70/$30 offers were rejected.

So fairness considerations are more powerful motivators than might have been thought. However, I do not assume that fairness considerations are a more powerful motivator than self-interest. They do not have to be more powerful than self-interest to make a big difference in politics. The reason is that, on most political issues, there will typically be a large group of people who have no strong personal interest in the outcome. Call them the *impartial audience*. Because their self-interested motives will not be very powerful, judgments of fairness may well be their strongest motive. Even if their judgments of fairness are only strong enough to motivate them to incur small costs to promote fairness, if the impartial audience is large, the sum of the small costs they are willing to pay can be so large as to make the force for fairness irresistible.

How the Moral Standpoint Protects Rights and Helps to Solve the Reliable Feedback Problem

Because human beings are not angels, external enforcement of solutions to n-person prisoners' dilemmas is necessary. Because they are not devils, they are willing to incur at least small costs to support fairness in cases in which they have no strong countervailing personal interest. For example, most people are willing to support taxes to finance a system of external enforcement of basic rights and to finance solutions to collective action problems. Because human beings are not devils, rights-respecting democracies not only prevent famines, they are the most effective way known of preventing and eliminating oppression.

Consider some examples. When members of the New York Police Department physically and sexually abused a Haitian immigrant, they probably thought that most people would not care. Certainly, the majority would realize that violations of the rights of a poor immigrant would not pose any threat to *their* rights. The resulting popular uproar was not the result of the mistaken judgment that violating the rights of Haitian immigrants was a threat to the rights of the majority. It was largely a reaction to the unfairness of the treatment in that case.

This sort of bottom-up social protection of rights has achieved many important victories, none greater than the consensus on the elimination of slavery in the nineteenth century. As would be predicted, the antislavery movement was strongest in places where there were no slaves, for example, in England and the northern United States. Few slaveowners were able to overcome their self-interested motives to take the moral standpoint on the practice. As discussed in chapter 4, outsiders must be careful not to impose their own cultural understandings on the practices of other cultures (e.g., by classifying rituals of human sacrifice as cannibalism). However, often outsiders are in a better position to morally evaluate the practices of a culture than insiders, because they are not subject to the distorting influences of socially enforced self-serving justifications of the practices.

This bottom-up process of promoting fairness has given rise to a new kind of political movement: movements of nonviolent resistance. Gandhi was the founder of this new kind of movement. Gandhi's strategy of nonviolent resistance shows how, when dealing with a rights-respecting democracy, weakness can become a political strength. To an impartial observer, the more force a government must use to enforce its authority, the less legitimate it will seem to be. By being willing to suffer violence at the hands of the British without threatening violence themselves, Gandhi and his followers made a powerful appeal to those who had no strong personal stake in colonization and who thus were able to adopt the moral standpoint.

Although Gandhi himself did not limit the applicability of his strategy to rights-respecting democracies, it is clear that to be effective, the strategy depended on its being addressed to them. Hitler or Stalin or Mao would have swiftly crushed Gandhi's independence movement without any reports of it in the press. Gandhi's strategy depended on a free press to report on it to voters in England and on the support of English voters who did not have a strong stake in maintaining India as a colony.

Martin Luther King, Jr., adapted Gandhi's strategy to the civil rights movement in the United States. Again, weakness became a strength. Had the United States not been a rights-respecting democracy, the nonviolent civil rights movement would have been crushed and few outside the movement would have even known of its existence. In addition, if the southern United States had been an independent country, the civil rights movement would almost surely have failed for lack of an impartial audience of voters without a stake in the oppression to whom the movement could appeal. In the South, socially enforced self-serving justifications for the system of segregation made it unlikely that whites would be able to attain a moral standpoint on the system. It was voters outside the South, who had no stake in the system, who provided the federal government with the necessary support to enact and enforce civil rights laws.

For the Gandhi-King strategy of nonviolent resistance to oppression to be successful, there has to be a relatively free press that will report on it in spite of pressure not to do so and a relatively impartial audience to respond to the reports, with a relatively low-cost option for opposing the oppression. Apartheid in South Africa was ended in part because of the pressure from those in rights-respecting countries outside South Africa who could rely on a free press to report on apartheid and who were willing to bear small costs (e.g., supporting trade sanctions) to oppose the oppression.

Because human beings are not devils, because they are able to adopt the moral standpoint, and because they are willing to incur at least small costs to promote fairness as judged from the moral standpoint, rights-respecting democracies can be stable and can improve themselves over time. I have focused on the importance of the bottom-up process of moral transformation that depends on the exercise of moral judgment by voters in a democracy, because this is the most significant way that the exercise of moral judgment makes a difference in politics. However, it is also important to realize that democracies benefit from the exercise of moral judgment by those at the top. The exercise of moral judgment is important at every level of society.

An Addition to Democratic Rights:
An Independent Judiciary to Enforce Rights

When a majority has a powerful interest that conflicts with the rights of a minority, legislators can come under almost irresistible pressure to go along with the majority. When the government's chief executive has an interest that conflicts with individuals' rights, there will be a strong temptation to ignore their rights. No democratic system will reliably protect basic human rights unless it includes an independent judiciary to enforce them. So in addition to the usual democratic rights, a rights-respecting democracy must also include a reasonably independent judiciary.

If the *Dred Scott* decision showed the futility of relying solely on the judiciary to protect human rights, *Brown v. Board of Education* showed that the judiciary can sometimes play an important role in protecting them.[16] Thus, although I have emphasized how the moral judgment of voters can influence government officials in a bottom-up process, an adequate political system will also depend on some top-down influence. I have emphasized the influence that works in the bottom-up direction because it seems to me to be the most important.

The Consequentialist Case
for Basic Human Rights

If the claim of first-person authority is true, a government aiming to promote the (appropriately distributed) well-being of its citizens must guarantee development-of-judgment rights, exercise-of-judgment rights, and a sphere of autonomy free of government interference. Though at first glance it seems that the claim of first-person authority would eliminate any further role for government in promoting the well-being of its citizens, Hobbes's discovery of collective action problems that require externally enforced solutions (e.g., n-person prisoners' dilemmas) opened up a new kind of consequentialist justification for government action: social contract justification. Legal solutions to collective action problems typically require external enforcement. Where the law enforces a solution to a collective action problem, it does not overrule the judgment of those it coerces; it gives effect to it.

In combination with the other basic human rights, democratic rights provide governments with feedback on how best to solve their citizens' collective action problems. This sort of feedback is typically provided by voters when they simply vote according to their own interests. Where there are no serious questions of fairness at issue, voters usually should vote according to their own interests.

In addition to providing reliable feedback, democratic rights motivate the government to be appropriately responsive to that feedback, because its longevity depends on how well it promotes the well-being of its citizens. So a package of basic human rights, including democratic rights, enables a government to solve the consequentialist versions of the reliable feedback problem and the appropriate responsiveness problem.

There is another important role for democratic rights in the consequentialist justification of rights-respecting democracies. This is the role that they play both in preventing rights-respecting democracies from degenerating into one or another form of tyranny and in the improvement of rights-respecting democracies over time. Ultimately, the stability of rights-respecting democracies and their ability to improve over time depend crucially on there being enough voters who are able to adopt the moral standpoint to make fairness judgments in particular cases where issues of fairness are important and their willingness to bear at least small costs in order to promote fairness on issues in which they have no strong personal stake. It is only because ordinary people are willing to bear some cost to promote fairness that rights-respecting democracies are prevented from oppressing minorities and are able to improve themselves over time.

Mere legislation of democratic rights is not enough protection. An independent judiciary also plays a crucial role. For this reason, a right to an independent judiciary is an important part of the package of political rights that qualify as basic human rights.

If rights-respecting democracies depend on enough of their citizens developing and exercising their moral judgment, then it seems necessary to include in the package of basic human rights those rights that are necessary for the development and exercise of moral judgment. Does moral judgment require additional capacities beyond what is needed for people to make reliable judgments about their own good? Yes, it requires one further capacity: a capacity for empathic understanding. So it is important to specify that a child's right to what is necessary for normal emotional development should include what is necessary to develop empathic understanding. And the right to education should be understood broadly enough to include not only the information and skills necessary to make judgments about one's own good, but also training to develop empathic understanding.

The Nonconsequentialist Case
for Basic Human Rights

So far, I have focused most of my attention on the consequentialist case for basic human rights, because it seems to me that it is most in need of development. However, it is useful to consider the nonconsequentialist position also.

For the nonconsequentialist, the rights necessary for the development and exercise of autonomy do not have to be justified by their contribution to (appropriately distributed) human well-being. Autonomy itself is important enough to justify them. Thus, the development-of-judgment rights, the exercise-of-judgment rights, and rights to a sphere of autonomy free of paternalistic interference are directly justified on the nonconsequentialist account.

What about political rights, especially democratic rights? Do they have a nonconsequentialist justification? At the beginning of this chapter, I suggested three avenues for justifying them: an autonomy-based justification, a procedural justification, and a results-based justification. I suggested that the first two avenues were dead-ends. The third avenue is not. Although the nonconsequentialist does not agree with the consequentialist on the nature of the problems, the nonconsequentialist can point to the importance of democratic rights in solving the nonconsequentialist versions of the reliable feedback problem and the appropriate responsiveness problem.

The nonconsequentialist version of the reliable feedback problem is one of obtaining reliable feedback about how just (or unjust) the government's policies are. The nonconsequentialist version of the appropriate responsiveness problem is one of using the feedback to make the government's policies more just. The nonconsequentialist can take over my discussion of the role of fairness judgments in a democracy to explain why democratic rights are essential to solving both problems. On both the consequentialist and the nonconsequentialist accounts, it is possible to defend democratic rights for the role they play in making the system of government more just, including their role in protecting the other basic rights. So on both consequentialist and nonconsequentialist grounds, democratic rights qualify as basic human rights.

What divides the consequentialist and the nonconsequentialist is their conception of justice as applied to governments. For the consequentialist, a just government is one that promotes the (appropriately distributed) well-being of its citizens; for a nonconsequentialist, justice involves something more or something other than (appropriately distributed) well-being. Will a nonconsequentialist allow that a government should solve its citizens' collective action problems? Here the nonconsequentialists divide. *Libertarians* (e.g., Nozick 1974) assert that only the explicit consent of those who are taxed can justify a government's collection of tax money to solve a collective action problem. This would make it impermissible for a government to levy taxes to solve a collective action problem without the explicit consent of all taxpayers. However, most nonconsequentialists are not libertarians. Indeed, the largest category of nonconsequentialists are the *social contract theorists* or *contractarians* (e.g., Rawls 1993). They generally believe that a government's actions can be justified by the hypothetical agreement of its citizens under appropriate circumstances. Though the details differ, most social contract theorists hold that a government taxing its citizens to solve their collective action problems can pass the relevant hypothetical consent test.

Though consequentialists and nonconsequentialists differ on the nature of justice, it is important not to exaggerate the significance of the disagreement. If government policies are responsive to the fairness judgments of ordinary voters about particular cases, there is room for a considerable amount of agreement between consequentialists and nonconsequentialists. Often they will agree in many of their judgments on particular cases of justice and injustice. For example, they can agree that a rights-respecting democracy tends to become more just over time, even though they disagree about what justice is.

Rights-Respecting Democracies as Self-Improving Self-Regulating Systems

Some neoclassical economists had hoped to show that a rights-respecting democracy could be produced and maintained by an invisible hand process, even if the individuals involved were purely rationally self-interested. I have explained why I doubt this can be done. Rights-respecting democracies depend for their existence and stability on the ability of human beings to make judgments of fairness from the moral standpoint and on their willingness to incur small costs to promote fairness. For this reason, I do not believe they could arise or be maintained by an invisible hand process. Though it is not an invisible hand process, the process that makes rights-respecting democracies stable is itself an important kind of process worth investigating.

The process is one that makes a rights-respecting democracy more just over time, because it tends to be appropriately sensitive to reliable feedback that can be used to correct its injustices. Looked at in this way, a rights-respecting democracy is a special kind of *self-regulating system*. In chapter 2 I used the cruise control device in a car to illustrate the idea of a self-regulating system. A cruise control device can be quite complex, but from a theoretical point of view, it is a simple self-regulating system. It uses feedback from the speedometer to adjust the engine throttle to maintain the desired vehicle speed.

What is the goal of a rights-respecting democracy, understood as a self-regulating system? The goal is its own moral justification—that is, a just government. Rights-respecting democracies are different from simple self-regulating systems such as cruise control devices in two respects:

1. The goal is not well-defined. A cruise control device was designed by someone who understood the goal and how to achieve it. However, there is no agreement on exactly what makes a government just. Rights-respecting democracies would not be able to become more just over time unless their citizens were able to reliably identify justice and injustice in particular cases. That is enough to enable the system to improve itself over time, even though no one involved in the process has any direct rational insight into what justice is.

2. To be successful, the *system* must be able to improve itself. Cruise control devices do not have the ability to modify themselves to better achieve their goal. This is not true of rights-respecting democracies. As I mentioned in chapter 2, the original U.S. Constitution, with its recognition of slavery and its failure to recognize the rights of women, was far from a moral exemplar. Its saving grace was that it provided the framework for improving itself. In chapter 2, I mentioned the Article V provisions for amending the Constitution as one way it could be improved.

There is another process that has been almost equally important: the evolution of constitutional interpretation. The provisions of Article V have been used to amend the Constitution only twenty-seven times. At least as many important constitutional changes have been achieved through evolutions in interpretation. In chapter 6, I briefly reviewed the Supreme Court's development of the right to a sphere of individual autonomy. This is one of the most important developments in the legal protection of basic human rights in the United States since women's suffrage. Women's suffrage was accomplished by a constitutional amendment; autonomy rights have been accomplished by an evolution of interpretation. Both play a crucial role in the process of constitutional self-improvement.

The evolution of constitutional interpretation is sometimes portrayed as a top-down process, in which "elitist" judges have made their own moral judgments into law (e.g., Bork 2003). The process is almost never exclusively top-down. Supreme Court justices are influenced by social movements in the society at large. The development of the right to a sphere of autonomy would never have occurred without large-scale bottom-up social movements for such rights.[17]

In some cases, innovations in the Supreme Court's constitutional interpretation are really only a manifestation of bottom-up changes. An example of this sort of change is the change in the Supreme Court's standards for "due process" for property rights, which was necessary for Franklin Roosevelt's New Deal legislation to be judged constitutional.[18] When a government guarantees the package of basic human rights specified earlier, the legal system as a whole can be justified as a self-improving self-regulating system for promoting justice.

Understanding a rights-respecting democracy as a self-improving self-regulating system makes it easier to appreciate its advantages over an autocracy that does not respect basic human rights. To the extent that an autocracy is a self-regulating system, it will be aimed more at the autocrat's self-interest than at justice. Because there is no mechanism to correct for the distorting effects of self-interest, an autocracy will almost inevitably tend to become less just over time. There is no reason to expect the leaders of a rights-respecting democracy to be any less self-interested than an autocrat. However, considerations of self-interest will motivate the leaders of a rights-respecting democracy to give effect to the fairness judgments of their constituents, and this is enough to improve the justice of the system over time.

It is important not to overstate this conclusion. To say that rights-respecting democracies tend to become more just over time is not to say that they always become more just and never become less just nor that they always correct larger injustices before they correct smaller ones. However, there is also a tendency to underestimate the virtues of a rights-respecting democracy that must also be resisted. Because they guarantee freedom of the press, we know much more about the shortcomings of rights-respecting democracies than we know about any autocracy that has ever existed. And there is always the temptation, discussed in chapter 6, to think that if only I were in charge, I could correct in a day the injustices that democracies can take decades or centuries to correct.

In the United States, it was not until almost 100 years after the Declaration of Independence that Black slaves gained their independence. It took their descendants another 100 years to be freed from legally enforced segregation. Will it take another 100 years for their descendants to attain at least rough equality of opportunity? Looked at in this way, the pace of progress can seem glacially slow. And yet, the cumulative improvements in justice in the past 300 years are much greater than the cumulative improvements in justice for all of prior human history.[19] It is no accident that the pace of change has increased with the development of basic human rights. Guaranteeing basic human rights makes it much more likely that the fairness judgments of ordinary people will make a difference to the fairness of social institutions.

Thanks to the work of Sen (1999) and others, we now know that a government that respects the basic rights identified earlier for all of its citizens, women as well as men, will tend to eliminate famines, to reduce infant and child mortality, and to reduce fertility rates. In addition, in rights-respecting democracies, government opponents don't disappear, never to be heard from again, nor are they worked to death in prison camps. The contrast between twentieth-century autocracies and twentieth-century rights-respecting democracies could hardly be greater. While rights-respecting democracies were extending rights to minorities and women, twentieth-century autocracies in Russia, Germany, and China, among others, were committing some of the most heinous crimes ever committed in human history (Glover 1999). Finally, rights-respecting democracies almost never go to war with each other (Doyle 1997; Weart 1998). The best way to reduce the occurrence of wars, if not to eliminate them altogether, would be to make the basic human rights universal.

Additions to the List of Basic Rights

In the previous chapter, I proposed a list of eight basic rights. In this chapter I have made some additions to the list. Here is the final list:

1. a right to physical security
2. a right to physical subsistence (understood as a right to an opportunity to earn subsistence for those who are able to do so)
3. children's rights to what is necessary for normal physical, cognitive, emotional, and behavioral development, including the development of empathic understanding
4. a right to an education, including a moral education aimed at further development and use of empathic understanding
5. a right to freedom of the press
6. a right to freedom of thought and expression
7. a right to freedom of association
8. a right to a sphere of personal autonomy free from paternalistic interference
9. political rights, including democratic rights and an independent judiciary to enforce the entire package of rights

The list has been augmented in two ways. First, additions to items 3 and 4 make it clear that normal emotional development includes the development of empathic understanding and that education includes moral education focused on the further development and use of empathic understanding. Second, a new category of political rights has been added. Democratic rights include not only a right to vote, but also rights to engage in political opposition, to run for office, and so on. Political rights also include an independent judiciary, for without independent judicial review, laws protecting rights would be largely ineffective.

The rights on this list are not the only rights that should be universal. However, guaranteeing the rights on this list establishes a form of government that, over time, will tend to become more just by adopting other rights in addition to these basic ones. I discuss the other kinds of rights in the companion volume (Talbott forthcoming).

Conclusion

If human beings were devils, rights-respecting democracies would almost surely not arise and if they did, they would not last long. If human beings were angels, they would not need government to legally protect their basic human rights, because no one would violate them. They would still need a rights-respecting democracy to legislate solutions to collective action problems, though not to enforce them. Even if angels would never run a red light, they would need a government to decide where stop lights are needed, to decide on the best kind to use, and to pay for and install them.

Human beings are neither devils nor angels. Unlike devils, they can form and maintain stable rights-respecting democracies. Unlike angels, they need external enforcement of individual rights and of solutions to collective action problems.

For most of human history it has generally been believed that the only morally justified form of government was some form of autocracy. This is no accident, because most governments throughout history have been autocratic, and autocracies do not usually tolerate the opinion that other forms of government are morally justified.

Although the idea of a rights-respecting democracy is only a little more than 300 years old, it has profoundly changed history. It is possible for an autocracy to promote justice; however, the historical record makes it clear that autocracies have no general tendency to promote justice and avoid injustice. Based on the evidence from the twentieth century, autocracies seem to have a strong tendency in the opposite direction.

In a rights-respecting democracy, though not all changes are justice promoting, there is a clear historical trajectory in that direction. This is no accident. Respecting the basic human rights makes a government a self-improving self-regulating system that tends over time to promote justice.

The system does not depend on those in authority being moral exemplars. It works for two main reasons: (1) because such governments are more likely to act to promote the interests of their citizens (which is one important part of being a just government), and (2) because, when their personal interests are not directly involved, ordinary people are capable of making reasonably reliable fairness judgments and are willing to incur at least small costs to give effect to them. This largely bottom-up social process is the only known effective way of promoting justice over time.

8

CLARIFICATIONS
AND OBJECTIONS

These two centuries are most easily understood not as a period
of deepening understanding of the nature of rationality or
morality, but rather as one in which there occurred an
astonishingly rapid progress of sentiment, in which it has
become much easier for us to be moved to action by sad and
sentimental stories.

—Richard Rorty

In this chapter I address some potential questions and objections. One potential source of concern could be that the list of basic human rights I identified in the last chapter leaves them largely undefined. Shouldn't they be
specified more precisely?

In this book, my goal is to give the big picture, not to specify the precise
contours of the basic human rights. I have tried to articulate a framework
that enables us to understand why each of them is a basic human right and
why they should be guaranteed to all beings capable of autonomy, in my
nonmetaphysical sense. Understanding that the basic human rights are the
rights necessary for the development and exercise of autonomy does help to
define their contours. It also helps to identify gaps in the human rights
guarantees in existing human rights documents.

I would not want to convey the impression that I have direct rational
insight into what the precise contours of the basic human rights should be.
In my view, the contours of those rights are being defined by the same
bottom-up process of moral development I have discussed in previous chapters. However, I believe that we now have enough understanding of the
rationale for the basic human rights to project at least roughly where the
process should take us, and thus to make recommendations for how those
rights should be defined. I undertake this project in the companion volume
(Talbott forthcoming).

Moral Truth and Moral Progress

I believe we can discern in the development of human rights a process of discovery of moral truths about particular cases (e.g., that much of the European colonists' treatment of the American natives was wrong) and a process of developing moral principles that better approximate the truth (e.g., from versions of the Golden Rule to the utilitarian principle to human rights principles). Because I believe there are moral truths, I am a *moral realist.* Many philosophers deny that there are moral truths. They are *moral antirealists.*

There are many reasons to be a moral antirealist. The most influential argument for moral antirealism can be traced to David Hume. Hume distinguished between judgments that are true or false (which he attributed to reason) and judgments that simply express our own emotional responses, which he thought were neither true nor false. Hume's question was: Is moral judgment a product of reason or of emotion?

I think that Hume's question is based on a false presupposition, the presupposition that reason and emotion are totally separate psychological processes. Why would he believe this? This seems to me to be yet another unfortunate effect of the Proof paradigm. If reason is thought of as the austere, logical faculty used in mathematics, it is hard to see how that faculty would be involved in the emotions or how it would play much of a role in moral judgment. However, mathematics is a poor model for most determinations of truth, including moral truth.

An alternative is to expand our idea of reason to cover the variety of ways that we determine truth and falsity. On this expansive conception of reason, there need be no dichotomy between truth and emotion. Emotions can be understood as crucially involved in many of the most important determinations of truth and falsity, especially those that are necessary for social life (Nussbaum 2001). Understood in this way, emotions would often be a manifestation of reason, not an alternative to it.

In chapter 4 I discussed the role of empathy in moral judgment. There I emphasized that it is a mistake to think of empathy as a "mere" feeling. Empathy plays an essential role in our being able to determine important truths about other people. So I think of empathy as a capacity for judging something to be true or false. To capture the element of judgment in emotion, I favor thinking of empathy as *empathic understanding.* Empathic understanding plays an essential role in our ability to make reliable moral judgments from the moral standpoint.

Because I believe that emotions typically involve judgments of what is true and false, I can believe that emotions are an essential part of moral judgment and still be a moral realist. However, many philosophers explain moral judgments in terms of emotions or other related attitudes precisely because they believe that emotions *do not* involve judgments of what is true or false. Rorty (1993) makes a persuasive case for the antirealist position.

In chapter 2 I suggested that the history of moral inquiry is one of progress in the discovery of universal moral truths. In subsequent chapters, I have given many more examples of this sort of moral progress. But don't the victors always try to rewrite history so that their victory represents progress?

There is a tendency to think that any history, however arbitrary, can always be reconstructed as progress toward whatever result it eventuates in. This is not true of the history of moral development. There are many different ways that the history of moral development could fail to support the view that it is a history of progress in discovering universal moral truths. Suppose that moral inquiry almost invariably led to the conclusion that we should all do what most benefits ourselves; or suppose that different groups invariably reached the conclusion that they should always do what most benefits their group; or suppose that human moral inquiry seemed to be converging on some principle of maximizing the well-being of members of the species *Homo sapiens.* In all of these cases, it seems to me that we should conclude either that there are no universal moral truths or that human reasoning is too subject to biasing influence to be able to determine what they are.

However, this is not what the history of moral inquiry reveals. In chapter 2, I discussed how the Golden Rule and the utilitarian principle illustrate the development of moral principles that transcend parochial divisions of family, tribe, nation, and even species. The same is true of the basic human rights principles that I have discussed in the past three chapters. With the benefit of more than 300 years of historical development, we can see that there is a reason that the scope of human rights guarantees has been enlarged from white male property owners to normal adult white males and then to all normal adult males and finally to all normal adult humans, male and female. The reason is that human rights should be guaranteed to all beings capable of autonomy, in the nonmetaphysical sense in which I use the term. If human rights principles apply to any being capable of autonomy, then they provide us with another example of moral principles that transcend parochial divisions and achieve true universality.

In chapter 4, I tried to characterize a universal moral standpoint in terms of a combination of empathic understanding and reasonable agreement behind a veil of ignorance. Behind the veil of ignorance, differences of nationality, religion, race, sex, and even species are irrelevant. So it is the right kind of standpoint from which to reach universal moral truths.

This is why, when I look at the history of moral development, I see progress in the discovery of universal moral truths. Rorty (1993) does not see it this way. In the epigraph to this chapter, he gives an alternative, antirealist interpretation of this history, according to which the past 200 years is to be understood as a progress of sentiment that does not involve moral truth.[1] So there are two ways of looking at the history of moral development: one as a history of progress in the discovery of moral truths, one as a progress of sentiment that does not involve moral truths. How are we to decide between them?

To begin with, because I do not accept Hume's dichotomy between reason and emotion, I can agree with Rorty on the essential role of emotion in moral judgment. There remain two crucial issues between us:

1. Is there genuine moral progress? Rorty speaks of moral development as a "progress" of sentiments, but he cannot mean progress in its usual sense. In its usual sense, progress is not blind; it is directed toward something objective. I believe Rorty uses the term *progress* simply to express his approval of the process by which rights have been extended beyond the boundaries of race, religion, and gender. But why should it be regarded as progress, if there is nothing objective that the development is directed toward? I believe that Rorty's answer would be that our sentiments themselves determine the standards of progress, so that however they develop qualifies as progress. This seems to me to be an indirect way of saying that there really is no progress. In addition, it leads to a deeper problem for Rorty's view.
2. Is moral progress arbitrary? The deeper problem for Rorty's view is that it makes what we describe as *moral progress* too arbitrary. Rorty approves of the extension of human rights to all human beings. Where does he think we should draw the line? If there is no objective answer to this question, the only answer he can give is: wherever we decide, presumably on the basis of sympathy, to draw it.

This answer makes the line too arbitrary. To see this, suppose human beings were so constituted that they only could feel sympathy for beings who looked at least roughly human. One day extraterrestrial intelligent life is discovered in another galaxy. The extraterrestrials have much the same cognitive and emotional abilities as human beings, but they look like large cockroaches. Human beings find them repulsive and cannot feel sympathy for them. Having no sentiment of sympathy to oppose their sentiment of revulsion and no other faculty for determining moral truth, humans take great delight in squashing the cockroach people.

If the cockroach people had the same cognitive and emotional capacities as human beings, anyone who could access the moral standpoint and go behind the veil of ignorance would be able to see that it would be wrong to squash them. Instead, it would be apparent that they should be guaranteed the basic human rights necessary for the development and exercise of their autonomy. I believe that human beings have the ability to access this moral standpoint, so I would expect that at least some human beings would be able to overcome their revulsion to the cockroach people well enough to be able to access the moral standpoint and recognize that those people should be guaranteed the basic human rights.

However, on Rorty's view, there is no objective moral standpoint and there is no objective truth about how the cockroach people ought to be treated. On Rorty's view, if human beings could not feel sympathy for the cockroach people, and thus could not see anything wrong with squashing them, then there would not be anything wrong with squashing them. This seems to me to be a mistake. If the humans could not see what was wrong with squashing the cockroach people, that would not make their behavior right, any more than the inability of most Spanish colonists to see anything wrong with their treatment of the American natives made it right. Even if the Spanish colonists could not see anything wrong with their treatment of the American natives, I believe there is an objective moral standpoint from which it can be seen to be wrong, and the American natives themselves would easily be able to see that it was wrong.

Similarly, I believe that even if humans could not see that squashing the cockroach people was wrong, the cockroach people themselves might easily be able to access the moral standpoint and recognize its wrongness. Rorty's account of moral progress is too arbitrary, because it has no resources for explaining why the spread of the belief that it was not wrong to squash cockroach people would not qualify as moral progress.

I believe that Rorty has fallen into the trap set by Hume of thinking that morality must be based on either reason or sentiment. If I were forced to choose between an account of moral judgment based on reason, where reason was understood on the model of proof in mathematics, and an account based on sentiment, where sentiments were assumed not to involve judgments of what is true and false, I would choose sentiment. But it is a mistake to limit ourselves to those two choices. There is a third alternative: that sentiments themselves are often a manifestation of reasoning and can essentially involve judgments of what is true and false. To say that morality is based on sentiment in this sense does not exclude reason from moral judgment and does not lead to moral antirealism.

Moral Truth and Evolution

In chapter 7 I emphasized the importance of judgments of fairness made from the moral standpoint in making a rights-respecting democracy stable.

I used research on the ultimatum game to illustrate how fairness judgments can conflict with rational self-interest. Skyrms suggests that there may be an evolutionary account of the fairness judgments made by subjects in the ultimatum game and related contexts (1996, chap. 2). Skyrms's position qualifies as antirealist, because it is an attempt to explain how we could come to make such judgments without there being any objective truths about what is fair and unfair. For Skyrms, norms of fairness and unfairness are determined by our evolutionary history.

Skyrms's account has the same deep problem as Rorty's. It makes fairness judgments too arbitrary. If Skyrms's account were true, there would be no moral standpoint from which to morally criticize the fairness norms favored by evolution. From a logical point of view, the advocate of this sort of evolutionary account makes the same mistake as the cultural relativist. The cultural relativist denies that it is possible to morally criticize a culture's norms. An evolutionary account such as Skyrms's implies that there is no objective standpoint from which it is possible to morally criticize the norms of fairness favored by evolution. This is a mistake. Norms of fairness favored by evolution can be morally criticized.

Skyrms does not actually show how norms of even division for the ultimatum game could have evolved. However, we have good reason to believe that norms of uneven division in lots of contexts have also been favored by genetic or social evolution. In chapter 5, I reviewed some of the reasons for thinking that there is an evolutionary explanation of patriarchal norms. Those norms include norms of fairness between men and women that favor an unequal division of the benefits and burdens of social cooperation between them. Even though we ourselves are the products of that evolutionary process, it is possible for us to adopt the moral standpoint and to morally criticize the norms it has produced. From the original position, behind the veil of ignorance, the division of the benefits and costs of social cooperation between men and women in a traditional patriarchal culture is clearly unfair. Evolution may have favored our ancestors for accepting them. It has not prevented us, their descendants, from being able to morally criticize them. Even girls raised in rigid patriarchal families can recognize that they are not treated fairly, though they learn to resign themselves to it (Wainryb and Turiel 1994).

It is important to emphasize that my responses to Rorty and Skyrms are not veiled skeptical arguments. Anyone who, like me, holds that there are objective, universal moral truths or that there are objective, universal norms of fairness, but denies that we have direct rational insight into what they are, must acknowledge the possibility that our moral beliefs can be mistaken. I also believe that evolution could have made us so biased in favor of our own interests or the interests of our kin group or the interests of our community or so antipathetic to cockroach-like beings that we could never have discovered the truth about how we should treat others outside the favored category. It seems quite clear that evolution did produce powerful biases of these kinds. However, we have plenty of evidence that human beings have been able to transcend those biases and access a universal moral standpoint.

This is not an argument against evolution. Just as evolution gave us the ability to make progress in discovering truth in mathematics and truth in physics, evolution gave us the ability to make progress in discovering truths about how we ought to treat each other.

What Characteristic Grounds Human Rights?

I have tried to explain why the basic human rights should be guaranteed to all beings capable of autonomy, in my nonmetaphysical sense. Suppose we ask: What is the characteristic of normal human beings that makes it morally imperative that they be guaranteed the basic human rights? It is useful to be able to abbreviate this question as: What characteristic *grounds* basic human rights? On my account, the answer is: the capacity for autonomy.

Because the capacity for autonomy is a combination of the capacity for good judgment and the capacity for self-determination and the two capacities are almost always found together, it is only a slight simplification of my view to say that, according to it, the capacity for good judgment grounds human rights. The capacity for good judgment corresponds closely to Rawls's notion of rationality (1993, 72). So it is not inaccurate to say that, on my view, rationality grounds human rights.

Rorty (1993) ridicules the idea that a characteristic like rationality could ground human rights or any other kind of moral judgment. He thinks that moral judgments are simply expressions of sentiment that are not grounded in anything objective, unless it is just whatever we are disposed to respond to with sympathy. I will describe Rorty's view as the view that *sympathy grounds moral judgments*. How plausible is this view?

To evaluate this view, it is necessary to distinguish two kinds of moral judgments that need grounding: the judgment that I should hold others morally responsible for their acts and the judgment that I owe moral obligations to others. Call the first sort of judgment a *judgment of moral responsibility* and the second sort of judgment a *judgment of moral obligation*. I make the first sort of judgment when I assert that you should respect my rights. I make the second sort of judgment when I assert that you have rights that I should respect.

Let me begin with judgments of moral responsibility. What grounds them—that is, what characteristics make it appropriate to hold a being morally responsible? It cannot be membership in the species *Homo sapiens*, because there are many members of the species *Homo sapiens*—for example, those who are severely mentally retarded or who have suffered severe brain injuries—who are not held morally responsible for their actions. If Rorty thinks rationality is the wrong sort of characteristic to ground such judgments, what does ground them? It is quite implausible that sympathy grounds judgments of moral responsibility. Many people believe that they should hold their enemies morally responsible for their acts, even if they have no sympathy for them. Furthermore, many people who have great sympathy for their pets do not believe that they should hold them morally responsible for their acts. Even moral antirealists such as Rorty typically ground their judgments of moral responsibility in the capacity for rationality or autonomy.

What about judgments of moral obligation? Here there is room for more than one answer. Sentience is a characteristic that generates some moral obligations (e.g., an obligation not to cause unnecessary suffering). Let's focus on the central issue here. What characteristic grounds the basic human rights? Why is Rorty so sure that it is not rationality in the nonmetaphysical sense in which I use the term? If sentiment grounds the basic human rights, then the scope of human rights would be as arbitrary as Rorty's concept of moral progress. Is it reasonable to believe that human sentiments determine whether or not the cockroach people should be guaranteed the basic human rights?

Rawls identifies two moral powers as the ground of human rights: rationality—roughly what I refer to as the capacity for good judgment—and reasonableness, "the capacity for a sense of right and justice (the capacity to honor fair terms of cooperation)" (1993, 302). It seems to me that what Rawls calls "rationality" is enough by itself to ground the basic human rights.[2] Guaranteeing basic human rights is the appropriate policy for a government to adopt toward its citizens who have the capacity for good judgment.

The capacity for moral judgment (which corresponds to Rawls's reasonableness) plays a role in my account, though not as a ground for human rights. It is what distinguishes human beings from devils, and it is what makes rights-respecting democracies stable.

A Potential for Abuse

Won't a theory such as this one, a theory that makes the capacity for good judgment (i.e., the ability to make reliable judgments about one's own good) the ground of basic human rights, invite abuse by apologists for autocracy? They could justify denying basic human rights on the ground that most people are not reliable judges about what is good for them. Indeed, this has been a recurrent theme in the justifications offered for autocracies that deny basic human rights.

This is not an argument against my account of the ground of basic human rights. It is an argument for the importance of being on the lookout for self-serving justifications for autocracy. It is also an indirect argument for spreading the word that the claim of first-person authority is true. Under favorable circumstances (e.g., when the standard civil rights are protected) human beings with normal cognitive and emotional development really are reliable judges of what's good for them and much better judges of what's good for them than most autocrats are. The history of paternalism toward normal adults (e.g., paternalism toward aboriginal peoples, Blacks, and women) is a dismal one. I suspect there will always be new attempts to provide paternalist justifications for autocracy. I believe the explanation of this fact is that the *form* of justification is a good one. Paternalism toward children and toward human beings with severe brain injuries is justified. The problem is not with the *form* of the justification; the problem is with its *content*. It is a mistake to believe that normal, adult human beings are not reliable judges of what is good for them.

As I have reconstructed the history of the development of basic human rights, probably the most important discovery is the discovery that the claim of first-person authority is true. Couldn't I be mistaken about this? Perhaps what has been discovered is that autocracies and democracies both do a poor job of promoting the good of their subjects. Indeed, maybe the historical process I have invoked so often is a process in which democracy is just a temporary phase until the development of a new form of autocracy that corrects for the deficiencies of the previous ones. I think this is the best way of understanding Lee Kwan Yew's challenge to human rights.

Lee Kwan Yew's Capitalist Autocracy

This is not the way Lee's challenge is usually presented. It is usually presented as a cultural relativist defense of "Asian" values against "Western" human rights. In chapter 3 I explained why human rights are not a distinctively Western value and why paternalism is not a distinctively Eastern value. Lee's real challenge is the claim that he has discovered a better form of government than a rights-respecting democracy. It is this challenge that needs to be evaluated.

Here is the historical background to Lee's challenge. Though Singapore was nominally a democracy, Lee's rule from 1965 to 1990 was autocratic.[3] During the entire time that Lee was prime minister, his party (PAP) not only controlled the parliament, it ruled without any effective opposition.[4] There was no freedom to criticize the government. The government controlled the domestic media and censored international media. There was no independent judiciary. Trial by jury was abolished in 1969. When an appellate court in 1988 ordered the government to release four detainees held under the Internal Security Act, the parliament amended the constitution to eliminate judicial review of detentions under the Internal Security Act and made the amendment retroactive to 1971. This was not the only law for which judicial review was prohibited.

Lee never was an admirer of democracy and civil rights. Though he was an anticommunist, his models for governing were communist dictatorships and the Roman Catholic church. Lee had also learned the advantages of the ruthless use of force during the Japanese occupation of Singapore during World War II.[5] What distinguished Lee's autocracy from both fascist and communist autocracies was his championing of private ownership and capitalism. When Lee became Singapore's first prime minister in 1965, Singapore was one of the poorest cities in Asia. When he retired from the prime ministry in 1990, it was one of the most important economies in Asia, with practically no poverty, no homelessness, and one of the lowest crime rates in the world. There was practically no traffic congestion and air pollution was not a problem. Per capita income grew from $500 in 1965 to $12,000 in 1990 and to more than $24,000 in 2000.[6]

From the beginning, Lee adopted policies to encourage outside investment in Singapore. He also instituted a program of forced savings that could only be used for safe investments or housing. As a result, Singapore has achieved one of the highest rates of home ownership in the world—92 percent in 2000 (Singapore Department of Statistics 2002).[7] The Singapore experience raises the question of whether a new kind of autocracy—capitalist autocracy—is superior to a rights-respecting democracy.

Can Asians Think?

There are two ways of responding to Lee's challenge, one nonconsequentialist and one consequentialist. The nonconsequentialist reply is simple. It was wrong for Lee to limit the autonomy of his citizens, even if he did promote their (appropriately distributed) well-being. It is just wrong not to respect basic human rights. Although this reply has something to be said for it, I do not find it fully satisfactory. It seems to me that Hobbes was right about something: The existence of collective action problems (e.g., provision of government services, environmental protection, preventing pollution and traffic congestion) provides the basis for a potential justification for government coercion. Lee has done a better job of solving many of these collective action problems than have most rights-respecting democracies. So I am reluctant to dismiss his challenge out of hand.

The consequentialist response points to two main problems with Lee's capitalist autocracy. First, the benefits of a system of capitalist production or of individual home ownership, for example, are not evident a priori. Lee was able to learn from the experience of democratic governments in designing his capitalist autocracy, while blocking the feedback mechanism that would make possible improvements in the future.

In chapter 5 I reviewed the history of mistaken paternalist ideas about what is good for women. Lee does not have any better idea of what is good for them than any of the other paternalists. Rights-respecting democracies are going through one of the largest social transformations in history, the transformation to more equal opportunity for the female half of the population. Another example of this kind is the development of rights for gays, lesbians, bisexuals, and the transgendered. Under Lee, laws against homosexuals were harshly enforced. With no avenue for bottom-up social change, the substantial human costs imposed on gays, lesbians, bisexuals, and the transgendered by these policies were invisible.

Of course, by waiting until these worldwide transformations in women's roles and the transformations in the position of gays, lesbians, bisexuals, and the transgendered are complete and seeing the results, Singapore might be able to find a less traumatic way of getting there. This shows that there is potential for Singapore to free-ride on the rights-respecting democracies: Let the rights-respecting democracies go through the difficult social dislocations that often accompany bottom-up transformations, wait for the results, and then impose the results in a less traumatic top-down fashion. Understood this way, Lee's challenge is not so much a challenge to rights-respecting democracies as a way of benefiting from them.

There is a second problem with Lee's capitalist autocracy. Autocracies give rulers the power to do what they want, whether it benefits their subjects or not. For Lee's capitalist autocracy to be successful, it would, at a minimum, have to be able to reliably produce leaders who want to benefit their subjects. This is the benevolent motivation problem. No system of government has ever solved it. The reason is simple. Power attracts those who desire power, and benevolent motivation is not positively correlated with the desire for power. Even if by some chance Lee himself were good at choosing leaders with benevolent motivation, it is not at all plausible that he could reliably choose leaders who were themselves good at choosing leaders with benevolent motivation.

Instead, Lee worked to set the stage for his son to become prime minister. This is a common motivation in autocrats. There is overwhelming historical evidence from hereditary monarchies that genes do not produce either good leadership or benevolent motivation. So Lee has no solution to this problem. If Lee were a genuinely benevolent autocrat, he would have realized that there is no system for choosing leaders that can be relied on to select those with benevolent motivation. Instead of working to elevate his son to prime minister, he would have worked to assure that Singapore would become a genuine rights-respecting democracy.

However, even if he does not intend it, that will almost surely be the ultimate outcome of his rule. South Korea and Taiwan have shown how capitalist autocracies tend to be transformed into rights-respecting democracies. The only way to block the transformation is to become a totalitarian state. This is not a serious possibility for Singapore. In fact, Singapore has recently begun to allow political demonstrations and has officially adopted acceptance of gays and lesbians (Hoong 2003). So it seems that Lee's capitalist autocracy will not become an alternative to a rights-respecting democracy, but simply a new pathway to it.

Like many other autocrats, Lee Kwan Yew thought of himself as a stern father who must protect his children (the Singaporeans) from harm. A good father not only protects his children from harm when they are young, he prepares them to be able to exercise their own judgment to protect themselves when they grow up. Fortunately, though Lee probably did not intend for his children to grow up, he has made it almost inevitable that they will. When they do grow up, they will insist on having a genuine voice in their government, and they will insist that there be protections for the other basic human rights.

It is ironic that Lee's protégé Mahbubani (1998) gave his bestselling defense of Lee's views the provocative title *Can Asians Think?* In the book, Mahbubani makes it clear that he meant to be asking: Can Asian *leaders* think? Both Lee's and Mahbubani's criticisms of rights-respecting democracies implicitly assume that leaders can do a better job of solving people's problems than the people themselves can. Ironically, it is the defender of basic human rights, not Lee and Mahbubani, who insists that the answer to Mahbubani's title question is yes. Respecting human rights is the way that societies acknowledge that their *citizens* can think.

To be a true rights-respecting democracy, Singapore would have to guarantee all of the rights on my list of basic rights. It is important to see that respecting those rights is compatible with good faith disagreements about their exact contours. There will always be disagreement about the contours of human rights wherever the standard civil rights, including freedom of expression, are guaranteed. Thus, for example, Lee and Mahbubani have questioned whether there should be rights to use hate speech and rights to pornography. There are good faith disagreements in rights-respecting democracies on both of these issues. An epistemically modest advocate of basic human rights would expect the Singaporeans to enter into that debate and to contribute to working out the answers to those and other questions about how exactly to define the basic human rights.

Can Economic and Social Rights Be Basic Human Rights?

Cranston (1967) has argued that only the traditional political and civil rights can truly be regarded as universal human rights. He contrasts political and civil rights with social and economic rights. It is clear that the list of nine basic rights that I have identified includes rights from both categories. Here again is the list:

1. a right to physical security
2. a right to physical subsistence (understood as a right to an opportunity to earn subsistence for those who are able to do so)
3. children's rights to what is necessary for normal physical, cognitive, emotional, and behavioral development, including the development of empathic understanding
4. a right to an education, including a moral education aimed at further development and use of empathic understanding
5. a right to freedom of the press
6. a right to freedom of thought and expression
7. a right to freedom of association
8. a right to a sphere of personal autonomy free from paternalistic interference
9. political rights, including democratic rights and an independent judiciary to enforce the entire package of rights

Items 1, 5, 6, 7, 8, and 9 fit into the civil and political category. Items 2, 3, and 4 do not. Consider item 4, a right to an education (including a moral education), which Cranston explicitly mentions as something that should not be thought of as a human right. Why not?

According to Cranston, human rights must be universal and they must be of paramount importance. I agree with his criteria. I just don't understand why a right to an education does not qualify. Recall that the kind of education at issue is the kind of education necessary to enable people to develop their faculty of judgment so that they can make reliable judgments about what is good for them. It is the kind of education that Tostan brings to rural villages in Senegal. This sort of education enables villagers in Senegal to evaluate and make their own judgments about many issues of importance to them, including sanitation and health care, family planning, and traditional practices, such as female genital cutting. We know autocratic rulers and religious authorities often think that this sort of education is bad for people. However, it is essential if they are to be able to develop and exercise their own judgment.

Cranston is concerned that universal human rights not be extended from the realm of the morally compelling to include utopian aspirations. Why think that a universal right to education is utopian? One answer is that education costs money, and there is no way to guarantee that there will be enough money to pay for it. However, as Shue (1980) points out, police and a judicial system also cost money. If security rights should be guaranteed as universal human rights, someone will have to pay for the police and judicial system necessary to enforce them. So the mere fact that universal education would have to be paid for does not necessarily exclude it from being a universal right.

What if a country wants to provide a police/judicial system and a system of universal education, but cannot afford to pay for both? If the international community had no responsibility to help finance universal education when necessary, Cranston might be right that universal education would be too utopian to be a universal right. I disagree with him, because I do not see how it could be permissible for the developed nations to refuse to provide this sort of assistance, if asked to provide it by developing countries.

Education in the developing world is not expensive. Oxfam estimates that guaranteeing a primary education for every child in the world would cost an additional $8 billion (Skrlec 1999). In 2003, the United States spent approximately this amount on national defense every week. So the full amount could be funded by the developed countries. Do they have a moral obligation to fund it? To see how to answer this question, it is useful to consider it from the original position, behind the veil of ignorance. From this standpoint, on the supposition that the money would be well spent, what reason could be given by those in the developed countries for refusing to provide the relatively modest financing that would be required?[8]

The main impediment to universal education is not financial. It is the opposition of autocratic governments and religious leaders. Many oppose education for women. Even when they claim to support "education," what they usually support is indoctrination. This is a true impediment to universal education, but it is not the kind of impediment that makes universal education a utopian aspiration. All that is required to make a right to education universal is a consensus that it should be universal and relatively modest financial contributions from the developed countries.

I conclude that Cranston has drawn the line between morally compelling rights and utopian aspirations in the wrong place. The basic human rights that should be universal include some economic and social rights, not only political and civil rights.

Is the Development of Rights-Respecting Democracies Inevitable?

I have described the development of rights-respecting democracies as part of a historical process of moral development. Is this process historically inevitable? I think it is clear that the answer is no. As I have already mentioned, in parallel with the expansion of rights for aboriginal peoples, minorities, and women in the rights-respecting democracies, the twentieth century saw the development of autocracies that committed some of the worst crimes in human history. All over the world, fundamentalist religious movements (Islamic, Hindu, Jewish, and Christian) are increasing in power. Many of these fundamentalist religious movements would return women to the status of men's chattel. There are powerful evolutionary and social forces supporting these fundamentalist movements. So the direction of human social development—toward autocracies or toward rights-respecting democracies—is not inevitable. In addition, the development of weapons of mass destruction has thrown into question whether human civilization will continue to develop in any direction at all.

However, I am not pessimistic. Any impartial review of the development of rights-respecting democracies in the last 300 years would show that there is much reason for optimism. The progress that has been made is obscured by the fact that in a rights-respecting democracy with freedom of expression and a free press, there will always be an awareness of many problems. Because there are always many problems and democracies often solve known problems with known solutions more slowly than autocracies, it is easy to lose one's perspective and to feel that nothing ever gets better. That is why it is sometimes worthwhile to step back and look at the big picture. Three hundred years ago, how many would have predicted that a rights-respecting democracy could be stable? Two hundred years ago, how many would have predicted the development of a universal consensus to end slavery? One hundred years ago, how many would have predicted that in the United States each year more women than men would earn bachelor's degrees or that almost equal numbers of women and men would be admitted to medical school? Fifty years ago, how many would have predicted gays and lesbians would be able to marry in some countries (e.g., Belgium, the Netherlands, and Canada) and that they would be able to enter into civil unions in many others? Even thirty years ago, how many would have predicted that there would be a permanent International Criminal Court to punish serious violations of human rights? The list could easily be expanded.

All of these developments have depended at least in part on bottom-up social movements. They all involve providing the conditions to enable some people to develop and exercise their own judgment about what is good for them and, thus, their autonomy. They have all depended on enough people being able to recognize unfairness and being willing to incur at least small costs to promote fairness. This is the force that makes a more just world possible, if not inevitable.

Moral Progress Is a Collective Action Problem

As I have described it, the move toward greater justice in the world depends on enough people being willing to incur small costs to promote fairness. If they recognize that their own contribution to the elimination of any particular injustice is vanishingly small, why would it make sense for them to contribute? Ordinary citizens who supported the abolition of slavery in the nineteenth century could not reasonably have believed that the elimination of slavery hinged on their individual contributions. So wasn't it irrational for them to make a contribution?

This question illustrates how contributing to a social movement to eliminate an injustice often is a collective action problem. When we look at the world from our own personal point of view, what often matters to us is the effects of our own individual actions. Thus, from the personal point of view, contributing to the solution of a collective action problem can sometimes seem irrational. However, the decision to contribute to the elimination of an injustice is made from the moral standpoint. From the moral standpoint, it is not the effect of our individual contribution that matters. Instead, what is important is the effect of our joint contributions, where we recognize that we each should be willing to do our fair share to eliminate injustice (Murphy 2000). Other things being equal, if a successful boycott of certain products will help to improve wages and living conditions for exploited workers, the more other people there are willing to join the boycott, the greater the reason there is for me to join it. What is important from the moral standpoint is not the potential for *my* individual contribution to make a difference; it is the potential for *our* joint contributions to make a difference. If I depend on others to promote justice and don't contribute myself, I am free-riding on their contributions. From the moral standpoint, it would be wrong for me to do that.[9]

International Enforcement of Basic Human Rights?

When human rights are being violated on a large scale and intervention could end the violations with little collateral damage, is it morally permissible for one nation to intervene in the internal affairs of another? From the moral standpoint, the answer would clearly be yes, were it not for the danger that nations might use such a rationale as a self-serving justification for one nation to decide unilaterally to invade another. For the same reason that it is important to have an International Criminal Court to adjudicate rights violations, it is important that there be an international enforcement body with control over an international police force for the prevention and punishment of human rights abuses. This is a direction for potential progress in the future.

Why Wars Are Threats to Basic Human Rights

I have suggested that in a rights-respecting democracy one of the main safeguards of the basic rights of minorities is the existence of relatively impartial people who are willing to incur small costs to prevent injustice. If this is correct, then the greatest threats to basic human rights would be those that occur when there is no such impartial audience. When almost everyone has a powerful interest in violating the rights of a small minority, it will be difficult to develop a countervailing force to prevent the violations. This is the reason that basic human rights come under the greatest stress in times of war and when there are threats to national security.

The internment of Japanese Americans in World War II and the communist witch hunts of the McCarthy era involved violations of basic human rights that occurred because there was no substantial audience in the United States that could be impartial enough to object to the injustices. It is not surprising that the terrorist attacks of September 11, 2001, have made the U.S. government less concerned with respecting basic human rights, especially those of noncitizens. It *is* surprising that the U.S. government could take the position that noncitizens may be detained indefinitely outside the territory of the United States with no legal rights at all. Why was there so little public outcry in the United States over this classification of human beings as legal nonpersons? It is probably utopian to hope that someday the rationale for basic human rights might be so well understood that even in times of war or during threats to national security, governments would not be able to violate them without provoking powerful public opposition.

Consequentialist and Nonconsequentialist Justifications of Basic Human Rights

It may seem surprising that the consequentialist and nonconsequentialist accounts would justify much the same human rights. This would be surprising if moral reasoning were primarily top-down, because there would be no reason to expect two very different approaches to yield the same rights. However, if moral reasoning is largely bottom-up, the overlap is not so surprising. If moral reasoning is largely bottom-up, then both the consequentialist and nonconsequentialist accounts derive much of their support from their ability to explain our particular moral judgments. If they are both grounded by the particular moral judgments on which there is general agreement, it is not so surprising that their implications overlap to a great extent.[10]

9

CONCLUSION

I have proposed a list of nine basic rights that should be universal. It would be absurd to claim that these rights are self-evident or that they are timelessly universal. They had to be discovered. I have tried to explain why, in light of discoveries about human beings and human societies, they *should be* universal.

In previous chapters I have reconstructed the history of their discovery. An important step in the process was Las Casas's discovery of a group right to freedom of religion. The example of Las Casas opened up the possibility of a universal moral standpoint from which it is possible to make reliable judgments of the rightness or wrongness of particular acts. The Harsanyi-Rawls idea of an original position helps to explain what the moral standpoint is and how we are able to attain it. Our ability to attain a universal moral standpoint is what makes progress in moral discovery possible.

The discovery of basic human rights was made more difficult because it was not in the interests of autocratic governments or autocratic religious leaders that they be discovered. This discovery can itself be divided into two further steps: first, the discovery that paternalistic justifications of autocracy fail. I used Plato's defense of the beehive society as a framework for explaining this step. The crucial development in overcoming paternalistic justifications of autocracy is the discrediting of self-reinforcing paternalism, the sort of paternalism that prevents people from developing and exercising their own judgment about what is good for them on the grounds that developing and exercising their judgment is not good for them. I used the example of women's rights to illustrate how paternalism can be self-reinforcing and how such paternalism has been overcome.

The second step was the discovery that a rights-respecting democracy of autonomous individuals could be stable and could solve their collective action problems. I used Hobbes's defense of Leviathan to illustrate this step. The key to solving Hobbes's problem is the recognition that, though human beings are not angels, they are not devils either. A rights-respecting democracy can solve Hobbes's problem because it is a self-improving self-regulating system that tends to respond appropriately to reliable feedback to make itself more just over time.

The ground of basic human rights is the capacity of normal adult human beings to make reliable judgments about what is good for them. Enabling them to develop and exercise that capacity in their lives can be understood as guaranteeing them autonomy, in a nonmetaphysical sense. Basic human rights are the guarantees that enable people to develop and exercise their autonomy. This sort of autonomy has both nonconsequentialist and consequentialist value. Its nonconsequentialist value is to make it possible for people to be the authors of their own lives. Its consequentialist value is that it makes possible the design of a government that can be relied upon to promote the (appropriately distributed) well-being of all of its citizens, not just those in power.

How We Might Have Discovered That Judgment Really Was a Burden

Could we have discovered that autonomy was not so valuable? I believe we could have. Imagine a society in which normal adult human beings develop and exercise the faculty of judgment. They have the ability to form and evaluate life plans. However, exercising this faculty invariably makes them miserable. For example, they find making choices to be anxiety provoking. They much prefer not to have to make any.

One day, a scientist develops a chemical BF (Blind Follower) that disables the faculty of judgment and turns a person into a blind follower of authorities. The new chemical is tested in experimental trials (for which there are many more volunteers than there are available places) and is found to be completely successful with no side effects. A simple design for society is drawn up that requires only 1 percent of the population to continue to develop and exercise their faculty of judgment so that they can serve as authorities. It permits the other 99 percent to give up their faculty of judgment and simply be blind followers of the authorities. Everyone volunteers to be one of the followers, and no one volunteers to be one of the authorities. Everyone agrees on a fair lottery to select those who will have to be authorities. It is generally recognized that the 1 percent holding "losing" tickets will be condemned to a miserable life of autonomy and that the 99 percent holding "winning" tickets will be rewarded with a happy life on the chemical BF as a blind follower.

After the drawing, the winners celebrate and the losers console one another on their bad luck. The losers regard themselves as morally obligated to carry out their duties as authorities. However, if anyone gave them the opportunity to trade places with someone selected to be a blind follower, they would not hesitate to make the trade. From then on, children are separated by a lottery into authorities and blind followers at an early age. Being selected to be an authority is regarded as a misfortune by the authorities and will be so regarded by the children who become authorities, after they have developed the faculty that enables them to make such judgments.

How far is this scenario from the actual world where exercising coercive power over others is so far from being regarded as an unfortunate fate that there is never any shortage of candidates who eagerly compete for the privilege? In the actual world, autocratic rulers have an interest in preventing the large majority of their subjects from developing their faculty of judgment or, at least, preventing them from effectively exercising it. Their interest is not the benevolent one of promoting the subjects' well-being; it is the self-serving one of prolonging their own rule. It seems that Plato was right about one thing. One test of whether paternalistic autocracy is justified is whether the autocrats are reluctant to be autocrats. In our world, where potential autocrats eagerly seek such positions, they are themselves evidence against the moral justifiability of their rule.

Bottom-Up Progress

On the Proof paradigm, moral inquiry proceeds by top-down reasoning. On the alternative that I favor, the *Historical-Social Process of Moral Discovery paradigm*, moral inquiry proceeds primarily by bottom-up reasoning. From a social point of view, the process of moral discovery is also primarily bottom-up. Today there are still religious authorities who are regarded as infallible and who oppose equal rights for women. The example of Bartolomé de Las Casas is a reminder that even the dictates of moral authorities regarded as infallible can be modified by the process of bottom-up moral discovery.

If you are a moral philosopher in the sense that I explained in the introduction, your exercise of your moral judgment is part of this process of moral discovery. What do you think about assisted suicide or the legalization of drugs or marriage rights for gays and lesbians? Your opinion matters. It contributes to the historical process of discovering what rights should be universal. Not only your *opinion* matters. Your *actions* are needed to make progress in promoting basic human rights. Not necessarily heroic actions. Although heroic actions can be important, in the long run, what is most important is for enough people to be willing to incur small costs to promote fairness. If enough people are willing to do so, together we can make the world one in which basic human rights are universally respected.

Universal Moral Judgments

Probably the most implausible claim I have made in this book is the following: With no special equipment other than what is acquired through biological evolution and no special training other than the moral training most people receive in their culture, human beings have the ability to discern universal moral truths. We do this by being able to make reliable judgments about the rightness or wrongness of particular cases that are true universally—that is, true from any point of view. This is a metaphysically immodest position to take. Most people just assume that this sort of metaphysical immodesty would lead to moral imperialism. It does not have to. By being epistemically modest and antipaternalistic, it is possible to avoid moral imperialism.

Even if it is not morally imperialistic, metaphysical immodesty seems incredibly, well, *immodest.* It is one thing to think that human moral judgments can transcend the culture in which they are made, but how could they ever transcend the human species? The best way to see how they can is with an example. Suppose that beings from a different solar system invade earth looking for valuable minerals to enable them to make a profit on their interstellar voyage. Nothing crucial hinges on their making a profit; they just want to have more wealth. They decide that the most efficient way of obtaining those minerals is to enslave all human beings and put them to work in their mines. They recognize that we have the capacity to make reliable judgments about what is good for us, but they prefer not to develop that capacity in us, because it will make us less-docile slaves. They are not enslaving us to make life better for us; they are enslaving us to make life better for them.

Because the extraterrestrials have the ability to read minds, they can tell if any slave is having a rebellious thought. When they first arrived, many of us were able to access the moral standpoint and recognize that behind the veil of ignorance our masters would never accept a system of slavery on the grounds they used to justify it. So we judged that they were treating us wrongly. Because those of us who had such thoughts were summarily executed, over time, such thoughts became increasingly rare until they completely disappeared. Because the slaves have been convinced by their masters that they need their masters to take care of them and are not capable of living on their own, none of the slaves ever questions the moral justifiability of the system of slavery. None of the slaveowners ever questions it either, because the slaveowners are too blinded by self-interest to be able to attain the moral standpoint. If they were not so blinded by self-interest, they would recognize that behind the veil of ignorance, their justifications for the system of slavery would not be acceptable.

I believe that you and I can use the moral standpoint to understand why this system of slavery would be wrong, even if no one (slaveowner or slave) ever again had that thought. I am not claiming that no system of slavery could ever be morally justified. Perhaps in very extreme circumstances (e.g., if the survival of human life depended on it), some system of slavery could be morally justified. All I am claiming is that we can recognize that some systems of slavery, including this one, are morally wrong from any point of view. That is what it is like to make a universal moral judgment.

It is always possible that the impression that we are able to make universal moral judgments is an illusion. However, once we give up the Proof paradigm's standard of absolute certainty, it is no embarrassment to admit that we might be mistaken. The mere possibility of being mistaken is not a good reason for refusing to believe what seems to make the most sense. What do you think it makes the most sense to believe?

The Experiment Continues

Following Mill, I have suggested that a rights-respecting democracy is an experimental society, where people engage in experiments in living to try to better understand what makes for a good life. The experimental society is doubly experimental, because it not only encourages its members' experiments in living; the experimental society itself can be understood as part of a social experiment to determine the most appropriate kinds of social organization for human beings.

The experiment began recently, less than 300 years ago. This is not the end of history. The experiment has hardly begun.

NOTES

Chapter 1

1. The ancient Greeks and ancient Romans apparently had no concept of an individual human right. See Hart (1979, 126).

2. Though Singer professes to be a utilitarian, apparently not even he quite accepts all of its implications. See Specter (1999).

3. The top-down picture of moral development still exerts a powerful influence. Thus, for example, 58 percent of those polled in the United States believe that it is not possible to be moral without believing in God (Kristof 2003, A29). Unfortunately, the poll does not distinguish between those who think that belief in God is necessary for someone to believe that acts are morally right or wrong and those who simply think that belief in God is necessary to motivate people to do the right thing, when it conflicts with other desires.

4. The term *overlapping consensus* was originally used by Rawls (1993) for a different purpose. It is also used by Beitz (2001). As I use the term, it is intended to cover Beitz's "common core" and "overlapping consensus" interpretations (2001, 273).

5. Donnelly would undoubtedly agree, because he defends various rights for gays and lesbians even though he acknowledges that there is little prospect of an international consensus on such rights in the near future (2003, 238).

6. For a more fully developed argument that the overlapping consensus model cannot support truly universal human rights, see Kim (forthcoming).

7. The term *minimal legitimacy* used in the heading to this section is from Beitz (2001, 274).

8. To be precise, Rawls describes one kind of "decent peoples," which he refers to as "decent hierarchical peoples" (1999, 63). Decent hierarchical peoples

respect the human rights enumerated by Rawls. He leaves open the possibility that there might be other kinds of decent peoples, though he does not try to describe any other kinds.

9. I should say that I myself believe that autonomy is an important contributor to human well-being. My point here is simply that the case for autonomy rights does not depend on the intrinsic value of autonomy.

10. This suggests a fourth interpretation of human rights: the full justice interpretation, according to which human rights are the rights that are necessary to make any society fully just. I believe that the UN Universal Declaration of Human Rights and other documents of this kind are best understood on the full-justice interpretation, because I see no other way to account for the great variety of rights they include. These human rights documents are valuable, but it is obvious that all of the rights they enumerate are not equally important. In this book, I attempt to distinguish the basic from the nonbasic and to explain what makes the basic ones basic.

11. It seems clear that, if done to nonhuman animals, torture or foot binding would be regarded as extreme cruelty. Because of the analogy to spaying and neutering, infibulation may not seem so objectionable. However, spaying and neutering are not appropriate analogies for infibulation. Infibulation does not make pregnancy impossible. Among other effects, it makes sexual intercourse painful rather than pleasurable. I discuss infibulation more fully in chapter 5.

12. A justification also counts as paternalistic if the goal is to prevent autonomous adults from being persuaded to adopt a practice or from being influenced by an example. Burning those regarded as heretics at the stake was unlikely to save their souls, but it was advocated as a good way of preventing others from being influenced by their ideas. Where the influence is by persuasion or example, blocking the influence is paternalistic.

Chapter 2

1. Think of pragmatic reasoning as reasoning about how to promote one's own goals, unburdened by any truly moral constraints. For example, if someone is motivated to tell the truth solely out of the desire not to acquire a reputation for dishonesty, where the reputation is desirable because of the benefits one derives from it, then even if the act is morally correct, the motivation is purely pragmatic.

2. The *Requirimiento* is described by Las Casas ([1875], III.57), from which my quotations are excerpted. After quoting it, Las Casas notes that the statement was read to the natives in Spanish, not in any language they could understand.

3. In 1992, Pope John Paul II asked forgiveness for previous popes' endorsement of African slavery (Gutiérrez 1993, 330). The Roman Catholic church provides the best examples of religious fallibility, because it has the strongest doctrine of infallibility. See Wills (2000) for an informed discussion of how the

doctrine of papal infallibility has led the Catholic church to take positions (e.g., on contraception and on priestly celibacy) that are rejected by substantial portions of the Catholic priesthood and the laity. Wills argues that the greatest legacy of the doctrine of papal infallibility is the intellectual dishonesty required to uphold it. The best way to undo that harm would be for a pope to declare *ex cathedra* that popes are *not* infallible. For obvious reasons, the prospects for such a declaration are remote.

4. Epistemic justification is the kind of justification that a belief must have to qualify as knowledge, though it is possible for an epistemically justified belief to be false. In this book, I limit my attention to cases in which agent S's being morally justified in doing an act A depends on whether or not the agent has an epistemically justified belief that it is not wrong. The connection between the two notions has more logical structure than I discuss in the text. I set out my own view of the fuller picture here in a note because I expect it to be controversial, and nothing in the text depends on these details of my view. Imagine a situation in which a person S performs an act A, in part on the basis of a belief that it is not wrong. Consider the question of whether S is morally blameworthy for doing act A. When a person is epistemically justified in believing that an act is not wrong (i.e., when the belief is a reasonable one), and when she performs the act (in part) on the basis of that belief, then she is not morally blameworthy in doing it, even if A is objectively wrong. However, if the belief that A is not wrong is epistemically unjustified and act A is objectively wrong, then S doing A (in part) on the basis of that belief is blameworthy. For example, if I borrow your hammer and promise to bring it back within an hour, my failure to keep my promise may not be blameworthy if my mother's calling long distance causes me to lose track of the time and to forget to get the hammer back to you on time. Because I lost track of the time, I thought I was not doing anything wrong, and I was epistemically justified in believing that I was not doing anything wrong. In fact, an hour had passed, so I had broken my promise, which was objectively wrong.

5. The damage done by the Proof paradigm is not limited to moral philosophy. Due to the influence of the Proof paradigm, David Hume was able to argue that we can have no good reason for believing to be true any statement about the future, and a parallel argument leads to the conclusion that we can have no good reason to believe to be true any statement about the past. Similar arguments support the conclusion that we can have no good reason to believe to be true any scientific theory. So it is not surprising that similar arguments would undermine all moral claims. A surprising number of philosophers agree with these conclusions, and an even larger number (I am thinking here of pragmatists and deconstructionists) believe that there is no point in believing *anything* to be true. I am not claiming here that these kinds of skepticism are simply bad consequences of the Proof paradigm. I am claiming that the Proof paradigm has led to such misunderstanding of the nature of epistemic justification that it has led to serious misunderstandings about what makes a belief epistemically justified even by those who reject it.

6. My discussion here applies to what might be referred to as *classical versions* of the Proof paradigm, which required the premises of justificatory arguments to be rationally unquestionable, and thus infallible. None of my criticisms directly applies to recent versions that are fallibilistic about a priori insight (e.g., BonJour 1998). Fallibilism about a priori insight seems to give up most of the motivation for the Proof paradigm in the first place. Would mathematics have been chosen as the model for knowledge if it were thought to be a fallible kind of knowledge?

7. To contrast with the Proof paradigm's *deductivism*, I take the term *inductivist* from Millgram (1997). I use inductivist simply to indicate the bottom-up direction of the reasoning. I do not mean to imply that inductivist reasoning always involves generalizing from observed instances. Bottom-up reasoning can include what are called *abduction* and *inference to the best explanation.* Jonsen and Toulmin (1988) have emphasized the importance of bottom-up epistemic justification on moral matters. They refer to this sort of reasoning as "casuistry." Because of the pejorative connotations of casuistry, I prefer the more neutral term inductivism.

8. In the literature on scientific explanation, this model of explanation is referred to as the *deductive-nomological model,* after Hempel (1965), though the main idea can be traced back to Aristotle. Of course, not all deductions are equally good explanations of their conclusions.

9. Actually, the arguments I give here do not address a less extreme form of inductivism, which is fallibilistic about particular moral judgments. I should confess that I used to be an inductivist of this less extreme kind until my students, especially Jason Baehr, talked me out of it. Fortunately, nothing crucial hinges on this issue. The main arguments of the book are compatible with either a fallibilistic inductivist or a fallibilistic equilibrium model for the epistemic justification of moral beliefs.

10. By "substantive moral principles," I mean to set aside principles such as whatever is right is not wrong.

11. Mill emphasized the necessity of hearing and responding to contrary opinions if our own opinion is to be epistemically justified or rational ([1859], 42–46). The term *equilibrium* is from Rawls (1971, 49).

12. Rawls's favored notion of reflective equilibrium was not narrowly intrasubjective, but widely so, because Rawls required that the individual consider alternatives to his own moral views and the arguments for them (1971, 49). See the next note for a reference to a place where Rawls seems to move beyond wide reflective equilibrium to a general (i.e., interpersonal) reflective equilibrium.

13. Indeed, in one place, Rawls seems to extend his intrapersonal notion of reflective equilibrium to make it an interpersonal one, when he says, "The overall criterion of the reasonable is *general* and wide reflective equilibrium" (1995, 141; emphasis added). For a moral belief to be in *wide* reflective equilibrium requires considering all relevant alternatives to it with the arguments in support of them. *General* reflective equilibrium on a moral belief is interpersonal, because it requires a consensus in the relevant population on the given belief. Moreover,

there is a sense in which Habermas's view is ultimately individualistic, because each person, though she should be open to the opinions of others, must ultimately make her own judgment about whether others' opinions qualify as "noncoercive rational discourse among free and equal participants" (Habermas 1995, 117). It is important not to conflate the notion of interpersonal equilibrium with interpersonal agreement. It is possible to have an interpersonal equilibrium in which 80 percent of the population believes that torturing a suspected terrorist is wrong and 20 percent does not. To say that it is in equilibrium is to say that the division is a stable one. For there to be a significant shift of opinion, some new factor would have to be introduced.

14. Dworkin (1996) makes this argument.

15. Rawls expresses his metaphysical modesty by saying that his liberalism is "political not metaphysical" (1993, 10). On his disavowal of claims to truth for his political liberalism, see Rawls (1993, xx, 60, 128–129).

16. See, also, Habermas (1993, 29). Habermas uses the term *validity* rather than *truth* to avoid the metaphysics of a correspondence theory of truth for normative claims. He has no objection to understanding the validity of normative claims "[b]y analogy with a nonsemantic concept of truth purified of all connotations of correspondence" (1995, 124).

17. See McCarthy (1994, 47), where he claims that Habermas's notion of universality is not culture- but species-specific. In correspondence with the author, McCarthy has indicated that he now agrees with what I have called the *strong* interpretation of Habermas.

18. This is different from claiming that it is always wrong to torture the innocent. That norm may also be true, but its status is much less certain than clear-cut examples of wrongful torture of the innocent.

19. Moral judgments are not the only judgments that have this strong universality. I believe that all normative judgments, including judgments about what it is rational to believe or do (in nonmoral situations), also have this strong universality and that our epistemic justification for believing them fits the same equilibrium model, which I develop further in chapter 4.

20. A classic example of the historical development of the interpretation of the Golden Rule is Jesus' use of the story of the Good Samaritan (Luke 10: 25–37).

21. On the problems for utilitarianism, see, for example, Rawls (1958 and 1971). The main problem with all versions of the Golden Rule is that they make morality too dependent on individual preferences. For example, both "Love your neighbor as yourself" and "Do unto others as you would have them do unto you" would seem either to justify a masochist causing pain to others (on the grounds that he would like other people to cause him pain) or to require others to cause him pain (on the grounds that they would want to be caused pain if they were in his position).

22. The same thing can be said about the sciences. Even though it was not completely correct, Newtonian physics was a great scientific advance.

23. Article V of the Constitution gives the procedures for amending it. The

same procedures apply to the entire Constitution (including Article V), except that "no state, without its consent, shall be deprived of its equal suffrage in the Senate." Thus, it is allowed that even the equal suffrage provision can be amended, but the procedure for amending it is different. Note that there is a logical defect in the Constitution, since it permits a two-step procedure for depriving a state of its equal suffrage in the Senate without its consent. To do so, it would first be necessary to amend Article V to eliminate the consent condition on amending the equal suffrage provision. This could be done by a two-thirds vote in both houses of Congress, with the approval of three-quarters of the states. Then the equal suffrage provision itself could be amended in the same way. Obviously, it would be possible to obtain the required approvals without having the consent of all of the states that would be deprived of equal suffrage in the Senate by the change. This seems to me to be merely a logical problem, not a practical one, because the obvious unfairness of this way of circumventing the intent of Article V would almost surely prevent it from ever being approved.

Chapter 3

1. Perhaps the most influential statement of the Singaporean position is that of Lee's protégé Mahbubani (1998).

2. In Confucianism, the relation of a son to his father is the model for the relation of a subject to his ruler. Thus, for example, there is a political implication to Confucius's remark that if a child believes that his parents are wrong, he may try to dissuade them in the gentlest way, but if they ignore his advice, he should remain reverent and should not be disobedient to them (Analects II: 7). Some scholars question the translation of the Chinese term *bu wei* as "disobedient," but their questions are not enough to change the clear tenor of the passage. See Chan (1999, 223–224). There are some elements of Confucianism that would provide support for respecting human rights, especially in Confucius's opposition to the use of force to promote the virtue or well-being of another person (Analects II:20). See Chan (1999, 225–237).

3. Fifty years later the American Anthropological Association (1999) adopted a new statement endorsing universal human rights.

4. Recall from chapter 1 that I use "universal" in the strong sense that does not limit it to *human* cultures. As I use the term, a universal moral norm would apply to all cultures, terrestrial and extraterrestrial, actual and hypothetical.

5. This incoherence in relativist views was first pointed out for epistemological relativism by Socrates in Plato's *Theaetetus*.

6. Here and throughout this book, I understand criticizing the norms of a culture to involve claiming that the members of the relevant culture should not follow them. The American Anthropological Association's (1947) defense of cultural relativism about human rights seems to be based on cultural relativism about internal norms. Also, although he does not use the term, Walzer (1983)

can be read as defending a version of cultural relativism about internal norms: cultural relativism about internal norms of justice.

Chapter 4

1. To Isabella's credit, she later reversed her opinion and ordered the slaves in Spain returned to their former homes. See Pagden (1982, 31). I should also mention that, although I discuss the Spanish treatment of the American natives extensively here, I do not mean to imply that they were any worse than any of the other European colonizers. I agree with Stannard's verdict that all of the European colonials were equally genocidal (1992, 98). I have chosen to discuss the Spanish because of the remarkable work of Bartolomé de Las Casas, both in documenting the atrocities and in devoting his life to opposing them.

2. See, for example, Sale (1990, 132–135). Although the Spaniards did transport some natives to Spain and sell them in slave markets, by far the greatest number of natives were forced to work on Spanish estates in the colonies under a practice referred to as *encomienda*, in which the natives could not be legally bought and sold, but were regarded as part of the landholder's estate. I follow most commentators in regarding both practices as forms of slavery. For more on the practice of *encomienda*, see Pagden (1982, 36).

3. The examples are legion. See, for example, Todorov (1984, 21, 150); and Sale (1990, 201–203).

4. Saco (1879, I:158), quoted in Thomas (1997, 105).

5. Stannard continues the quotation: "When the Indians were thus still alive and hanging, the Spaniards tested their strength and their blades against them, ripping chests open with one blow and exposing entrails, and there were those who did worse. The straw was wrapped around their torn bodies and they were burned alive. One man caught two children about two years old, pierced their throats with a dagger, then hurled them down a precipice" (1992, 72).

6. Letter from a group of Dominicans to M. De Xeries, quoted in Todorov (1984, 139).

7. The obvious source would be the Decalogue, where idolatry is clearly forbidden by the First Commandment ("Thou shalt not have false gods before me") and cannibalism as a part of human sacrifice is forbidden by the Fifth Commandment (or Sixth, depending on the numbering) ("Thou shalt not kill").

8. For classic statements of this sort of relativism, see J. Mackie (1977) and MacIntyre (1984).

9. It is important to emphasize that I do not claim that the structure of epistemic justification is only bottom-up. As discussed in chapter 2, an equilibrium model allows for the transmission of epistemic justification in both directions, top-down and bottom-up.

10. Ecclesiasticus 34:21. Las Casas reports that reading these words caused his conversion to the cause of the American natives. See Todorov (1984, 134–135).

11. Closely related to this puzzle is the puzzle of how human beings can make judgments about what it is rational (or not rational) to believe or rational (or not rational) to do. I think that all of these puzzles have the same sort of solution, but for present purposes, I simply take it for granted that we do have these abilities. The alternative requires us to accept that no act (not even the awful tortures inflicted by the Europeans on the American natives) really is wrong, or that no belief (not even a belief based on wish fulfillment or self-deception) really is irrational, or that no action (not even the act of someone who, due to a momentary urge, throws himself off a cliff) is irrational. These conclusions seem to me to be too implausible to accept.

12. Perhaps the most important disanalogy is that in a scientific experiment, it is easy to see how the state of the physical world plays a role in determining the outcome of the experiment. Therefore, it is plausible to think that a good explanation of the experimental result might well tell us something about what that world is like.

In our moral observations there is no corresponding role played by an objective moral world. In our moral observations there is only *our* moral response to an objective physical world. Why should we think that our responses are any guide to objective moral truths, rather than just the more or less parochial responses of an idiosyncratic individual, or of the members of a cultural group with the same type of moral training, or of the members of a species with the same sorts of inherited capacities and dispositions? Harman (1977) and Williams (1985) make arguments of this kind.

This is an objection that is better answered in a book on epistemology than in a book on human rights. Here I can only mention that there are many areas of inquiry that take us beyond the way things are in the actual world—for example, abstract mathematics and normative theories of rational belief and rational, nonmoral choice. It is not at all obvious that even the practice of science would make sense in the absence of an objective grounding for such theories, for if there were no objective truth about what it is rational to believe, there would not really be any good reason to accept a scientific theory on the basis of experimental evidence; and if there were no objective truth about what it is rational to do in at least some situations, there would be no truth about how best to proceed to test a scientific theory. The practice of science would be ultimately arbitrary. The alternative is to believe that we are sensitive to objective truths about what it is rational to believe and what it is rational to do in some situations. If we are sensitive to normative truths in these cases, then it is not such a stretch to think that we might be sensitive to normative moral truths. Indeed, I think it is plausible to think that evolution would have made us sensitive to all three kinds of normative truths, but the argument would take me too far afield.

13. It is easy to see how universal moral reasons for driving on the same side of the road as everyone else would support different rules in different societies.

14. David Hume ([1734]) famously attempted to reduce moral judgment to a feeling in us. Many philosophers have defended Humean views. I discuss Rorty

(1993) in chapter 8. For the contrary view—that emotions involve intelligence, not blind feeling—see Nussbaum (2001).

15. When unconscious bias is at least in part due to interests or desires, it is referred to as *hot bias*. I regard self-deception as a paradigmatic example of hot bias. In the text I only briefly outline what is involved in self-deception. For a fuller discussion of what is involved, see Talbott (1995).

16. Enforcement was extremely brutal. Lynchings were common. See Tolnay and Beck (1995).

17. I am indebted to Paul C. Taylor for clarifying this distinction.

18. For another example, even though Lyndon Johnson was one of the most powerful men in the Senate, he confessed to one of his Black employees that he had to be rough in his treatment of Blacks because he did not want to be called a "n—r lover" (Caro 2002, 61). Caro also provides an account of how Johnson's compassion for victims of racial discrimination made him aware of the powerful pressures that socially enforced segregation in Texas (64–75).

19. Thus, it seems to me that without federal law and the use of federal troops, segregation would not have ended in the South in the 1960s. Similarly, without international sanctions, I do not believe that apartheid in South Africa would have ended in the 1980s. Of course, I could be mistaken about these claims.

20. Las Casas was threatened with physical harm and denounced to the Inquisition (Gutiérrez 1993, 289, 369).

21. I discuss this phenomenon more fully in Talbott (1995).

22. See Harman (1977) and Williams (1985) for skeptical arguments of this kind.

23. This is not the place to pursue the important epistemological issues raised by this paragraph. Here I can only note that the kind of defense of the objectivity of moral judgment I give here is the kind of defense I would expect for any kind of objectivity—for example, the objectivity of a belief about physical objects, the objectivity of a belief in a proposition from a scientific theory, or the objectivity of a mathematical belief—as well as the objectivity of a normative belief, for example, a belief about what it is rational to believe or to do.

24. I repeat here my earlier disclaimer that even if the distinctively human rights are not appropriate for nonhuman animals, that does not imply that non-human animals should have no rights. The fact that it would be absurd to hold nonhuman animals morally responsible for their actions shows that their moral status is different from the status of normal human beings.

25. And corresponding demands lead to other kinds of skepticism. Suppose you are an advocate of the Proof paradigm. You want to know whether your judgments of kind K are reliable. Someone offers you a proof that they are. Before you can evaluate the proof, you would seem to need to be justified in trusting that you are reliable in evaluating a proof. How could you be justified in that? Not by a proof. I believe the Proof paradigm sets standards for epistemic justification that cannot be met in any domain.

26. Here the most influential work has been Singer's (1975).

27. I must add that merely asserting that another person's moral beliefs are due to self-serving bias does not make it true.

28. My account of Las Casas's change near the end of his life follows Todorov (1984, 186–201).

29. The crucial transition comes when Las Casas, arguing against Sepulveda, concludes: "Therefore nature itself dictates and teaches those who do not have faith, grace, or doctrine, who live within the limits of the light of nature, that, in spite of every contrary positive law, they ought to sacrifice human victims to the true God or *to the false god who is thought to be true*" (1974, 234; emphasis added).

30. It seems to me that Todorov, who refers to the change as a change to "perspectivalism" (1984, 189), is inclined to interpret it relativistically, because he describes the change this way: "There is no longer a true God (ours), but a coexistence of possible universes: if someone considers it as true" (190). Here Todorov is focusing on the religious beliefs. It is the moral beliefs, including the belief that the American natives' cannibalistic and idolatrous religious practices were not wrong, that I claim to be universal. Todorov does not take a position on this issue, so I am not sure whether he is a moral relativist.

31. Exodus 20:3.

32. What I am calling here the discovery that different cultures should be allowed to worship in their own way is a difficult and hard-won discovery in intolerant cultures, such as those of Western Europe. It is not such a difficult discovery in more tolerant cultures, including many of the Native American cultures. The Seneca warrior Sagoyewatha (also called Red Jacket) admonished the missionaries: "Brother, the Great Sprit has made us all; but he has made a great difference between his white children and his red children; he has given us a different complexion, and different customs. . . . Since he has made so great a difference between us in other things, why may we not conclude that he has given us a different religion? . . .

"Brother! We do not wish to destroy your religion, or take it from you. We only want to enjoy our own" (Josephy 1994, 283).

33. Here I follow Todorov (1984, 170–171).

34. See Gutiérrez, who explains Las Casas's removal of his moral blindspot about the Africans this way: "[A]s we know, nothing stimulated Bartolomé's thinking more effectively than what came from experience" (1993, 326).

35. My answer would be Peter Singer, though I believe that it is his particular moral judgments (for example, about the mistreatment of animals) rather than his moral principles (utilitarianism) that have had such a large impact on prevailing moral views. Interestingly, not even Singer himself lives completely by his principles. See Specter (1999).

36. I agree with Scanlon that there is no reason to expect that choosing in accordance with nonmoral standards of rationality will yield morally acceptable results (1998, 190–191).

37. Though not the first. Cyrus the Great, king of Persia, who lived in the sixth century B.C.E., is the first so far as I know.

Chapter 5

1. See, for example, Maynard Smith (1982) and Axelrod (1984). When applied to the evolution of male and female social roles, the idea of evolutionarily stable strategies must be extended to cover strategy combinations that include more than one strategy.

2. "Honor killings" are murders of women for "immoral" behavior that dishonors the family. A woman can be killed for any behavior that lowers her perceived value as a wife. The UN Population Fund (2000) reports that women are killed for the "dishonor" of having been raped, often by a family member. Perpetrators of honor killings are typically male relatives of the murdered woman. They often go unpunished or receive lenient sentences.

3. Including Shirin Ebadi, the Iranian women's rights advocate and winner of the 2003 Nobel Peace Prize (C. S. Smith 2003).

4. This idea is found in G. Mackie (1996). My discussion is greatly indebted to his analysis.

5. So-called because it is a generalization to more than two players of Sen's (1974) assurance game. This classification is only meant to be suggestive. A detailed discussion of the formal requirements of an n-person assurance game would show that some of the requirements are not strictly satisfied, but the approximation is close enough to make the classification analytically valuable.

6. For more information on the calculations and on the continuing disparity, see Sen (2003b).

7. It might be thought that the increase in the male-female ratio would make females more valuable and, thus, improve their status. This prediction is half right. Females have become more valuable as commodities, with the result that it is now estimated that more than 4 million girls and women each year are sold into marriage, prostitution, or slavery (UN Population Fund 2000, chap. 3).

8. In Saudi Arabia, only male births are recorded in family or tribal records (Sasson 1992, 23). Although in Western societies, girls count, they don't count as much as boys. Lundberg and Rose (2002) report, for example, that, in the year following birth, fathers of sons work longer hours and have a higher hourly pay rate than fathers of daughters. In addition, they (Lundberg and Rose 2004) report that single mothers of sons are 11 percent more likely to eventually marry than single mothers of daughters (and 42 percent more likely to marry the child's biological father).

9. See, for example, Riding (2003), for a report on the criticism of Seierstad.

10. And yet, organizations, such as the Bangladesh Rural Advancement Committee, that have attempted to provide educational opportunities for women and organizations, such as the Grameen Bank, that have tried to provide occupational opportunities for women, have been targeted by Islamic fundamentalists (Weaver 1994, 50).

11. Victor Davis Hanson, a military historian, thinks there may have been a brief interval of world peace between A.D. 100 and A.D. 200 (Angier 2003). If

the definition of *war* is restrictive enough, perhaps there was a period without war. If war is understood broadly enough to include violent hostilities between groups, then it is hard to believe there has been a time of world peace in all of recorded history.

12. My discussion of the elimination of foot binding follows G. Mackie (1996).

13. My discussion of Tostan is based on information from the Tostan Website (URL: www.tostan.org) and from conversations with Molly Melching, the organization's founder.

14. It is not inconceivable that there might be a voluntary movement for a less extreme form of female genital cutting. It should also be mentioned that the desire to be able to wear stylish high heel shoes has resurrected a milder version of foot binding. Some women now undergo expensive cosmetic foot surgery procedures to shorten toes or narrow or reshape their feet, sometimes with disastrous consequences (Harris 2003).

Chapter 6

1. Nonconsequentialist defenders of human rights include the historical figures Locke and Kant as well as many recent authors, including Nozick (1974), Gewirth (1978), J. Thomson (1990), and Donnelly (2003). In my sense of the term, the early Rawls (1971) was a consequentialist, because he attempted to justify the priority of basic rights on the basis of their contribution to appropriately distributed well-being. In Rawls's terms, he believed that the priority of liberty is part of a narrower conception of justice, which could be justified as a special case of a general conception of justice based on maximin (see the next note for an explanation of this concept) (1971, 300, 541–548). Also see the next note for more on the relation between Mill and the early Rawls. The later Rawls disavowed his earlier attempt to derive the special conception from the general conception (1993, 371–84).

2. John Stuart Mill ([1859]) was the first to attempt to give a consequentialist justification for rights to develop and exercise autonomy. Mill was a utilitarian. He thought that the rights necessary to protect individual autonomy could be justified by their contribution to overall well-being. Because overall well-being is measured as a sum or average, maximizing it does not guarantee that everyone will have a high level of it. Even if some people were at the low end of well-being, average or total well-being could be high (even maximal) if there were enough other people at the high end who counterbalanced those at the low end. Call this utilitarianism's *distributional blindspot*. The early John Rawls (1958 and 1971) was disturbed by utilitarianism's distributional blindspot, so he proposed an alternative principle, *maximin*, that required maximizing the expected well-being (measured in terms of what he called *primary goods*) of the least well-off group. The early Rawls's account was not utilitarian. However, as I use the term, his account was consequentialist, because it made the justification of basic rights dependent upon their helping to promote *appropriately distrib-*

uted well-being. The later Rawls (1993) abandoned this consequentialist project. In this book and the companion volume (Talbott forthcoming) I attempt to resuscitate the consequentialist project in human rights. I agree with the early Rawls that basic human rights can be justified by their contribution to (appropriately distributed) well-being, though I believe that Rawls's maximin principle is too extreme.

3. For many more examples, see Aron (1957), Hollander (1981), and Lilla (2001).

4. In Plato's *Republic*, the main character is Plato's teacher Socrates. It is Socrates who, in the dialogue, defines and defends the ideal society of the *Republic*. A vexed issue, which I cannot pursue here, is the extent to which the character in the dialogue represents the views of Socrates and the extent to which the character in the dialogue represents the views of Plato himself. Because I agree with those authors who find more of Plato than of Socrates in the *Republic*, in this book I attribute the views expressed by Socrates in the dialogue to Plato.

5. For Aristotle's discussion of slavery, see *Politics* (I.4–7, 13); for his discussion of women, see *Politics* (I.12–13).

6. For the ruler/shepherd analogy in the *Republic*, see 343–346. The ruler/shepherd analogy is the central analogy in Plato's *Statesman*. See, for example, 275a1–5. Aristotle employs the analogy in the *Nichomachean Ethics* (VIII.11).

7. I favor "philosopher-autocrat" over the usual "philosopher-king" not as a superior translation of the term employed by Plato, but as a more appropriate description of the sort of ruler Plato advocates. For example, although the ruler of the *Republic* exercises absolute rule, the position is not hereditary.

8. As one of the earliest proponents of equality of the sexes, Plato allows that the philosopher-autocrat may be male or female (*Republic*, 540c5–9). Plato makes it quite clear that there are no limits on the powers of philosopher-autocrats, when he says they will "take the city and the characters of men, as they might a tablet, and first wipe it clean" (*Republic*, 501a3–4), so as to fashion the city and the characters of its citizens according to their ideal model. A partial list of aspects of life that would be regulated by the philosopher-autocrat includes literature and music (398–403), sexual activity (457–459), and property ownership (464–465).

9. The beehive metaphor is not unfair to Plato, for he himself employs it (*Republic*, 590).

10. Plato is not the only paternalist to claim there is an infallible source of knowledge about how to promote human well-being. Many religious traditions claim to have a direct pipeline to God's infallible knowledge on the subject. Their great disadvantage is that they are prevented from learning from their mistakes, because they can never acknowledge making any.

11. Readers familiar only with the recent history of existing communist governments (e.g., China, North Korea, Vietnam, and Cuba) or with the recent history of former communist governments (e.g., the Soviet Union, the Eastern European communist bloc, and Cambodia) might justifiably believe that communist dictatorship has always been identified with the cynical exercise of totalitar-

ian power. This would be a mistake. In the 1920s, the communist dictatorship in Russia was regarded as a model government by prominent intellectuals throughout the world. By the end of the 1930s, most intellectuals in the West had become disillusioned with the Soviet model, but not necessarily the communist ideal. In the 1950s and especially the 1960s, intellectuals in the West championed the communist dictatorship of Mao Zedong in China. By the end of the 1970s, most intellectuals in the West had become disillusioned with the Maoist model. Some of the history of Western intellectuals' infatuation with twentieth-century totalitarian regimes, fascist as well as communist, can be found in Aron (1957), Hollander (1981), and Lilla (2001).

12. My account of Lysenko follows Medvedev (1969) and Tucker (1990, 560–561, 571).

13. Reported in an editorial in a Soviet newspaper, quoted in Medvedev (1969, 165).

14. On Khrushchev, see Medvedev (1969, 196). On Mao, see Glover (1999, 285).

15. Things did not go well for the assistant principal who blew the whistle. Winerip (2003) reports that he was assigned to a windowless office with nothing to do. The prospects were not good for his being rehired when his contract expired.

16. To speak of a free market of ideas is to take an idea from economics to illuminate epistemology. I believe Hayek (1960) was the first to see that the explanation also goes in the other direction—that the advantages of free markets can be explained in epistemological terms.

17. This is the lesson of Nozick's experience machine thought experiment (1974, 42–45). Most people would not choose to hook up to an experience machine for life, even if they were sure it would guarantee them a life of bliss. Most people care about having interactions with the real world (even though on the experience machine they would believe they were having interactions with the real world). Sober and Wilson (1998) argue, in addition, that there are good reasons to expect evolution to have favored beings with a combination of altruistic and egoistic (or hedonistic) motivations.

18. I make no claim to originality here. What I am calling the *constitutive element* in a person's judgment of what is good for her is probably the central idea in Rawls's account of "goodness as rationality" (1971, chap. 7).

19. Shue's third basic right is a right to liberty with two parts: a right to political participation and a right to freedom of movement (1980, chap. 3). A right to political participation is included in the political rights I discuss in chapter 7. A right to freedom of movement would be included in my right to security, as a right against imprisonment. Shortly, I will add a much broader liberty right than Shue's to my list of basic human rights.

20. J. Thomson (1990) has argued that rights protect only against certain harms, not the threat of harm. I explain why I disagree with her in Talbott (forthcoming).

21. Martha Nussbaum (2000) has emphasized the importance of emotional

development as part of the basic capabilities essential to normal human development.

22. One big presumption I discard is the presumption that autonomy requires a special metaphysics according to which autonomous choices cannot be causally determined. To defend a nonmetaphysical conception of autonomy would take me too far afield, so I simply note here, as I use the terms, that neither good judgment nor self-determination require an absence of causal determinism.

23. Could one autonomously choose not to shape one's life according to one's judgment? Not completely, because that very decision would give it some shape.

24. A nonconsequentialist justification of autonomy rights need not be so direct. See Scanlon (1972) for an *indirect nonconsequentialist* defense of autonomy rights on the grounds that they are necessary for a government to be legitimate. It was Scanlon's paper that first gave me the idea of giving the sort of *indirect consequentialist* justification of autonomy rights that I develop in this book and the companion volume (Talbott forthcoming).

25. I focus here only on paternalistic interference. I take it for granted that any acceptable government will guarantee security rights that will include laws against murder and other forms of direct harm to others. For more on these sorts of security rights, see the companion volume (Talbott forthcoming).

26. *Griswold v. Connecticut*, 381 U.S. 479 (1965).

27. *Planned Parenthood v. Casey*, 505 U.S. 833, 851 (1992).

28. *Lawrence v. Texas*, 156 L. Ed. 2d 508, 514 (2003). The sphere also includes decisions about whether to prolong one's life or to refuse life support. See *Cruzan v. Director, Missouri Dep't. of Health*, 497 U.S. 261 (1990).

29. I attempt to answer this question in the companion volume (Talbott forthcoming).

30. *Loving v. Virginia*, 388 U.S. 1, 87 S. Ct. 1817 (1967).

Chapter 7

1. This thought experiment comes from Nozick (1974, 282–292).

2. Technically, 50,000 votes would not be a majority if there were 100,000 votes cast. Suppose that, because it is your life, if there is an exact split in the vote, your vote is the tie breaker.

3. It is unknown whether the author of *Federalist* No. 51 was James Madison or Alexander Hamilton.

4. This simplified example can be modified to explain how groups larger than individual families (e.g., tribes, ethnic groups, nationalities, or religions) can provide similar solutions to problems of deterrence and how each such solution can generate potentially endless cycles of retaliation. This is not a mere abstract possibility. These sorts of cycles can be observed throughout history and in many places today.

5. The general characterization of a collective action problem is a situation in which, even if everyone acts rationally, the outcome may be worse for everyone in their own estimation than it would have been if they had all chosen differently (M. Taylor 1987, 19). It is easy to see how, in such a situation, a law requiring everyone to choose appropriately could make everyone better off. Although technically a collective action problem requires that there be an outcome that makes *everyone involved* better off, in the real world, it is good enough if *almost* everyone is made better off. In Talbott (forthcoming) I weaken this requirement still further, to require only that a majority be made better off, because, under certain circumstances, a *rule* permitting legal solutions to a majority's collective action problems would be expected to make *everyone* better off.

6. M. Taylor (1987) shows how it would be possible for a smaller community to solve such problems by convention, but even then it would not be easy.

7. Technically, the situation is closer to an iterated n-person prisoners' dilemma (n-person prisoners' dilemma supergame). This is true of the other examples that I discuss also. Because my discussion of these examples is informal, I abstract away from the details that would be important if I were trying to precisely model the interactions. It is enough for my purposes that both the one-shot and the iterated n-person prisoners' dilemmas are collective action problems. For more on the differences between the two, see M. Taylor (1987).

8. Hobbes allowed that the sovereign could be "a man or assembly of men" ([1651], 143). For simplicity, I focus on the case where the sovereign is an individual autocrat.

9. In its more sophisticated forms, it can be used to explain how evolution could select for behaviors that seem to reduce fitness. See, for example, Frank (1988) and Skyrms (1996).

10. Buchanan's (1975) mistake was to think that cooperative game theory could be used to explain the derivation of contracts. It is now generally agreed that cooperative game theory only applies to situations where contracts are enforced.

11. To appreciate some of the difficulties, see M. Taylor's discussion of a related problem: the possibility of a stable cooperative solution to an n-person prisoners' dilemma supergame (1987, chap. 4). Taylor titled his book *The Possibility of Cooperation*, but the force of the book is to convince the reader of how unrealistic a possibility it is.

12. Downs (1957) first made the argument and drew the conclusion that it would not be rational for voters to inform themselves on the candidates and issues, but he was not able to bring himself to draw the final conclusion that it would also not be rational for them to vote.

13. Sen (2003a) is a collection of essays he has written over two decades including several in which he challenges the economic orthodoxy that identifies rationality with rational self-interest. He continues the challenge in Sen (1999). Another Nobel Prize–winning economist who has emphasized the importance of moral ideas in politics is North (1990). It would be valuable to have a comprehensive review of all of the winners of the Nobel Prize in economics to determine

how many of them think that rational self-interest is sufficient to explain all human behavior. I have not attempted such a review.

14. Years ago I saw a film clip of a news interview with Snow on his return from China in which he stated emphatically that he had not seen anyone starving. I do not know if that film clip still exists.

15. Researchers on the simultaneous ultimatum game, where both players decide on what they will offer and what they will accept simultaneously, report similar results (Kahneman, Knetsch, and Thaler 1986).

16. *Dred Scott v. Sandford*, 60 U.S. 393 (1857) (the Court ruled that slaves had no rights). *Brown v. Board of Education*, 347 U.S. 483 (1954) (the Court overruled "separate but equal" justification for segregation in schools).

17. I am not advocating that judges routinely overrule majoritarian legislation or legal precedents based on their own moral judgments. A strong consequentialist case can be made for generally respecting legal precedents and the will of the majority. However, where, as in prohibitions of sodomy and of gay and lesbian marriages, the law conflicts with basic human rights, the courts should protect basic human rights.

18. The leading case was *West Coast Hotel v. Parrish*, 300 U.S. 379 (1937).

19. In my lifetime, legally enforced racial segregation has been ended in the United States and in democracies throughout the world. Unprecedented educational and occupational opportunities have opened up for women. The rights of aboriginal peoples have been recognized throughout the democratic world. When I was a child, homosexuality was classified as a disease. Laws against homosexual activity were severely enforced. Now gay and lesbian marriages are recognized in Belgium, the Netherlands, and Canada. Gay and lesbian civil unions are recognized in many others. Almost every international human rights document has been adopted since my birth in 1949, or shortly before it. As autocracies, Germany and Japan were two of the most militaristic countries in the world. As rights-respecting democracies, they have become two of the most pacific. After centuries of strife, European countries have not gone to war against each other for more than fifty years. Former enemies are now allies in the European Union. And the first permanent international court for human rights prosecution (the International Criminal Court) was established in 2002 and began operation in 2003. Many more changes could easily be added to this list.

Chapter 8

1. Rorty gives credit to Baier (1987) for having articulated the position he endorses, but Baier has since expanded upon her interpretation of Hume in such a way as to make him a revisionist about reason. On her reading, Hume's project is "not so much to dethrone reason as to enlarge our conception of it" (Baier 1991, 278). This is the sort of change in the understanding of what reason is that I, too, would endorse. I have focused on Rorty, because, unlike Baier, he

continues to dichotomize reason and sentiment. I should also mention that Rorty identifies the central moral sentiment as "sympathy," probably because that is the term Hume uses. In my discussion, I follow Rorty in taking the central moral sentiment to be "sympathy." However, it should be noted that both Hume and Rorty use that term in a way that more closely corresponds to what is ordinarily meant by "empathy."

2. On my account, exactly the same characteristic also grounds moral responsibility, but that is too large a topic to be addressed adequately here.

3. Even after relinquishing the position of prime minister in 1990, Lee continued to be influential as senior minister and head of the majority party (PAP). Unless otherwise noted, the facts of Lee's rule are taken from Sesser (1992).

4. The parliament did not have a single opposition member from 1966 to 1981. The opposition never had more than four of eighty-one seats during Lee's time as prime minister (Sesser 1992, 61).

5. As prime minister of Singapore, Lee faced a genuine threat of violent confrontations between the Chinese and the Malay population of Singapore. This was one of the reasons he gave for not permitting freedom of speech or assembly. In 1965, when Singapore declared its independence, the potential for ethnic violence was real. But Lee continued to use this justification for his autocratic rule long after the threat had abated.

6. For comparison, per capita income in the United States in 2000 was $34,000.

7. By comparison, the home ownership rate in the United States reached 68 percent in 2002. See U.S. Census Bureau (2002).

8. For more on how the original position thought experiment applies to relations between developed and developing countries, see the companion volume (Talbott forthcoming).

9. I do not mean to imply that there can never be a justification for not contributing when most others are, only that any such justification would have to be made from the moral standpoint, where it would have to be justifiable to everyone behind the veil of ignorance. Free-riding cannot be justified from the moral standpoint behind the veil of ignorance.

10. In the companion volume (Talbott forthcoming), I attempt a more careful comparison of their differences.

REFERENCES

American Anthropological Association. 1947. "Statement on Human Rights."
American Anthropologist 49: 539–543.

———. 1999. "Declaration on Anthropology and Human Rights." URL: http://
www.aaanet.org/stmts/humanrts.htm.

Angier, Natalie. 2003. "Is War Our Biological Destiny?" *New York Times* (Nov.
11): D1, D12.

Aristotle. *Nicomachean Ethics*. In McKeon 1941: 935–1112.

———. *Politics*. In McKeon 1941: 1127–1316.

Aron, Raymond. 1957. *The Opium of the Intellectuals* (London: Secker & War-
burg).

Axelrod, Robert. 1984. *The Evolution of Cooperation* (New York: Basic).

Baier, Annette. 1987. "Hume: The Women's Moral Theorist?" In Eva Feder Kit-
tay and Diana T. Meyers, eds., *Women and Moral Theory* (Totowa, N.J.: Row-
man and Littlefield): 40–55.

———. 1991. *A Progress of Sentiments* (Cambridge, Mass.: Harvard University
Press).

Barkow, Jerome H., Leda Cosmides, and John Tooby, eds. 1992. *The Adapted
Mind* (New York: Oxford University Press).

BBC News. 1998. "Millions Dead from Starvation Says North Korean Defector"
(Feb. 18). URL: http://news.bbc.co.uk/2/hi/asia-pacific/57740.stm

Beitz, Charles R. 2001. "Human Rights as a Common Concern." *American Political Science Review* 95(June): 269–282.

BonJour, Laurence. 1998. *In Defense of Pure Reason* (Cambridge: Cambridge University Press).

Bork, Robert H. 2003. *Coercing Virtue: The Worldwide Rule of Judges* (Washington,
D.C.: AEI Press).

Brennan, Geoffrey, and James M. Buchanan. 1985. *The Reason of Rules: Constitutional Political Economy* (Cambridge: Cambridge University Press).

Brickman, Philip, Dan Coates, and Ronnie Janoff-Bulman. 1978. "Lottery Winners and Accident Victims: Is Happiness Relative?" *Journal of Personality and Social Psychology* 36: 917–927.

Brownmiller, Susan. 1975. *Against Our Will* (New York: Bantam).

Buchanan, James M. 1975. *The Limits of Liberty: Between Anarchy and Leviathan* (Chicago: University of Chicago Press).

Buchanan, James M., and G. Tullock. 1962. *The Calculus of Consent* (Ann Arbor: University of Michigan Press).

Camerer, Colin, and Richard H. Thaler. 1995. "Anomalies: Ultimatums, Dictators, and Manners." *Journal of Economic Perspectives* 9 (Spring): 209–219.

Caro, Robert A. 2002. "The Compassion of Lyndon Johnson." *New Yorker* (Apr. 1): 56–77.

Chan, Joseph. 1999. "A Confucian Perspective on Human Rights for Contemporary China." In Joanne R. Bauer and Daniel A. Bell, eds., *The East Asian Challenge for Human Rights* (Cambridge: Cambridge University Press): 212–237.

Chang, Jung. 1991. *Wild Swans* (New York: Simon & Schuster).

Cosmides, Leda, and John Tooby. 1992. "Cognitive Adaptations for Social Exchange." In Barkow, Cosmides, and Tooby 1992: 163–228.

Cranston, Maurice. 1967. "Human Rights, Real and Supposed." In D. D. Raphael, ed., *Political Theory and the Rights of Man* (Bloomington: Indiana University Press): 43–53.

Dhimgjoka, Merita. 2002. "Blood Feuds Spark Call for Revised Killing Rules." *Seattle Times* (May 20): A8.

Donnelly, Jack. 2003. *Universal Human Rights in Theory and Practice*, 2d ed. (Ithaca, N.Y.: Cornell University Press).

Downs, Anthony. 1957. *An Economic Theory of Democracy* (New York: Harper).

Doyle, Michael W. 1997. *Ways of War and Peace* (New York: Norton).

Dworkin, Ronald. 1996. "Objectivity and Truth: You'd Better Believe It." *Philosophy and Public Affairs* 25 (Spring): 87–139.

Eckert, Allan W. 1992. *A Sorrow in Our Heart* (New York: Bantam).

Frank, Robert H. 1988. *Passions within Reason* (New York: Norton).

Gannon, Kathy. 2001. "Kabul Women Welcome Return to Human Race." *Seattle Times* (Nov. 29): A3.

Gewirth, Alan. 1978. *Reason and Morality* (Chicago: University of Chicago Press).

Gittings, John. 2002. "Growing Sex Imbalance Shocks China." *Guardian* (May 13). URL: http://www.guardian.co.uk/international/story/0,3604,714412,00.html.

Glover, Jonathan. 1999. *Humanity* (New Haven, Conn.: Yale University Press).

Goodwin, Jan. 1994. *Price of Honor* (New York: Little, Brown).

Gutiérrez, Gustavo. 1993. *Las Casas* (Maryknoll, N.Y.: Orbis).

Habermas, Jürgen. 1990. *Moral Consciousness and Communicative Action*, trans. Christian Lenhardt and Shierry Weber Nicholsen (Cambridge, Mass.: MIT Press).

———. 1993. *Justification and Application*, trans. Ciaran Cronin (Cambridge, Mass.: MIT Press).

————. 1995. "Reconciliation through the Public Use of Reason: Remarks on John Rawls's Political Liberalism." *Journal of Philosophy* 92 (Mar.): 109–131.

————. 1996. *Between Facts and Norms: Contributions to a Discourse Theory of Law and Democracy*, trans. William Rehg (Cambridge, Mass.: MIT Press).

Hamilton, Edith, and Huntington Cairns, eds. 1961. *The Collected Dialogues of Plato* (Princeton, N.J.: Princeton University Press).

Harman, Gilbert. 1977. *The Nature of Morality* (New York: Oxford University Press).

Harris, Gordon. 2003. "If Shoe Won't Fit, Fix the Foot? Popular Surgery Raises Concern." *New York Times* (Dec. 7): A1, A24.

Harsanyi, John C. 1953. "Cardinal Utility in Welfare Economics and in the Theory of Risk-Taking." *Journal of Political Economy* 61: 434–435.

Hart, H. L. A. 1979. "Bentham on Legal Rights." In David Lyons, ed., *Rights* (Belmont, Calif.: Wadsworth): 125–148.

Hayek, Friedrich. 1960. *The Constitution of Liberty* (Chicago: University of Chicago Press).

Hempel, Carl. 1965. "Aspects of Scientific Explanation." In *Aspects of Scientific Explanation and Other Essays in the Philosophy of Science* (New York: Free Press).

Hobbes, Thomas. [1651] 1958. *Leviathan* (Indianapolis, Ind.: Library of Liberal Arts).

Hoffman, Elizabeth, Kevin A. McCabe, and Vernon L. Smith. 1996. "On Expectations and the Monetary Stakes in Ultimatum Games." *International Journal of Game Theory* 25: 289–301.

Hollander, Paul. 1981. *Political Pilgrims* (New York: Oxford University Press).

Hoong, Chua Mui. 2003. "It's Not about Gay Rights—It's Survival." *Straits Times* (July 9). URL: http://straitstimes.asia1.com.sg/columnist/0,1886,84–198784,00.html.

Hume, David. [1734] 1888. *A Treatise of Human Nature*, ed. L. A. Selby-Bigge (Oxford: Clarendon).

Jonsen, Albert R., and Stephen Toulmin. 1988. *The Abuse of Casuistry* (Berkeley: University of California Press).

Josephy, Alvin M., Jr. 1994. *500 Nations* (New York: Knopf).

Kahneman, Daniel, Jack L. Knetsch, and Richard H. Thaler. 1986. "Fairness and the Assumptions of Economics." *Journal of Business* 59 (Oct.): S285–S300. Reprinted in Robin M. Hogarth and Melvin W. Reder, eds., *Rational Choice* (Chicago: University of Chicago Press, 1987): 101–116.

Kant, Immanuel. [1795] 1957. *Perpetual Peace*, trans. Lewis White Beck (New York: Liberal Arts Press).

————. [1797] 1996. *The Metaphysics of Morals*, trans. and ed. Mary Gregor (Cambridge: Cambridge University Press).

Kelley, Steve. 2002. "Title IX Saved Dunn; She's Ready to Return Favor." *Seattle Times* (May 31): D1.

Kim, E. Katherine. Forthcoming. "Human Rights and Consensus." In *Theoretical Foundations of Human Rights: The Conference Proceedings of the Second International Conference on Human Rights*.

Kristof, Nicholas. 2003. "Believe It, or Not." *New York Times* (Aug. 15): A29.

Kymlicka, Will. 1996. "The Good, the Bad, and the Intolerable: Minority Group Rights." *Dissent* 43: 22–30.

Las Casas, Bartolomé de. [1875] 1971. *History of the Indies*, trans. and ed. Andrée Collard (New York: Harper & Row).

———. 1974. *In Defense of the Indians*, trans. S. Poole (DeKalb: Northern Illinois University Press).

Lilla, Mark. 2001. *The Reckless Mind* (New York: New York Review of Books).

Lundberg, Shelly J., and Elaina Rose. 2002. "The Effect of Sons and Daughters on Men's Labor Supply and Wages." *Review of Economics and Statistics* (May): 251–268.

———. 2004. "Investments in Sons and Daughters: Evidence from the Consumer Expenditure Survey." In Ariel Kalil and Thomas DeLeire, eds., *Family Investments in Children: Resources and Behaviors That Promote Success* (Mahwah, N.J.: Erlbaum): 163–180.

MacIntyre, Alasdair. 1984. *After Virtue*, 2d ed. (Notre Dame, Ind.: University of Notre Dame Press).

Mackie, Gerry. 1996. "Ending Footbinding and Infibulation: A Convention Account." *American Sociological Review* 61: 999–1017.

Mackie, John. 1977. *Ethics: Inventing Right and Wrong* (New York: Penguin).

Mahbubani, Kishore. 1998. *Can Asians Think?* (Singapore: Times Books International).

Maynard Smith, John. 1982. *Evolution and the Theory of Games* (New York: Cambridge University Press).

McCarthy, Thomas A. 1994. "Kantian Constructivism and Reconstructivism: Rawls and Habermas in Dialogue." *Ethics* 105 (Oct.): 44–63.

McCullough, Marie. 2003. "Report: Medical School Applications Down" (Sept. 2). URL: http://www.philly.com/mld/philly/news/nation/6675640.htm.

McGirk, Tim. 2003. "Asma Jahangir." *Time Asia* (Apr. 28). URL: http://www.time.com/time/asia/2003/heroes/asma_jahangir.html.

McKeon, Richard, trans. 1941. *The Basic Works of Aristotle* (New York: Random House).

Medvedev, Zhores. 1969. *The Rise and Fall of T. D. Lysenko* (New York: Columbia University Press).

Melching, Molly. 2000. "You Are an African Woman" (Nov. 16). URL: http://www.tostan.org/news-mollym.htm.

Mill, John Stuart. [1859] 1986. *On Liberty* (New York: Prometheus).

———. [1869] 1970. *The Subjection of Women* (Cambridge, Mass.: MIT Press).

Millgram, Elijah. 1997. *Practical Induction* (Cambridge, Mass.: Harvard University Press).

Moore, Molly. 1994. "Push for Change in Hindu Castes Brings Violence." *Seattle Times* (Feb. 17): A2.

Murphy, Liam. 2000. *Moral Demands in Nonideal Theory* (New York: Oxford University Press).

Myrdal, Gunnar, with the assistance of Richard Sterner and Arnold Rose. 1944.

An American Dilemma: The Negro Problem and Modern Democracy (New York: Harper).

Nelson, Soraya Sarhaddi. 2003. "Mother Kills Raped Daughter to Restore 'Honor.'" *Seattle Times* (Nov. 17): A8.

North, Douglas. 1990. *Institutions, Institutional Change and Economic Performance* (Cambridge: Cambridge University Press).

Nozick, Robert. 1974. *Anarchy, State, and Utopia* (New York: Basic).

Nussbaum, Martha C. 2000. *Women and Human Development* (Cambridge: Cambridge University Press).

———. 2001. *Upheavals of Thought: The Intelligence of Emotions* (Cambridge: Cambridge University Press).

Pagden, Anthony. 1982. *The Fall of Natural Man* (Cambridge: Cambridge University Press).

Perrin, Ellen C., and Committee on Psychosocial Aspects of Child and Family Health. 2002. "Technical Report: Coparent or Second-Parent Adoption by Same-Sex Parents." *Pediatrics* 109 (Feb.): 341–344. URL: http://www.aap .org/policy/020008t.html.

Plato. *Republic*, trans. Paul Shorey. In Hamilton and Cairns 1961: 575–844.

———. *Statesman*, trans. J. B. Skemp. In Hamilton and Cairns 1961: 1018–1085.

———. *Theaetetus*, trans. F. M. Cornford. In Hamilton and Cairns 1961: 845–919.

Rawls, John. 1958. "Justice as Fairness." *Philosophical Review* 67 (Apr.): 164–194.

———. 1971. *A Theory of Justice* (Cambridge, Mass.: Harvard University Press).

———. 1993. *Political Liberalism* (New York: Columbia University Press).

———. 1995. "Reply to Habermas." *Journal of Philosophy* 92 (Mar.): 132–180.

———. 1999. *The Law of Peoples* (Cambridge, Mass.: Harvard University Press).

Raz, Joseph. 1986. *The Morality of Freedom* (Oxford: Clarendon).

Riding, Alan. 2003. "Bookseller of Kabul v. Journalist of Oslo." *New York Times* (Oct. 29): B1, B8.

Rorty, Richard. 1993. "Human Rights, Rationality, and Sentimentality." In Stephen Shute and Susan Hurley, eds., *On Human Rights: Oxford Amnesty Lectures* (New York: Basic): 111–134.

Roth, A., V. Prasnikar, M. Okuno-Fujiwara, and S. Zamir. 1991. "Bargaining and Market Behavior in Jerusalem, Ljubljana, Pittsburgh and Tokyo: An Experimental Study." *American Economic Review* 81: 1068–1095.

Rousseau, Jean Jacques. [1762] 1979. *Emile*, trans. Allan Bloom (New York: Basic).

Saco, José Antonio. 1879. *Historia de la Esclavitud Africana en el Nuevo Mundo*, 3 vols. (Paris).

Sale, Kirkpatrick. 1990. *The Conquest of Paradise* (New York: Knopf).

Sandel, Michael J. 1982. *Liberalism and the Limits of Justice* (Cambridge: Cambridge University Press).

Sartre, Jean-Paul. 1956. "Existentialism Is a Humanism." In Walter Kaufmann, ed., *Existentialism from Dostoevsky to Sartre* (New York: Meridian): 287–311.

Sasson, Jean. 1992. *Princess: A True Story of Life behind the Veil in Saudi Arabia* (New York: Morrow).

Scanlon, T. M. 1972. "A Theory of Freedom of Expression." *Philosophy and Public Affairs* 1: 204–226.

———. 1998. *What We Owe to Each Other* (Cambridge, Mass.: Belknap).

Seierstad, Asne. 2003. *The Bookseller of Kabul* (New York: Little, Brown).

Sen, Amartya. 1974. "Choice, Orderings, and Morality." In Stephan Korner, ed., *Practical Reason* (New Haven, Conn.: Yale University Press): 54–82.

———. 1990. "More Than a Hundred Million Women Are Missing." *New York Review of Books* (Dec. 20): 61–67.

———.1999. *Development as Freedom* (New York: Knopf).

———. 2003a. *Rationality and Freedom* (Cambridge, Mass.: Harvard University Press).

———. 2003b. "Missing Women—Revisited." *British Medical Journal* 327 (Dec. 6): 1297–1298.

Sesser, Stan. 1992. "A Nation of Contradictions." *New Yorker* (Jan. 13): 37–68.

Shue, Henry. 1980. *Basic Rights* (Princeton, N.J.: Princeton University Press).

Singapore Department of Statistics. 2002. "Key Indicators of the Population and Households." URL: http://www.singstat.gov.sg/keystats/c2000/population.pdf.

Singer, Peter. 1975. *Animal Liberation* (New York: Random House).

Skrlec, Jasminka. 1999. "World's Schools Received Poor Grades from Oxfam" (May 3). URL: http://www.findarticles.com/cf_dls/m1571/16_15/54543047/print.jhtml.

Skyrms, Brian. 1996. *Evolution of the Social Contract* (Cambridge: Cambridge University Press).

Smith, Adam. [1759] 1976. *The Theory of Moral Sentiments*, ed. D. D. Raphael and A. L. Macfie (Oxford: Clarendon).

———. [1776] 1976. An Inquiry into the Nature and Causes of the *Wealth of Nations*, ed. W. B. Todd (Oxford: Clarendon).

Smith, Craig S. 2003. "In Speech, Nobel Winner Rebukes the U.S." *New York Times* (Dec. 11): A18.

Smith, Vernon. 1991. "Rational Choice: The Contrast between Economics and Psychology." *Journal of Political Economy* 99 (August): 877–898.

Sober, Elliott, and David Sloan Wilson. 1998. *Unto Others: The Evolution and Psychology of Unselfish Behavior* (Cambridge, Mass.: Harvard University Press).

Specter, Michael. 1999. "The Dangerous Philosopher." *New Yorker* 75 (Sept. 6): 46–55.

Stannard, David E. 1992. *American Holocaust* (New York: Oxford University Press).

Stuttaford, Andrew. 2003. "Prize Specimen: The Campaign to Revoke Walter Duranty's Pulitzer" (May 7). *National Review Online.* URL: http://www.nationalreview.com/stuttaford/stuttaford050703.asp.

Talbott, William J. 1995. "Intentional Self-Deception in a Single, Coherent Self." *Philosophy and Phenomenological Research* 55 (Mar.): 27–74.

————. Forthcoming. *Human Rights and Human Well-Being* (New York: Oxford University Press).

Tamir, Yael. 1996. "Hands Off Clitoridectomy." *Boston Review* (Summer 1996): 21–22.

Taylor, Charles. 1996. "A World Consensus on Human Rights?" *Dissent* (Summer): 15–21.

Taylor, Michael. 1987. *The Possibility of Cooperation* (Cambridge: Cambridge University Press).

Thomas, Hugh. 1997. *The Slave Trade* (New York: Simon & Schuster).

Thomson, Judith Jarvis. 1990. *The Realm of Rights* (Cambridge, Mass.: Harvard University Press).

Thomson, Susan. 2003. "Skipping School." *Seattle Times* (Aug. 15): A3.

Tjaden, Patricia, and Nancy Thoennes. 1998. "Prevalence, Incidence, and Consequences of Violence against Women: Findings from the National Violence against Women Survey." National Institute of Justice and Center for Disease Control and Prevention. URL: http://ncjrs.org/pdffiles/172837.pdf.

Todorov, Tzvetan. 1984. *The Conquest of America*, trans. Richard Howard (New York: Harper & Row).

Tolnay, Stewart E., and E. M. Beck. 1995. *A Festival of Violence: An Analysis of Southern Lynchings, 1882–1930* (Urbana: University of Illinois Press).

Tucker, Robert C. 1990. *Stalin in Power* (New York: Norton).

United Nations. 1948. "Universal Declaration of Human Rights." In J. Paul Martin and R. Rangaswamy, eds., *Twenty-Five Human Rights Documents* (New York: Columbia University Center for the Study of Human Rights, 1994).

UN Economic Commission for Europe. 2003. "Crime and Violence: Perpetrators and Types of Crime" (Apr. 25). URL: http://www.unece.org/stats/gender/web/genpols/keyinds/crime/violence.htm.

UN Population Fund. 2000. "Lives Together, Worlds Apart: Men and Women in a Time of Change." URL: http://www.unfpa.org/swp/2000/english/index.html.

————. 2003. "Missing . . . Mapping the Adverse Child Sex Ratio in India." URL: http://www.unfpa.org.in/publications/16_Map%20brochure_English.pdf.

U.S. Census Bureau. 2002. "Housing Vacancy Survey: First Quarter 2002." URL: http://www.census.gov/hhes/www/housing/hvs/q102tab5.html.

Wainryb, Cecilia, and Elliot Turiel. 1994. "Dominance, Subordination, and Concepts of Personal Entitlements in Cultural Contexts." *Child Development* 65 (Dec.): 1701–1722.

Waldron, Jeremy. 1999. "How to Argue for a Universal Claim." *Columbia Human Rights Law Review* 30: 305–314.

Walzer, Michael. 1983. *Spheres of Justice* (New York: Basic).

Wattles, Jeffrey. 1996. *The Golden Rule* (Oxford: Oxford University Press).

Weart, Spencer R. 1998. *Never at War: Why Democracies Will Not Fight One Another* (New Haven, Conn.: Yale University Press).

Weaver, Mary Anne. 1994. "A Fugitive from Justice." *New Yorker* (Sept. 12): 48–60.

Williams, Bernard. 1985. *Ethics and the Limits of Philosophy* (Cambridge, Mass.: Harvard University Press).

Wills, Gary. 1990. "Goodbye, Columbus." *New York Review of Books* 37 (Nov. 22): 6–10.

———. 2000. *Papal Sin* (New York: Doubleday).

Wilson, Margo, and Martin Daly. 1992. "The Man Who Mistook His Wife for a Chattel." In Barkow, Cosmides, and Tooby 1992: 289–322.

Winerip, Michael. 2003. "A 'Zero Dropout' Miracle: Alas! A Texas Tall Tale." *New York Times* (Aug. 13): A19.

Wollstonecraft, Mary. [1792] 1967. (New York: Norton).

Zagorin, Perez. 2003. *How the Idea of Religious Toleration Came to the West* (Princeton, N.J.: Princeton University Press).

INDEX